# Think on These Things

By Esther B. King

With the assistance of: Glenda S. Munos

Order this book online at www.trafford.com
or email orders@trafford.com

Most Trafford titles are also available at major online book retailers.

Printed in the United States of America.

ISBN: 978-1-4269-6997-3 (sc)
ISBN: 978-1-4269-6996-6 (e)


Trafford rev. 07/15/2011

 www.trafford.com

North America & international
toll-free: 1 888 232 4444 (USA & Canada)
phone: 250 383 6864 ♦ fax: 812 355 4082

*"….whatever things are true, whatever things are honorable, whatever things are just, whatever things are pure, whatever things are lovely, whatever things are of good report; if there be any virtue, and if there be any praise, think on these things."*

Philippians 4:8

# Forward

Esther Black King came into the El Campo Leader-News office in 1982 to see if I would be interested in running a religious column. It just so happened that I had been considering looking for some religious copy to run on our Saturday church directory page. So I told her I would run it on a trial basis for at least six weeks and ask our readers to let me know if the Leader-News should continue to carry her column.

I did get a few responses in the affirmative, and I liked what she wrote and enjoyed editing it. Mrs. King never missed a deadline in the more than seven years that she wrote "Think on These Things" for the Leader-News.

Her columns are always philosophical and thought provoking. An aunt of mine who lives in Austin used one of Mrs. King's columns as a program topic at a club meeting. An El Campo businessman told me his secretary would sometimes clip Mrs. King's columns, make copies, and pass them around the business for others to read.

In 1989 Mrs. King decided to retire "Think on These Things". But I'm glad the Leader-News had the opportunity to print it during most of the 1980's. I'm sure it made a difference in the lives of some of our readers.

Christopher F. Barbee
Managing Editor
El Campo Leader-News
El Campo, Texas

This writer, who dearly loves to write and even more dearly loves to write about inspiring things (things that will make readers feel better and happier for having read them), has been searching diligently for a title for this column.

The inspiration came last week while reading from the writings of Paul of Tarsus these words: "Finally, my brothers, whatever things are true, whatever things are honorable, whatever things are just, whatever things are pure, whatever things are lovely, whatever things are of good report; if there be any virtue, and if there be any praise, think on these things." (Paul's letter to the Philippians 4:8)

Thank you, Paul of Tarsus! Why only think about them, when one can also write about them? The subjects discussed in this column may be of science, society, general happenings, international news items, work, play, school, family, theology, psychology, philosophy, or merely reminiscing. However, the writing standard and code of ethics will be the requirements as listed by Paul of Tarsus.

We are living in such a hectic age and time is an uncertain part of life. The following is a quote from Marcus Aurelious Antoninus (a Roman scholar):

"Time is a sort of river of passing events, and strong is its current; no sooner is a thing brought to sight than it is swept by and another takes its place, and this too will be swept away."

He also said, "The universe is change; our life is what our thoughts make it."

Time **is** a rare commodity. We should use it wisely. Reading only the best and writing only the best; and giving of our time and talents to subjects beneficial to everyone.

Having finished a study of Dr. Crane's textbook on psychology, the subjects of self-control, self-respect, way of life, encouragement, the generation gap and others are appealing. (George W. Crane, PhD, MD)

Now – have a happy day! Which is the modern way of saying: Be of good cheer! The sun WILL shine again. It's darkest just before dawn. Greet the new day! "Sufficient unto the day is the evil thereof" – but don't think about it. Think good and joyful thoughts. The evil will take care of itself. And it is known that even evil has been turned into good.

(Editor's Note: Esther Black King, whose philosophical column will be carried by this newspaper each Saturday for at least a six week trial period, is a journalist and retired Sunday School teacher. She is a professional member of The National Writer's Club and has written "Comments on the International Sunday School Lessons" and other columns, all having a religious over-tone.)

• • • • • • • • • • • • • • • • • • • • • • • • • • • • • • • • • • • • • • • • • • •

This year (1982) an exhibit from Cairo, Egypt, will tour the farm states in the U.S.A. These exhibits will show how the ancient Egyptians farmed and tilled the soil in the fertile Nile Valley. Also on display will be seeds of wheat and barley that were found in King Tut's tomb.

According to Mrs. Sheryle D. Ameen, who is representing a group of Arab-Americans participating in the program, the first exhibition early in 1981 will be in the Heritage Hall, Bismarck, North Dakota. This Egyptian Museum of Agriculture is not to be confused with the Egyptian Museum that is the home of the famous King Tutankhamen collection that has already toured the United States and was in Houston for its Texas showing. However, and again, according to Mrs. Ameen, the two museums have combined for this exhibit and are offering 60 items that are 3,500 to 7,000 years old.

The link between Egypt and North Dakota goes back to the year of 1975 when the governor of N.D. visited Cairo. At that time the governor of Giza, site of the Sphinx and Egypt's most famous pyramid just outside of Cairo, declared themselves to be "sisters". So it is only natural that Cairo's sister state (N.D.) would be chosen for the first farm exhibit.

North Dakota is planning a reciprocal exhibit for Egypt. Its focus will be on how the American Indians and early pioneer settlers lived and worked in farm communities in the U.S.A.

Speaking of the exhibit exchange between the sister states, Mrs. Ameen said, "The exhibits are intended to be a cultural exchange that illustrates how the ancestors of both people lived centuries ago."

The Egyptians believed in many gods. (Sphinx was the old Egyptian Pharaoh's cat-like sun god.) The farm exhibit will include many statues of men farmers at work, plowing, planting, irrigating, and harvesting. Statues of Egyptian women doing their chores and cooking their food will be a part of the exhibit. Included are also statues of their deities; the most impressive being the medium height, gilded bronze statue of Osiris, their god of agriculture.

It would seem that the sister states consider these things as objects of art and relics from the past.

The Bible has always headed the list of best-selling books and because more people prefer the majesty, rhythm, and intangible quality of the King James Version, there is going to be a new King James Bible on the market soon. It is to be published in 1982.

The 1611 "authorized" King James Bible has been quoted for centuries in protestant cathedrals and churches but its language is so sprinkled with "thee" and "thou" and obsolete words, it seems almost a different language. However, as we have seen, in some of the translations, it is very difficult to revise the Bible without changing the meaning in some instances.

Thomas Nelson Inc., the world's largest Bible publisher, with home in Nashville, Tenn., is making the biggest publishing venture it has ever undertaken. It has just spent $3.5 million in its effort to update the 370 year old English in the world's best-selling book. A team of scholars are finishing seven years of sifting through the obsolete words of the archaic language to produce a Bible whose same meaning will remain intact.

The advertising director for Thomas Nelson is Ed Liden. Ed said, "We don't like the term 'revised' so we're calling it the New King James. It's not a translation; it's not a paraphrase; it's just a reworking of updating of the original." The 27 books of the New Testament have already been published and in the bookstores in August of 1982.

To show how the original meaning has been kept in the new edition, the publishing house gave two examples. One being John 3:16, "For God so loved the world, that he gave His only begotten son, that whoever believes in Him should not perish but have everlasting life." This verse is the same in both editions except for one word: whosoever was changed to whoever.

The other example was the 23rd Psalm which was practically the same in both editions.

"May the good Lord watch between you and me (not thee and me) while we are absent one from the other."

• • • • • • • • • • • • • • • • • • • • • • • • • • • • • • • • • • • • • • •

Some years ago we (my husband and I) attended a class in safe boating that was being taught in El Campo, Texas by Robert Melanson, commander of Flotilla number 69 of the U.S. Coast Guard Auxiliary.

For a few weeks we studied a textbook, took tests and listened to his instructions on navigation and safe-boating. One point he stressed: "If you see threatening clouds, head for home or the shore immediately."

One day we left the pier, in front of our summer home on Carancahua Bay, went through the pass into Matagorda Bay and then around Sandy Point into Lavaca Bay. The weather was beautiful, balmy – just enough breeze to be comfortable. Then we noticed a cloud over toward Port Lavaca. We decided that it was not a dangerous cloud. It wasn't dark enough and there was a hazy mist surrounding it. Just a small shower, we thought.

Soon a gust of wind hit us hard, then another and another. If it had not been a small cloud and blown over so quickly, we would surely have capsized; we almost did several times and the steering was difficult. The boat was a 20 ft. seven passenger Glasspar, and it was tossed about like a cork. The flotation bottom (a layer of thick Styrofoam between the bottom of the boat and the floorboards) may have helped to keep us on top of the water.

Life has been referred to as a sea by song writers and poets. The sea of life also gets stormy occasionally, and we need built-in protections as well as instructions on how to weather the storms that beset us. We have a textbook, the Bible, and we have a Teacher-guide who has promised to be with us "even to the end of the world". The scriptures describe the snares and pitfalls that tempt us in life if we don't take measures to prevent them.

Sometimes, like the small cloud, the dangers are not apparent until we are overwhelmed. The storms of life can sink us if we are not prepared to withstand the buffeting. Keep the harbor lights burning! Or, as the scriptures tell us, keep your lamps trimmed and filled with oil and "Watch therefore, for you know neither the day nor the hour when the Son of man will come again". (Matthew 25:13)

When choosing a boat, get one with safety features.

When choosing a pilot, remember the hymn: "Christ will my pilot be". He will steer you on a course so straight and narrow that many will never find it. (Matthew 7:14)

Self-control is marvelous! Self-control is strength! Self-control is power! That strength and power can belong to anyone who really and truly tries. Strength and power, once attained, must be shared because in giving strength to others, we become stronger; in using our power to help others, we gain contentment and a spirit of caring and sharing that will build self-esteem which is important to self-control.

If you are content to be a nobody, you can fritter away the days; just lie back and let the rest of the world go by, and forget about self-control. Instead, look deeply inside yourself in the mornings and say, "I am waking up to a beautiful, marvelous day". Set your mind in a pattern with positive thinking, and you are ready to have the best day of your life, a day in which you can make wonderful things happen, all through the art of self-control.

By maintaining a spirit of caring and sharing, plus the strength and power of self-control, we are equipped with the tools for building a better world.

Although some people have self-control and others don't, no one is born with it. It is learned; and with practice, can be self-taught. Environment is a contributing factor. Children who have frustrated, screaming-meemies for parents are not good candidates for self-control. But even unlikely candidates can, with personal dedication and use of full potential, gain a certain amount of self-control and chart a personal plan of action that will make a better life possible.

One cannot expect to encompass everything good, success in business, personal fulfillment, exceptional financial opportunities, without some tangible manifestation of self-control.

Self-control is a wonderful attribute but it doesn't mean that everything you want will be handed to you on a silver platter. It doesn't mean that you are a natural born leader. Self-control is just something that you must have for your own peace of mind, your emotional health, for keeping commitments, and for cooperating with the family, friends, and other inhabitants of this world.

• • • • • • • • • • • • • • • • • • • • • • • • • • • • • • • • • • • • •

Encouragement!  What would life be like without an encouraging word or a congratulatory slap on the back?  The id and the ego must be fed!  Not to make us prudish or arrogant, but to boost our self-respect, so that we may "love our neighbors as we love ourselves".

If you feel that you must give constructive criticism, make double-sure that is constructive and begin with a compliment and end with encouragement.  This applies to men, women, and children; whether business associates, school personnel, relatives afar, or the neighbors next door.

Will Rodgers said, "I never met a man I didn't like."  And none of us has ever met a person that we couldn't find something nice or complimentary to say and be truthful about it.  When you talk to a person about his, or her, good qualities, that person is apt to try and enlarge those attributes.

Let's remember the three parts of constructive criticism:
1.  True but not excessive compliments.  Too much will sound insincere.
2.  Constructive criticism.  Be brief and use a very kind voice.
3.  Encouragement.  All you can give, a world full is not too much.

Encouragement is spiritually healing for the person to whom it is administered.  Sometimes a little encouragement is all it takes to make one feel vibrantly alive.

Ruth Stafford Peale, in her book about Daily Living, wrote one chapter entitled, "How to Bend a Twig".  Her advice on rearing children is solid.  She put _time_ first and _encouragement_ second.  "Most parents," she said, "don't give enough of their time and themselves to their children, and they don't give them the encouragement they need."

Adults need encouragement too.  Back between A.D. 46 and 120, Plutarch was giving encouragement (to help avoid conflict) to the adult population of his day  when he said, "Perseverance is more prevailing than violence; and many things which cannot be overcome when they are together, yield themselves up when taken little by little."  One wonders if maybe Martin Luther King wasn't a student of Plutarch.

The youth of this country are encouraged, at least publicly, by sponsors and leaders of youth fairs, rodeos, fryer sales, animal shows, 4-H and FFA, Little League, and other sporting events, to keep them at their best.  But, do we, as good citizens, applaud and encourage these youth leaders to keep them enjoying their work and knowing that they are appreciated?

. . . . . . . . . . . . . . . . . . . . . . . . . . . . . . . . . .

Everyone wants to look better, feel better, and live longer. Americans are still looking for this panacea. Every newspaper, magazine and TV ad proves this. We have come a long way since pioneer mothers were satisfied if their houses were tidy and their families were neat and clean.

We are grateful for our American way of life and readily acknowledge that people should look and feel the best they can; but honestly now, don't you think it is being carried a little too far?

The first books on beauty care are still selling and new ones are continually being published. Newspapers and magazines have articles in every issue on self-improvement. There are columnists who write weekly, or daily, on only one aspect of beauty, such as hair care, eye care, skin care, care of the nails, feminine hygiene, clothing styles, and anything else you can think of, and some things you never would.

Make-up was first used on actresses by the make-up artists in Hollywood; but now anyone can look like a movie star if they take the time and effort (what make-up can't do, plastic surgery can).

While watching the Miss America pageant this week, and noting the apparent perfect features of each beautiful face, the thought occurred to me that the continuous smiles must be a strain. There was this wish, to see them with their faces relaxed. The smiles looked real until they were required to hold them for some time. In my imagination, Bob Barker was in a policeman's uniform, pointing a gun at them, and shouting, "Freeze"!

Beauty, real or applied, is only skin deep, according to mothers. Grandmothers would say: "Beauty is a beauty does." At least mine did back in 1930.

My theory has always been: A person should look the best that he or she can with the least amount of effort. Also, a person should feel the best that he or she can without drugs and with proper nutrition and exercise.

Of course, everyone wants to live forever and indeed we shall, with the little transition called death in between.

One should not spend too much time and effort in worrying about the way one looks, because worry and frustration can affect the way one looks and feels! But God has supplied us with doctors who can, sometimes, repair the damage that we do when we don't have enough sense, or enough incentive, to take care of ourselves.

When are we going to learn, America, that there is only one place to search for perfection? When are we going to learn to "let go, and let God"?

• • • • • • • • • • • • • • • • • • • • • • • • • • • • • • • • • • • • • • •

In 1929 Harper & Brothers published a book of 23 chapters, written by 23 different people. The title is <u>If I had Only One Sermon to Preach on Immortality</u>. Immortality is a fascinating word, and it is seldom expressed except by poets and preachers. It has multiple meanings: hope, faith, expectancy, and yearning all rolled into one.

The oratorical authors of this book, representing various doctrines and beliefs, were each asked the question: "What would you preach if you had only one sermon to preach on immorality?" Each one that was questioned wrote a sermon, not defining the word but giving his best thoughts and convictions on the subject. The answers were varied according to the individual's beliefs.

Immortality pertains to eternity, and the subject of eternity is too profound for man's mind. How many persons have cried out, as did Job: "If a man die, shall he live again?"

W.E. Biederwolf, president of Lake Winona Bible Conference and school of theology, says this is the all-absorbing question of the ages and that Buddhists, Mohammedans, Christians, Theosophists, Agnostics, Infidels, and men of every faith, and men who say they have no faith at all, will sit around the table and discuss for hours the question, "Are the dead alive?" and "Do we survive the chemical change called 'death'?"

Only one man (God-man) has ever answered this question with authority, and He spoke as no man ever had when He said, "I came that you might have life and have it more abundantly." Christ also said, "….I go to prepare a place for you….if it were not so, I would have told you."

Whether we believe in immortality hinges on whether or not we believe the Easter message and Jesus. We remember that Job's wife told him to "….curse God and die." But Job said, "Even though He slay me, I will still trust Him." And the outcome of Job was that his later days were better than his first.

This writer believes there is no such thing as death for the Christian. The Christian spirit in man (made in the image of God) when departed from the earthly clay body is changed "in the twinkling of an eye" and exists in what to us is the unknown but will become known to us when our time comes. We get a foretaste of what awaits us by the way we live here. Death belongs to the devil and his followers. The writer sincerely believes that to be separated from God is the hell we make for ourselves here and in the hereafter.

Dr. Norman Vincent Peale teaches the right way of living is to indulge in positive thinking; that positive thoughts can rule over the environment and early training if the individual persists and uses his full potential trying for a positive life factor.

Dale Carnegie (deceased) whose courses in public speaking have been universally taught, and are still being taught, also dealt with positive thinking. (This writer attended such a class twice a week for several weeks, not that she wanted to become a public speaker, but the training was food for creative thinking and writing).

English teachers in high schools and junior high schools, who also teach public speaking, should try some of the Carnegie methods. There are methods suited to debates and extemporaneous speeches.

Party games have been played where two speakers are chosen and each given a list of words. The negative speaker may be given the following list of adjectives: ugly, dirty, untidy, repulsive, short-sighted, colorless, contemptible, unappreciative, and cowardly. The positive speaker may have the following words: tall, handsome, intelligent, polite, friendly, interesting, capable, truthful and likable. Now each speaker has nine adjectives, and the leader says, "Finish this sentence with the words given you: I met (name) who was …."

Of course this is an over-simplified example, but the results are just as bizarre when more sophisticated words and subjects are used. And there is no happy medium to be obtained by mixing the positive and negative adjectives. The negative words remain negative and cast a shadow over the pleasant, positive words.

Observe the man, woman or child who lives on the negative side of life by using many negative or unpleasant words. What do you see? Probably a person whose bodily carriage is droopy and bent-over, a person who walks in a lackadaisical manner, a woe-be gone expression out of unsmiling eyes and the corners of the mouth turned downward. Of course, it depends on the degree of negativism as to how pronounced the characteristics will be.

The positive or pleasantly optimistic person walks with a spring in his or her step, the carriage is erect, the head and chin are up as well as the corners of the mouth, usually tiny laugh wrinkles around the eyes, and always a friendly greeting or handshake is forthcoming. Be positive!

Prayer: that ultimate ecstasy of oneness with God our Father and creator of all things both great and small.

There are all kinds of prayers; the request prayer: Father I want this or that, please give it to me. The bargaining prayer: Father, if you will grant me thus and so, I'll do thus and so for you. The prayer for healing with a promise of commitment: Father, if you will heal me, I'll spend the rest of my life doing things for you.

The above types of prayers often get no higher than the ceiling because God knows the hearts of people and can judge the sincerity of their intent.

The prayer for forgiveness is the important prayer: "Father be merciful to me, a sinner." "Father, forgive them for they know not what they do." If you want to build a "hotline" for private communication between you and the Father, you must first get forgiveness for any unforgiven sins. The Father commands this. If the request is sincere, He says that He will remember them against us no more. They will be cleansed "whiter than snow."

The atheistic world belittles the Christians. One well-known atheist writer said that Christians were weaklings and that they have invented a father and big brother upstairs to take care of them. Were there any weaklings among the Christians in Rome who went out into the arena of lions singing God's praises?

All they had to do, to keep the lions from tearing them limb from limb and devouring them, was to deny Christ and give allegiance to Caesar, and they would have been rescued. Those who were burned at the stake and others who were set on fire and used as torches could have been saved the same way. Through their great strength our Christian heritage was preserved.

Some prayers aren't answered because an answer isn't really expected. If you awake restless, and ask "God, help me back to sleep," are you also wondering where you left the half-finished book or what is there to eat in the refrigerator? When the friend you called didn't answer, you kept on trying until the call went through. Is the Father a lesser friend?

Pray with the right attitude, beginning with true worship and praise, have a contrite heart and talk as a child of God, remembering that He is our father, with a persistence that doesn't give up until the Holy Spirit is right there in the room with you. God wants us to: Ask! Expect! Receive!

Repent! For the kingdom of heaven is at hand.

This doesn't mean that the world is going to end tomorrow, although it's possible; neither does it mean that God's time is limited. It's our time that is limited. The kingdom is at hand for this generation. That is our life's span: one generation! And if we don't accept salvation in our generation, what will happen to future ones?

Could it be that Christians grew lax and indifferent in the last generations and because of this we have violence, war threats and a lack of peace in our time? We understand the need and the urgency to accept the gospel message when we realize the extreme shortness of our limited earthly existence. The interval between birth and death is short indeed. What person has accomplished all that he, or she, wanted to do in one lifetime?

The devoted Christian knows and feels, with heart, mind and soul, and has the instinct of a homing pigeon about his future home in the kingdom of heaven. The non-Christian has the instinct of a homing pigeon gone blind. He wants to go back from whence he came but he can't see the way. He is forever searching, seeking a more joyful and satisfying way of life that also relieves the craving of his spirit.

To all lost souls, Jesus is still saying: "Behold, I stand at the door and knock." To those having eyes but still can't see the way, He says: "I am the Way, the Truth, and the Life: no man cometh unto the Father, but by Me."

Voltaire said, "We never live; we are always in the expectation of living." And it was Zimmermann who said, "There appears to exist a greater desire to live long that to live well!"

Ludwig Tieck, the German poet and novelist, 1773-1853, wrote: "He is not dead who departs from life with a high and noble fame, but he is dead, even while living, whose brow is branded with infamy. Measure not life by the hopes and enjoyments of this world, but by the preparation it makes for another; looking forward to what you shall be rather than backward to what you have been."

Repenting and becoming a Christian does not mean wearing a long and sour expression, nor even a pious one. It's a joyful experience filled with a new and satisfying kind of happiness.

In the beginning God created the heavens and the earth and everything in them. Then, to climax His mighty work, He created man. He made him from the substances that He had used to create animal and vegetable life: the same chemicals, the same elements, the same life and death process of multiplying and decreasing cell structure.

God then did a most wonderful thing. He said, "Let US make man in our own image." Whenever and wherever this statement is read, there are always those who call attention to the plurality of the sentence and ask, "Who helped God?"

What difference does it make? All we need to know is in the first sentence: "In the beginning God...." In the beginning God created. He is behind all things and the pattern of his handiwork is in all things. If it were necessary for us to know exactly when or how, He would have revealed it to us. But the nature of man is to be curious.

Some say that He was talking to His angels. Others say that He was talking to the second and third part of the Trinity (which is another way of saying that He was talking to Himself). Some go so far as to say that He was talking to Lucifer (Satan or Devil) whom, the scriptures tell us, He later threw out of heaven.

Did He have a helper or was He talking to Himself? The answer is unessential and the questions only serve to take our minds from the real purpose of the book of Genesis.

An illustration (not a comparison by any means) would be the accomplishment of Charles A Lindberg who made the first non-stop flight to Europe. In telling of his flight, he spoke of his airplane as though it were a person, saying, "We left...." And "We arrived...." And "We were over the ocean at a certain point." The future generations of a few thousand (or maybe hundreds) years from now may doubt that Lindberg made a solo flight and vow that he had someone with him because he used the plural pronoun "We".

The evidence that there is a higher intelligence than man is evident in the things we see, hear, taste, smell, and touch every day.

Bacon said, "They that deny a God, destroy man's nobility; for clearly man is of kin to the beasts by his body, and if he be not of kin to God by his spirit, he is a base and ignoble creature."

"God is great and therefore, He will be sought: He is good and therefore, He will be found," stated John Jay.

. . . . . . . . . . . . . . . . . . . . . . . . . . . . . . . . . . . .

The most challenging concept in the Hebraic-Christian faith is the fact that man is made in the image of God. This being so, we should try to be more like Him. Man has learned to fly through the air, to orbit the earth, and to accomplish many other feats that are astounding; but has he learned to think, speak, and act as a child of God?

Our faith and belief is that God has formed us and redeemed us, therefore, we are His. We believe that God knows our name, our needs, our desires, and that He offers Himself as our help in time of trouble.

Man is the only animal who can use, creatively, his memory and his imagination. He can use memory of past experiences for corrective purposes. He can use historical and scientific knowledge to better the welfare of himself and others. It is the stated will of God that man "subdue the earth and have dominion over it." But somewhere along the way, he seems to have gotten the idea that he must subdue his fellowman and have dominion over him too. The natural result of this is rebellion and war.

What man is and what he is capable of doing is more often two entirely different things. Man rarely uses the full potential of those rare qualities with which he was endowed and which set him entirely apart from the rest of creation.

Under the glass top of this writer's desk is a clipping of a "Today's chuckle" taken from a front page of The Houston Post newspaper some years ago, "Man has twelve billion brain cells, and if he gets in an especially tight place he'll use a dozen or so of them as a last resort."

Man has the rare privilege of deliberately trying to improve himself, his skills, his ability to think, his speech, his personal and public relations, his morals and his faith – first of all in God, and then in himself and his fellowman.

Let us not forget that God's great gift to man, at the time of his creation, was a **spirit** made in the image of His own likeness. God is a spirit. He is not black, white, red, or brown, but He is the father and creator of all. (In this article, the word "man" is used as mankind, including women.)

. . . . . . . . . . . . . . . . . . . . . . . . . . . . . . . . . . . . . . . . . . . . .

Have you had a good case of the "blues" lately? The components most often found in the blues are self-pity, frustrations, and fears. These are not healthy attitudes for anyone. So dispose of them at once.

While the three above mentioned components are the most likely culprits, they are not the only things that can cause the "blues".

The artist, with his paints, palette and brush, makes all shades of blue by mixing in white. As he mixes, you can see dark blue become sky blue, then baby blue, and with still more white, it will become white altogether. There are two other colors on the painter's palette that are sometimes associated with people's attitudes. They are yellow and green. Yellow is a word used for cowardice and green is used for jealousy and envy; these are mental states comparable to the downhearted despondency of the "blues". Just as dark shades are diminishable when mixed with white, so will our wrong attitudes diminish when mixed with God's light.

Self-pity is self-centeredness and a forgetfulness of others and a person afflicted with it should say to himself, or herself, constantly: "I must not think of what others can do for me, but about what I can do for others." This is not to say that you never have cause for grievance; it is to say, don't dwell upon it! It will only get you down with a good case of the "blues".

Charles Haddon Spurgeon (1834-1892), an English clergyman, said: "Beware of no man more than yourself; we carry our worst enemies within us." And G.B. Cheever said, "As a man goes down in self, he goes up in God."

Frustrations may be caused by many things but mostly by worrying about problems that you can't solve and you won't ask God's help because you think He won't or can't, or maybe you had forgotten about Him.

A story is told of a man asking a preacher to help him with a problem that he had worried with for months and couldn't solve. The good pastor said, "I can't solve your problem, but God can. Go home and pray every day this week. Tell God what you've just told me and ask Him to help you. Come back next week and tell me if He helped you."

The next week the man came back and said, "Preacher, I did what you said. I prayed every day and night last week, but it didn't do any good. However, I don't have the problem anymore. When He wouldn't help me, I thought of what to do about it myself."

Do we forget to thank God and give him the credit for lifting us out of self-pity, solving our frustrating problems, and calming our fears?

• • • • • • • • • • • • • • • • • • • • • • • • • • • • • • • • • • • • • • • • • • • • • •

It was a very sad day, in ancient history, when the king of Judah gave himself up to the king of Babylon. How dearly rulers and nations must pay for listening to false teachers and poor advisors! If it were only the king, or ruler, who paid for his mistakes, but life is not like that; the whole nation suffers the consequences of the leader's mistakes, the same as reaping the benefits of his good judgments.

It is also true of individuals. Our lives are such that everyone who might be made proud by our accomplishments, also are the ones certain to be hurt and ashamed by our failures. "Man cannot live unto himself alone…." Parents, relatives, friends, and neighbors share our joys and our sorrows, our good fortune or our disgrace.

Early history shows prophecies fulfilled and others made, and always the sins of the people find them out. Prophets and the crucifixion cannot persuade every evil heart to turn from its wicked way. Only when we let the love of God (the love that is God) come into our hearts and lives, can it light the fires of faith that will illumine the darkness of despair and desolation.

It is said that "God reveals Himself through tragic events." Why would this be true? Especially, when He said, "Behold, I stand at the door and knock…." Perhaps it's because sometimes it takes a tragedy to make people receptive to God.

It is characteristic of the human race to want to be "do-it-your-selfers", even to seeking their own salvation. But it doesn't happen that way. Man must be permissive and let God have full sway in his life to gain the highest state of perfection available in this world.

Adolf Hitler sought perfection by having the greatest military might of all time. Nations have made the mistake of putting brute force in charge, instead of the more powerful God, since the beginning of nations. A nation rising to prominence in this way is causing her own defeat and fall from power. It was so with Babylonia. Fifty years after invading and destroying Jerusalem, Babylon herself was conquered.

It isn't military might that determines the fate or future of a nation; it's a decline of honor and integrity that results in moral decay. It's the primary cause of every fallen nation. But first, however, there was a turning away from God, or a matter of not accepting Him and His laws.

A Christian nation may protect itself but never provoke an attack.

Who are angels?  The Bible tells us that "God made man just a little lower than the angels." Mankind may reach sainthood on this earth, but he can never become an angel because they will always be a little above human beings.

Some say they are heaven's messengers, and the Bible tells us they were to the shepherds on that first Christmas Day.  Others think there is an angel assigned to each of us to watch over and care for us.  Billy Graham believes in Guardian Angels.  In fact, he has written a book about them. Infants and maidens have been incorrectly called angels by poets, parents, and lovers.

How fortunate that God has angels to do His bidding because He surely can't depend on earthlings.  The Bible is full of scriptures about angels doing the will of God.  Nebuchadnezzar, said, "God hath sent his angel, and delivered His servants that trusted in Him…."  Also, Daniel said, "My God hath sent His angel, and hath shut the lions' mouths, that they have not hurt me…."

Angels were also seen in the empty tomb of Jesus, one standing at the head and the other at the foot of the place where Christ's body had lain.  The angels were seen by local people, and the angels spoke to them saying: "Why seek ye the living among the dead?" (Luke 24:4&5, John 29:12)

An angel must be very powerful because 2nd Chronicles 32:21 says: "And the Lord sent an angel, which cut off all the mighty men of valor, and the leaders and captains in the camp of the king of Assyria."  And when the king returned shamefaced to his own country and to his heathen god, his own sons slew him with swords.  Isaiah tell us (37:36) the number of Assyrians the angel of the Lord "smote" a hundred and four score and five thousand "early in the morning, behold, they were all dead corpses."

If America remains a Christian nation, she can truthfully say to the heaviest armed of countries, "If God and His angels be for us, who can stand against us?"

We cannot become angels in this life, but we will reach that status after death (Mark 12:25) "For when they shall rise from the dead, they neither marry, nor are given in marriage; but are as the angels which are in heaven." (that is, spiritual)

Modern writers shy away from the subject of angels, early writers did not:  "The angels may have wider spheres of action and nobler forms of duty than ourselves, but truth and right to them and to us are one and the same thing." (E.H. Chapin, American clergyman, 1814-1880)

What's in a name? This question is meant in more ways than literally. One may be well up the ladder toward "making a name for himself" or he may be roaming the country "trying to find himself" and wanting to find God. If you already know Him, then strive for a closer walk with Him and increase your faith.

The Bible tells us that "a good name is rather to be chosen than great riches…." (Proverbs 22:1) What is a good name? Is your word as good as your bond? Does your tongue ever slip into idle gossip? Are you "hot-headed" and unable to hold your temper? How about those "little white lies" told to save hurt feelings when it wasn't necessary to say anything at all? Can one depend on you to act with courtesy, dignity, and integrity in most situations?

There are lots of ways that we can ruin our own good names. A bad name isn't always dependent on the other fellow's smear-campaign. Names are synonymous with reputations and both should be kept clean and honorable.

Not only do our friends know us by name, but also God knows our names and the number of hairs on our heads as well, and according to John, wants to record our names in heaven. In speaking of heaven and the New Jerusalem, John said, "But nothing unclean shall enter it, nor anyone who practices abomination or falsehood, but only those who are written in the Lamb's book of life." (Revelation 21:27, Revised Standard Version)

What's in a name? Everything! Would you rather your name be selected as a candidate for high office, drawn as winner of a large sweepstakes prize, placed in The Hall of Fame, or would you rather be recorded in the Lamb's book of life for all eternity?

You can make for yourself a golden name or you can make it mud, and once a name is soiled it can only be cleaned by the "blood of the Lamb" through the grace of God. For a fee the courts will change a name, but the person will still be the same person. Shakespeare said that you can give a rose another name but it will still have the same sweet fragrance of a rose.

J. Hawes said, "A good name lost is seldom regained. When character is gone, all is gone and one of the richest jewels of life is lost forever."

But with God all things are possible, and He controls the destiny of our souls.

How does one recognize a good person? Or distinguish between a good person and the "wolf in sheep clothing" of which the scriptures speak? (Matthew 7:15) Wolves are mentioned three times in the Old Testament Bible and three times in the New Testament, always in contrast to sheep and about them destroying the lambs.

Matthew, Mark, and Luke speak of the "ravenous wolves". Symbolically the wolf was used to denote evil and evil people in the world. Sheep or lambs were applied to the good people. Ravenous means: "giving to seizing prey in order to devour it, as animals". Therefore, the evil is always trying to "gobble-up" the good in this world. Yet we are told that we must overcome evil with good; that is the only way. We cannot combat evil with evil lest the whole world become evil and be destroyed.

The Old Testament says, "an eye for an eye and a tooth for a tooth", but the New Testament says, "a soft answer turns away wrath", and "do good to them that hate you and despitefully use you."

We have been taught from childhood that here is good and bad in all of us. One of my mother's favorite sayings was the quote: "There is so much bad in the best of us and so much good in the worst of us that it scarcely behooves any of us to talk about the rest of us."

We are told not to judge; we are told how to recognize good people by the deeds they do, the words they speak, and the way they live. The Bible says we can tell a good tree by the fruit it bears. The fruit is either good or bad. The same is true of a person.

Some think that those who kill and rape and destroy for "kicks" have never had good associates to influence them, yet Judas Iscariot associated with 11 good men and Jesus said of him that "he was a devil from the beginning."

We must recognize the fact that God can take the evil in this world and make it fit into His plans for good.

Some people seek acclaim and worldly recognition and never find it; others have it heaped upon them by living an exemplary life. There is a lot more good than evil in the world, that's why bad things are news. It's the rare and unusual that makes headlines. Let's hope that good news stories never predominate because that would mean evil has taken over the world and goodness is rare and unusual.

News does well in exposing crime. Napoleon said, "I fear three newspapers more than a hundred thousand bayonets."

Whether you believe that Christ was the Son of God, a prophet, an inspired teacher or merely a good man, you must surely agree that He accomplished His mission which is the same as that of Abraham, Isaac, and Jacob: "....to draw all men unto God." (Atheists are fewer than believers.)

Surely we are all tested and tried at some point in our lives. Why? To prove our worth? To prepare us for a more perfect world to come? Abraham's life, after he had given it over to God, was one cruel test after another. His first, at age 75, was to give up his home, country, kinsmen, and friends to go into an unknown land. Another test was to find peaceful solutions for the quarrels between his herdsmen and those of his nephew, Lot. Then, there was the test of waiting and wondering in a strange land for 24 years. A man of lesser faith would have been tempted to think that God had forgotten him. One of the hardest lessons to learn is to have patience and wait, especially upon God whose time element is quite different from ours.

When God confided that he was going to destroy the wicked cities of Sodom and Gomorrah, Abraham passed the test of "personal intercession for others". But the supreme test was when God told him to sacrifice his son Isaac. We must remember that this was only a test, and God "stayed his hand" because by acquiescing, he had already passed the test.

If this seems unbelievable, just remember that God didn't ask Abraham to do anything that He wouldn't do Himself. At Calvary, God offered His son on the cross, and He didn't stay the hand of death because Christ submitted Himself willingly for sacrifice and was "obedient unto death". God's covenant with Abraham was fulfilled in this terrible event that was for the good of all mankind, even those as yet unborn, until the day of final judgment.

Was God cruel to destroy women and children of Hiroshima and Nagasaki? Does God, who is "no respecter of persons", place emphasis on women and children or is it only men who do that? Anyway, if both of these events were to prevent further and far-reaching bloodshed, and therefore prevent delay of redeeming the human animal, then it was not cruelty at all but a kindness to the human race.

This is our Father's world, and we can all be happy in the knowledge that He is in full charge of it. And although we may feel our faith to be sorely tried and tested, we know that everything, even the wrongs of this world, can be used for good to those who love God. (Romans 8:28)

• • • • • • • • • • • • • • • • • • • • • • • • • • • • • • • • • • • • • • • • •

The books in the New Testament Bible affirm that Christians are a peculiar people. One wonders if the word "peculiar" wasn't given a different connotation in those early days. In this modern age no one wants to seem peculiar. Today we think of "peculiar" as strange, odd, or weird. We give the word a negative meaning, therefore, it's considered undesirable. If that civilization thought it meant being "different", then it accurately described the early Christians. They certainly were different from the other people of that day.

An unbeliever once said to a Christian, "You're living in a world of make-believe! You should be a realist like me. I want to live now! You're just a dreamer!"

The Christian replied, "You may think of yourself as a realist, but I don't see you as such. You can't be a realist because they see what is real and true. You are a conformist, conforming to the ways of this world."

A minister once told the following story to illustrate his point. A very wealthy woman died. She had loved life, not as a realist, but as a conformist, until her late years when she repented of her worldly ways and did some good deeds; but she was old then, and there was not enough time left to make up for all the wasted years. At the pearly gate to heaven she was admitted, and a guide was sent to take her to her new home. They walked down a golden street where the homes were large and beautiful. In the center of the next block was the most splendid house of all.

"That surely must be mine!" she exclaimed.

"No," replied the guide, "that is the home of your former maid."

My goodness, she thought, if that quiet, peculiar, little woman can have a mansion like this, mine must be a castle. They walked on for many blocks, and the houses became smaller and smaller until the street came to a dead end and one desolate, little shack was pointed out as her new home. "Why?" she gasped in astonishment.

The guide explained patiently, "The homes here are built with the things each owner sends to us, and dear sister, this is all the material you sent up."

"Where your treasure is, there will your heart be also." (Luke 12:34)

Having just a small amount of faith is like having only a little money. How far can you get on a smattering of faith? How much can you buy with a few small coins? It seems to take both for a quality existence, but of the two, one has priority. In fact, if we can obtain the first, we are promised the second: "Seek ye first the kingdom of God and His righteousness and all these things shall be added unto you." (Matthew 6:33)

First, we must build a faith so strong and unshakable that it won't waver or crumble, causing us to become bankrupt spiritually and financially. And if we are seeking the first, only to obtain the latter, it will profit us nothing. We won't have either one. If we seek with all our heart and soul to obtain the first, the goods of this world that we need, will come to us as promised.

The greatest faith comes when studying and believing the Bible and developing a better relationship with God. A closer walk and better communication with God is helped by associating with other Christians.

When we enjoy fellowship with Christians, we are unconsciously depending upon their influence, thinking that we have none of our own? You may think you have no influence, but you cannot do one little misdeed without leading others astray. God's word says, "None of us liveth to himself."

Faith improperly focused can be a very dangerous thing. Everyone has faith in something or someone. Faith in itself is neither good nor bad; it is where we place our faith that counts. Some put their faith in communism and some in atomic power and modern weapons. Many have faith in their own objectives and abilities.

Teachers, administrators, and all advisors ask that we have faith and a steadfastness of purpose to reach life's goals, but are vague and hazy about what or in whom that faith must be placed.

If we gather the truth from the Bible, then it is clear that the acceptable faith to God is faith in Jesus Christ.

Faith is the most powerful force in the world! And faith in Christ is a spiritual force for good that is unequaled on earth.

"Above all, take the shield of faith, which will enable you to quench all the fiery darts of the evil ones." (Ephesians 6:16)

• • • • • • • • • • • • • • • • • • • • • • • • • • • • • • • • • • • •

Are serenity, calmness, and tranquility disappearing from modern society? Think of the entertainment available today, especially of television, which is the most common and is in nearly every home. Could the following adjectives apply to TV programs: Serene, calm, tranquil, quiet, peaceful, placid, unruffled, motionless, restful, composed, self-possessed, etc.?

Both children and adults need a clear mind and a cool head to study lessons, solve daily problems, meditate, read, and especially to pray. Do we, amid the noise and irritations, forget to pray, even at mealtime, to thank God that we still live in a land of plenty and where Christians love and help the underprivileged.

It is regrettable that so many people take the fatalist's way of looking at life. The fatalist is not calm. He accepts his life as though he were drifting at sea with no compass and no knowledge of his destination. His constant surrender to his environment makes him restless and recklessly indifferent to his future.

The person who is calm and self-possessed usually has great plans for the future, is in harmony with himself and his ideals. That person charts a straight course and stands ready to meet any crisis.

A calm and serene person has learned to adopt or acquire the more favorable attributes of life. He has an aura, or moral atmosphere of self-reliance, self-control, and self-respect. Do not confuse serenity with a dead spirit or a passive and inactive individual because no one lives life more fully, more intensely, and more consciously than the man or woman who is calm.

No, serenity cannot be acquired of itself and by itself; it comes as the aftermath of a series of cultivated attributes, or virtues, which raises one to a higher standard of living and to a greater sense of appreciation for the privilege and dignity of higher and nobler concept of life.

What is worry? It is the forerunner of insomnia. It is a traitor to thoughts of happiness. It is the dragon that slays mental energy and dulls the mind, reducing it to a vague, restless, unsatisfied and fearing state. Worry zaps our strength and feeds us mental poison that causes indigestion and irritates our disposition as it changes our character.

It can put one in the hospital because worry, if not conquered, will in time stimulate diseases that fill our hospital beds. Many patients' charts could have the words "worry caused" written above the name of the diagnosed illness. If the organs of the body do withstand disease while worrying, the brain might develop a chronic depression and a pessimistic attitude.

Continuous worrying becomes a habit. There are people who must have something or someone to worry about before they can make conversation. They can talk only about their "pet peeves".

Just as the liquor and tobacco habits are hard to break, so is the worry habit, and equally so. It is also hard on the rest of the family. There is not, to my knowledge, an organization such as worriers anonymous for worried individuals. In fact, anonymousness would not help at all.

No one can cure the habitual worrier except himself, and he must convince himself of one of two things: that he can prevent the evil he fears from happening, and that it's useless to worry about something he isn't going to let happen, or he can tell himself that if what he fears actually happens there isn't anything that he can do to stop it. There's no need to worry about something over which he has no control.

Habitual worriers have not learned to "let go and let God".

A minister once said, "If a man does, day by day, the best he can by the light he has, he has no need to fear, no need to regret, no need to worry. No amount of agony and worry would help him. Neither man nor angel can do more than his best."

If you are prone to worry, read the following three scriptures:

Cure of worry: Psalms 37:1-5

Result of worry: Job 7:3-7, 14, 15

Uselessness of worry: Psalms 127:2, Matthew 6:25-34, Luke 12:22-23

Has the man or woman ever lived that thought they had too much money and too much of this world's goods? No, because it's typical of human nature to want things and the more one acquires the more one wants.

It is logical to believe that God wants us to have enough of this world's goods to be adequately sustained, if the material assets are obtained honestly and means of others are not ignored.

When Jesus told "the rich young ruler" to go and sell what he had and give it to the poor, He was not setting an example or saying that everyone should do that. He knew the heart of the rich young ruler, how he felt about his possessions, and in his case that was the only way he could be saved.

An English Bishop, George Horne (1730-1792), must have known what was in the mind of Christ, regarding the rich young ruler, when he wrote in the 18th century: "Riches, honors and pleasures are the sweets which destroy the mind's appetite for heavenly food; poverty, disgrace, and pain are the bitters which restore it." The French priest and philosopher, Pierre Charron (1541-1603) had the same trend of thought when he wrote: "Riches should be admitted into our homes, but not into our hearts; we may take them into our possession, but not into our affections."

Extreme wealth is a danger because "There is a burden of care in getting riches; fear in keeping them, temptation in using them, guilt in abusing them, sorrow in losing them, and a burden of account at last to be given concerning them." (M. Henry) And Shakespeare said, "If thou bearest thy heavy riches but a journey, and death unloads thee."

Other men cater and kowtow to the rich man, but their respect is only for his philanthropy. Riches used wisely can provide a fully, happy and beneficial life. Many of the men in the Old Testament were rich: Abraham, most of the kings, with King Solomon the richest of all. The three wise men from the east didn't let their great wealth keep them from making a long, tiresome journey to see the Christ child, and they brought Him expensive gifts which may have financed the little family's flight into Egypt.

Riches are good or evil, depending on the attitudes of those who possess them. All riches belong to God and can be bestowed or taken away; He has the whole world in His hands.

Should we determine a person's success by his wealth and social standing, or by the number of adversities that he has overcome? "There goes Mr. Doe; he is worth millions!" Is that really his worth? How can one know the worth of a person? The Bible tells not to judge the outward appearances because the inner man is the true character that reflects success and not the outward "show".

In a palatial home, in the best part of the city, lived a family of six. The mother was a social butterfly who put her needs and commitments above family unity and responsibilities. The father had made it to the top of the corporate ladder and his time was filled with out-of-town, and often out-of-the-country, business trips, board meetings of which he was chairman of several and an important member of others. He was rarely at home.

The older boy and girl have been dismissed from colleges but were still buying their way into other schools. The younger boy and girl were having trouble in high school with drugs, wild parties, drag-racing and getting other young people into trouble. Anytime two or more were at home together, there were accusations and bickering.

To the outside world, this family appeared to be successful because each member had an expensive car, a personal expense account, could buy whatever he or she wanted, and could go whenever and wherever he or she wanted to go.

Compare this home with one that has good family relationships. Where, more often than not, they take their meals together with witty conversation and each relates personal experiences that brings sympathy, encouragement, helpful hints or advice, laughter, enjoyment and a loving atmosphere of caring. Therein lies true success.

Too much money or the lack of enough of it for comfort is detrimental to success. Why would a fair and just God want the rich to become richer and the poor to become poorer? One is convinced that He does not, but He gave man a free spirit to control his own destiny. There will not be equal distribution of chances for success as long as there is corruption in high places, in governments, and unscrupulous people in the world.

An English novelist wrote: "The man who succeeds above his fellows is the one who, early in life, clearly discerns his object, and towards that object habitually directs his powers. Genius is but fine observation strengthened by fixity of purpose…." Bulwer (1803-1873)

To be steadfast in the Christian faith takes prayer, self-denial, immunity to criticism, a burning desire to further the good in the world, an abhorrence of the existing evils, no matter what seductive form the Devil may take, a sure knowledge that the Holy Spirit is there to help every step of the way, and above all, do not allow yourself to be yoked with an unbeliever: "For what fellowship hath righteousness with unrighteousness? And what communion hath light with darkness?" (2 Cor. 6:14)

The wife who taught school before marriage had roomed and boarded with a rural Christian family. The oldest son in that home (now her husband) was a college graduate, working on his Ph.D. degree. She fell in love with him while listening to him read Bible stories to his younger brothers and sisters. They now have a Christian home, teenage children, all taking part in church work and civic affairs.

A young couple, much in love, was married. The girl knew that the boy was taking drugs, but thought their great love would help him to break the habit. Later the boy was arrested for possession of drugs and hanged himself in his jail cell. The girl gave birth to a deformed baby and her aged parents were burdened with the care of them.

Another unequally yoked couple was the Biblical characters, Job and his wife. Job was a firm believer and loved God, but his wife did not. The story of Job isn't legendary. The man was a real person who dwelt in the land of Uz on the borders of Indumaea. He was a descendant of Aram, son of Shem, and possibly was contemporary with Abraham who also lived in the land of Uz.

The Bible says of Job's character: "He was upright, feared God and eschewed evil." (Job 1:1) But he didn't obey God when he became unequally yoked with a pagan woman. Job was afflicted with sores and illness and although he remained kind, patient, and righteous; his friends left him and his wife and told him to "Curse God and die!" Job replied: (verse 13:15) "Though He slay me, yet will I trust in Him." After Job's friends and family left him, his health, wealth, and honor were restored.

Everything works for good to them who love the Lord with steadfastness.

. . . . . . . . . . . . . . . . . . . . . . . . . . . . . . . . . . . . . . . . .

When ghosts and goblins from the dark past come back to haunt us, we must do as did Paul of Tarsus: "Forget the things that have gone before and press on toward the high calling of God."

When Paul was a very young man he was on the side of those persecuting Christians but after he saw the light, one day on the road to Damacus, his life was changed completely. As he began his new life, there must have been many instances when things from his past came back to haunt him.

Life is like reading a book; when you turn a leaf over, you go on to the next one – ever forward. Paul was learning this, also the fact that God's revealing light was the only thing that could dispel the darkness. Just as the wicked witches and evil spirits of Halloween disappear with morning's light, so will black deeds from the misty past "melt into thin air" when they are obliterated by God's grace and powerful light.

Lowell said, "Light is the symbol of truth" and Plato said, "Light is the shadow of God." If sunlight is a shadow compared to God's light, small wonder Paul was blinded by it. Because we are made in the image of God, His light is reflected in the enlightenment of our intelligence.

J.K. Lord, (1810-1894) an American historian, tells us where we get our enlightenment: "The light of nature, the light of science, and the light of reason, are but as darkness, compared with the divine light which shines only from the word of God."

As a child, the sunflowers that grew on one side of my grandmother's vegetable garden held a fascination for me. The big yellow heads always turned toward the sun whether early or late in the afternoon. Grandmother said, "We can all learn a lesson from the sunflower. They help me to stand tall with head erect and to search for God's guiding light."

It has been said that when God was building the earth He first gave man the light of day and on the last day He gave him the light of reason.

It has been said, "Opportunity knocks once only." This may be true of one particular plan or goal, however, the opportune time may differ with each endeavor and one must learn to recognize it when it comes.

Sometimes we set our goals too high for beginning and we don't recognize, or if we do, we don't take advantage of the smaller opportunities that would be stepping stones to our higher goals. It is like wanting to step to the ladder's top without touching each rung on the way up.

Johnson said it best when he said, "It is common to overlook what is nearby keeping the eye fixed on something remote. In the same manner present opportunities are neglected and attainable good is slighted by minds busied in extensive ranges, and intent upon future advantages. Life, however short, is made shorter by waste of time."

Shakespeare also spoke of opportunities, "There is a tide in the affairs of men, which, taken at the flood, leads one to fortune; omitted, all the voyage of their life is bound in shallows and in miseries; and we must take the current when it serves, or lose our ventures."

We must acknowledge one thing that is more important than opportunity and that is education and preparedness that enables one to recognize and cope with the opportunity when it presents itself. In fact, the more knowledgeable one is of his ultimate goal, the less time is spent in waiting because often one can make opportunities with what the experts call "know-how".

Some of the opportunities that come to us are not for ourselves and these are the hardest to see. Paul of Tarsus, in Galatians 6:10, gives this admonition, "As we have therefore opportunity, let us do good unto all men, especially unto them who are of the household of faith."

Each of us have opportunities for our own ambitions, also for helping others, and now is an opportune time to make new commitments for a closer relationship with God who has said, "My spirit shall not always strive with man…"

Paul made his calling and election sure. Before he died he wrote to Timothy: "I have fought a good fight, I have finished my course, I have kept the faith…." And "….lay hold on eternal life, whereunto thou are also called…."

In today's hectic world patience is a rare virtue, a vanishing commodity that is necessary for a well-balanced and regulated life.

It could well be that God is trying to teach us patience when He does not answer our prayers right away. Excerpts from two scriptures seem to warrant this deduction: "….in the full of time…." And "Wait upon the Lord…."

Patience is an attribute well worth striving for, but it takes much practice, determination and daily application to acquire it. Prayer and meditation are essential helps too. "Patience strengthens the spirit, sweetens the temper, stifles anger, extinguishes envy, subdues pride, bridles the tongue, restrains the hand and tramples upon temptation," said Bishop Horne in the 18th century. If patience can indeed accomplish all of the above, it can terminate many evils.

When God put man upon the earth He told him to do good and warned against evil. Is the world combating evil today or embracing it? The prophet Isaiah in the Old Testament Bible (14:12), and in the book of Luke in the New Testament, tell of Satan being an angel that was cast out of heaven because he became evil and a trouble-maker (Satan means Devil, fallen angel).

God is good and we are made in His image; therefore, it is up to us to banish Satan from the earth? We are told to "overcome evil with good." Immediately, we think that if all the goodness in heaven couldn't influence Satan, while he was there, what chance do we have? Seemingly, none at all, but we are told to try.

Perhaps it's part of our testing to be tempted by the Devil and by telling him to, "get thee behind me, Satan" (Luke 4:8) we are proving ourselves worthy of heavenly citizenship.

A lack of patience is attributed to Satan's influence. He is often the cause of high temper and impatience. Patience is the product of a serene mind and is seldom present when the mind becomes anxious, agitated, depressed or worried.

We must practice patience by taking no thought for tomorrow. It is enough trying to overcome today's evils. Let tomorrow take care of itself. We can live only one day at a time if we are going to live patiently.

What a chaotic world it would be if we were all extremists. The person who goes to opposite extremes in every phase of life must be, of all people, the most miserable. It often causes nervous breakdowns because of stress and the resulting mental fatigue.

Arc you "long-suffering" one minute and "short-tempered" the next? Can you soar upwards from depression's valley to the top of cloud nine and then back down again in a matter of moments? Do things that most people consider trivial seem monstrous and out of proportion to you? There is an old nursery rhyme that accurately describes this type of person: "There was a little girl who had a little curl, right in the middle of her forehead. When she was good, she was very, very good; when she was bad she was horrid!"

We are not speaking here of life's natural rhythm of highs and lows, but of the highs that are way up, and the lows that are down, down, down. There are also extreme personalities that do not fluctuate between the ups and downs. These are the extreme introverts and extroverts. Everyone has the tendency to be slightly on one or the other. The mild introvert is never bored when alone, is usually occupied with handicraft, reading or otherwise engaged in things that interest him; the mild extrovert is happier talking and working with other people.

The extreme introvert is a loner who much prefers privacy, and most think that life is a battle between themselves and the rest of the world. They harbor "pet peeves" and resentments; a deep inferiority complex is common to the extremely introverted person.

A superiority complex is often seen in the extremely extroverted personality, but not always. They love crowds and being the center of attention. Some are known as gossips or neighborhood pests. They seem to have a need to share their every thought with others. Someone said that only business tycoons and extreme extroverts have telephones by their bathtubs.

It behooves all of us to take time out occasionally for self-analysis. It is only by knowing what we really are that we can avoid habits and keep patterns from forming that would lead to extremes.

Colton said, "Extremes beget extremes…." And the English historian, Aleyn (1590 – 1640) said, "No violent extremes endure; a sober moderation stands secure." My belief is that the French essayist and moralist, Jean de la Bruyere, said it best: "Extremes are vicious and proceed from men; compensation is just, and proceeds from God."

• • • • • • • • • • • • • • • • • • • • • • • • • • • • • • • • • • •

The person who doesn't try to hide his, or her, contempt of others is a contemptible human being himself. It is much easier to forgive the one who has wronged you, or even show some resentment toward you and your ideas, than it is to forgive the affronts of utter contempt.

Henry Fielding (1707 -1754), an English novelist, wrote: "There is not in human nature a more odious disposition than a proneness to contempt, which is a mixture of pride and ill nature. Nor is there any which more certainly denotes a bad disposition; for in a good and benign temper, there can be no room for it. It is the truest symptom of a base and bad heart."

Job's wife, in the Old Testament Bible, showed her contempt for Job when she told him to "curse God and die!"

Proverbs (18:3) tells us that "When the wicked cometh, then cometh also contempt and with ignominy reproach" and verse five gives this advice: "It is not good to accept the person of the wicked (the contemptuous person), to overthrow the righteous in judgment."

It is often quite easy to detect the flaws and imperfections in the character of other people; and to love them, despite these faults, is the will of God as expressed in the Ten Commandments and the Beatitudes; to hate them for these faults is contempt.

A good example of this can be seen and heard during election years when the candidates are out campaigning. They may not really hate their opponents but some certainly do express contempt for the other's ideas or way of life or party affiliation. It is this writer's opinion that "slinging mud" on another's reputation is the most contemptible way of showing contempt. May we soon see the day when those who engage in "smear campaigns" will be excluded from the race (contest) and when a president is elected, he will forget about party differences and serve all of the people equally without party favoritism.

Robert South, an English Minister in the 17th century, said, "Contempt naturally implies a man's esteeming himself greater than the person he contemns. He, therefore, that slights and contemns an affront, is properly superior to it." And in connection with the above quote, South told that Socrates, being kicked by a donkey, didn't think it a proper revenge to kick the donkey in return.

Returning good for evil will often squelch contempt. Try returning a compliment for unjust criticism. Is this hard to do? The results are worth it!

Excessive pride can be a monstrous force of evil. An insufficient amount of pride will make one a doormat who has no respect for himself or for those who walk over him.

"There is this paradox in pride; it makes some men ridiculous, but prevents others from being so," said Colton in the 17th century. And the Dutch scholar Erasmus, in the 15 century, wrote: "As Plato entertained some friends in a room where there was couch richly ornamented, Diogenes came in very dirty, as usual, and getting upon the couch, and trampling on it, said, ' I trampled upon the pride of Plato'." Plato mildly answered, "But with greater pride, Diogenes!"

Spurgeon reveals the deceiving power of pride, "None have more pride than those who dream that they have none. You may labor against vain glory 'til you think you are humble, and the fond conceit of your humility will prove to be pride in full bloom."

Pride is like a compass that always points to self, to a self that assumes more than it really knows. Thus, bringing truth to the old adage, "Pride cometh before a fall." He that desires knowledge must humble himself and become a dedicated servant of God, our only source for gaining wisdom and understanding.

If we are believers, and our spirits are striving to be as God-like as possible, then it is only natural that we understand others of the same purpose better than those who preach, teach, and talk with false pride that implies BIG I, little you. The mind is what counts. The mind that has been trained by the best schools in the land is no more knowledgeable than the alert mind that, on its own, seeks God's help for wisdom and finds it. The God-taught mind is ever-expanding, and has a heart to match.

Pride is the ointment with which the guilt-laden spirit soothes itself; it is used as an antidote by those bitten by jealousy; it is used as a virtuous coverlet for vice and evil. But the coverlet, the antidote, and the ointment defeat their own purpose, revealing the contemptibility of the one seeking self-esteem in that manner. Christians are taught to "judge not" but are given a gauge to determine the worth of a person: "By their fruits ye shall know them." (Matthew 8:20) Selfless means forgetting self but not discarding it, if we are to "love our neighbor as yourself" which is the second greatest commandment in the Bible. Yet we are not to think more highly of ourselves than we ought to think. God can help us to find the happy medium.

Pain, whether it is physical pain or the proverbial heartache, can be devastating.

What is pain? And why must people suffer? These are questions second only to the one about future life: "If a man dies, shall he live again?" We know that pain is associated only with life on this earth. The future life is one of eternal joy, without pain, without suffering of any kind. There will be no night or darkness there. We will bask in God's glorious light and love forever more.

We have a greater capacity for pain than we have for pleasure. Sensations of pleasure are brief, but pain is often prolonged and increases in intensity. Sometimes we think we cannot endure any more pain, and then discover that we can as it grows worse.

In ancient times people thought that anyone who was ill and in pain was demon-possessed. Later, in the days of Christianity, people asked, as they still do, "If God loves us, why does He cause us to suffer pain?" First, and foremost, God does NOT cause us to suffer pain. But He does allow it. Why? There can be any number of reasons why, and known only to God. Some think that God allows pain as a punishment for sin. Others believe that God, at the time of creation, made certain laws to govern the universe that He set into motion and when man breaks one of these rules or regulations, he automatically suffers the consequences.

This writer's thoughts on the subject of pain are these: If we didn't know pain, would we recognize good health? Would happiness mean anything to us if we never experienced unhappiness? Perhaps God allows us to feel the negative in order that we may appreciate the positive. Mankind was blissfully happy in the garden of Eden and could have remained so; but with his God-given gift of free choice, he chose to disobey and break the rules and the laws of God; therefore, his lot outside the garden was filled with pain and suffering.

Why does God allow people to suffer? Especially those who are good people? "We have all sinned and fallen short of the glory of God." There is none good except the Father (God). He makes the rain fall on the just as well as the unjust.

If this world is a testing ground, to prove our worthiness for heaven, perhaps we are rated by the way we cope with the stress, strain and strife of this life which includes pain and suffering.

The people living in 1982 and 1983 are just as hungry for practical psychological counseling as were those living in the 1940s when George W. Crane Ph.D. M.D., eminent psychologist and journalist, was making his radio talks and writing his two syndicated newspaper columns: "Test Your Horse Sense" and "The Worry Clinic".

We live in a mad, mad world according to one script writer; also in a sick, sick world, according to modern psychology. Yes, we live in an age when people do not trust in their own capabilities. The fact that there are so many self-improvement books on the market proves this to be true. Two such books are: <u>Return to Sanity</u> and <u>Don't Grow Old: Grow Up!</u> The bookstores are overflowing with good sellers pertaining to emotional stability, psychological intelligence, your tolerance level, your memory span, your physical stamina, motivation stimuli and various kinds of IQ tests.

Very few people can score 100 points on those tests. Yet, if we miss two or three questions, our wrong answers worry us and we begin a self-analysis. What is wrong with us? Are we of so much lower intelligence than the one who composed the test? Perhaps we go out and buy a book on brain power. There are many such books on the market. One that comes to mind is: <u>The Magic Power of Your Mind</u> written by Walter Germain

Germain claims that we not only have a subconscious mind, but also a supraconscious and that it has the power to reach beyond the limitation of the conscious mind, dealing with hypnotism, clairvoyance, telepathy and keeps in touch with the supraconscious minds of all other people.

After reading the book, we are so confused that we have forgotten all about the IQ tests and have something new to worry about. (Some of these far-out things written by psychiatrists may be responsible for people needing their services.)

For depressed people who are tired of life, Fulton J. Sheen has written the book, <u>Life Is Worth Living.</u> For those who want friends and don't know how to get them, read Dale Carnegie's book, <u>How to Win Friends and Influence People</u>. In 1958 over 4,126,000 copies had been sold and his <u>How to Stop Worrying and Start Living</u> was in its 29th printing.

The best counseling can be obtained from the Holy Bible. Choose one with a good concordance and index. Look for the subject that worries you. Then read all the scriptures pertaining to that subject. This is not only your best counseling but the least expensive and the most rewarding.

Many writers, at this time of year, are searching and researching their minds and all available literature on the subject, trying to find something new and different to say about Christmas. Sometimes it's more advantageous to stop the frantic search and keep still for quiet meditation and lend an ear to the thoughts of the supraconscience.

You may hear, or have the realization, that these words are worth repeating: "For God so loved the world that He gave His only begotten Son (on that first Christmas) that whosoever believes in Him shall not perish but have everlasting life."

No Christmas gift has ever excelled that great gift from our heavenly Father to His sinful and ungrateful children. No enlargement of the imagination, no play on words, or coining of new words and phrases, can tell the real meaning of Christmas as does this one verse of scripture.

We have all read or heard the Christmas story as told by Luke (2:1-16). We have seen it in pageants and plays put on by schools and church groups. There have been boys dressed in their dad's colorful bathrobes and their mother's turbans, as the wise men from the east; boys wearing shag rug sarongs as shepherds from the fields; little boys and girls in white, with white gauze wings hanging awry, singing "Glory to God in the highest and on earth, peace and good will to all men," the blanket-wrapped doll in the straw-lined manger, a bearded boy playing Joseph and little Mary leaning over the doll with loving care.

Yes, both Luke and Matthew gave us, in detail, the historical events of that first Christmas. But John 3:16, tells it all, simply and eloquently, in one sentence. He used the method of modern Digest Books and condensed the story to its basic truth. That one sentence tells us that God loves us, cares for us, sacrificed His most cherished possession that we would not perish but have everlasting life. And not only that we might have life, but also to have it more abundantly! That's what Christmas is all about.

Whether we're ready for it or not the New Year is here! The old one has gone and there is no chance of changing or preventing anything that happened last year. It will soon be recorded history. The historians will sift through the records and publish our accomplishments and our failures for future students to study. We hope they learn from our mistakes and make more headway toward world peace than we have.

As long as there are nations at war with each other, even though we are not directly involved, we cannot have world peace. We now know that war spreads like wild fire because the world is a much smaller place than formerly thought. Faster modes of travel and modern communication systems that show us battles and events of war, live – while it's happening – by satellite, and we judge which side is right and which is wrong.

Although there are many more people wanting peace, a handful of international war-mongers and rabble-rousers can upset an entire nation, paving the way to war, especially if some terrible crime or act of espionage is committed.

Each new year brings many changes, changes in lifestyles, changes in governments, in laws, in nation's responsibilities and in local civic and church affairs. The old adage that "nothing ever changes except change" may be true, but they are happening so fast that the present is outmoded before the next change is finalized.

Gone are the days when one could sit musing, listening to Guy Lombardo, and make resolutions for a better year. Resolutions (except those that deal with character) that seem right on Jan. 1 may be undesirable and self-defeating by the end of February. Such hectic changes are what inspire writers to write such things as, "Stop the World I want to get off."

Since time and change are interrelated, perhaps we should heed Baxter's admonition: "spend your time in nothing which you know must be repented of; in nothing which you could not review with a quiet conscience on your dying bed; in nothing which you might not safely and properly be found doing if death should surprise you in the act.

Nobility is a robe of distinction and all who wear it are honored and esteemed among men. We are speaking here of nature's noblemen; the ones endowed with knowledge and worth, with respectability and goodness, a liberal and benevolent mind that deals with all men impartially. Not the nobility of royalty of which the king of England, James the 1st (1566 – 1625), said, "I can make a Lord, but only the Almighty can make a gentleman."

Earls and dukes and lords and knights of the realm may sometimes be presumed to be noble when in reality they aren't. Many rulers have been mean and selfish and fit into the category of those spoken by W. H. Dollinger, the sage who said, "No man can ever be noble who thinks first and only of himself."

Of the nobility of royalty, John Ford said, "Titles of honor to his title." But Plato and Ruskin seem to say it best with: "If a man be endued with generous mind, this is the best kind of nobility." (Plato) "It is better to be nobly remembered, than nobly born." (Ruskin)

One remembers a lowly carpenter who was the essence of nobility. Every woman should recognize the fact that it was He who first showed respect for women, both in public and in the home. He was kind and protective to the woman at the well who was considered an enemy of his people; He respected Mary Magdalene and raised her standard of living; He was a good friend to Mary and Martha, the sisters of Lazarus; and on the cross, just before dying, He provided for His Mother – a home with John. How can any woman ignore Him?

He set an example for the men of the world to follow, and it is not wealth, nor ancestry, but good conduct and a noble disposition. It is man's willingness to know and obey the laws of God that make him truly great and noble. Also, the world is slowly learning that because two men think differently, neither may be wicked.

Nobility is not a lost cause, it needs incentive and promoting.

The thoughts that we harbor have more to do with shaping our lives than does our social relations, our training, our environment , or our closest circle of friends and advisers. Our thoughts cause our successes or our failures, as they form our character.

The nutritionist says, "You are what you eat." But God said that we are what we think, when He said, "As a man thinketh in his heart, so is he." He also said, "it is not what goes into the mouth that defiles a man, but that which comes out of the mouth." And the words that come out of the mouth depend on the nature of the thoughts.

Clear thoughts promote understanding, but understanding cannot cleanse an impure and prejudiced heart; neither can it impart goodness to an evil heart unless the thoughts are pure as well as clear.

Domergue, a French grammarian (1745 – 1810) said, "Some people study all their lives, and at their death they have learned everything except to think."

Just as we must learn to conserve and use energy wisely, so we must learn to harness our thoughts and not let our thinking run wild in unguided confusion. An unbridled mind is the Devil's workshop, and if we don't control our minds, he will come in and try to force his ideas upon us.

Computers are not new. God has endowed each of us with a personal computer (brain). When fed properly, its memory contains the solutions to most of our problems. If there is a problem it can't solve, we can always call on its manufacturer for help with the problem, and if necessary repair the machine.

The human brain also needs rest and if it is properly in tune with its maker, it will, at this time, become a receiver instead of a transmitter.

Most of us need the warning of Bacon, "A man could do well to carry a pencil in his pocket, and write down the thoughts of the moment. Those that come unsought for are commonly the most valuable, and should be secured, because they seldom return."

One cannot kill time without injuring eternity, according to Thoreau. This is what we complain of having the least of, yet we don't make the most of what little we have. Wasted time is the blot that cannot be removed because time, once lost, can never be regained.

Mrs. Lydia H. Sigourney, American author (1791 – 1865), expressed her feelings about lost time this way, "Lost, yesterday, somewhere between sunrise and sunset, two golden hours, each set with 60 diamond minutes. No reward is offered, for they are gone forever!"

What is time? Is it dates on a calendar? Is it the interlude between sunset and sunrise or vice versa? Is it the four seasons of the year? Or is it the distance between birth and death? We know that time is a part of eternity, and that eternity is the life of the soul.

What's the beginning and ending of the soul? When God finished molding man, from the clay on the earth, He breathed into him the breath of life that became a living soul. As far as man is concerned that's when his soul began, but this is not to say that it didn't exist somewhere before it was given to him.

This spiritual breath and soul is the part of man that is in the image of God. It is the only part that survives the physical death and will live forever. We, with our finite minds, cannot comprehend the real meaning of the words "forever" and "eternity".

How does God see time? Surely not as a creation-to-destruction epoch! We are not privilege to that information, but one cannot imagine God's thinking of time as being past, present or future as man does. Man has those three points of view regarding any object in time, however, he is still handicapped because he knows only the immediate past and can learn only the immediate future that fall within his limited range of three score and 10 years (maybe a few more, and maybe a lot less). We cannot compare our few years of time with God's eons.

Time is a rare commodity and opportunity can't knock on the door of lost time.

Science is knowledge and it is certainly not the enemy of religious teachings that most people think it to be. Oliver Wendell Holmes, American poet and author who died in 1894, said, "As knowledge advances, science ceases to scoff at religion; and religion ceases to frown on science. The hour of mockery by the one, and of reproof by the other, is passing away. Henceforth they will dwell together in unity and good will. They will mutually illustrate the wisdom, power, and grace of God. Science will adorn and enrich religion; and religion will ennoble and sanctify science."

Tyron Edwards wrote, "It has been said that science is opposed to, and in conflict with, religion. But the history of the former shows that the greater its progress, and the more accurate its investigations and results, the more plainly it is seen not only not to clash with the latter, but in all things to confirm it. The very sciences from which objections have been brought against religion have, by their own progress, removed those objections, and in the end furnished full confirmation of the inspired word of God."

We sometimes expect too much of science and scientists. Because they have discovered so many things, it encourages us to think that, maybe someday soon, they will solve all of life's mysteries for us. Men of science have walked, or floated, in space and also on the moon, but they have not yet determined origin and therefore, they cannot determine destiny. Only God knows the answer to that.

Men like to think of God as being a man, but the Bible says that He is a spirit. To some people the word "spirit" implies the supernatural, which they consider the same as voo-doo-ism. One person said, "I won't believe what I can't see!" Yet he does. He believes in tomorrow when all he can see is today. And he sees today for only one second at a time.

Dr. J.G. Holland said, "God pity the man of science who believes in nothing but what he can prove by scientific methods; for if ever a human being needed divine pity he does."

• • • • • • • • • • • • • • • • • • • • • • • • • • • • • • • • • • • • • • • • •

Throughout cities, towns, villages, around the world, there are buildings called churches. Some are imposing structures, others are more modest. We call them churches, but the name is a misnomer.

A local pastor told his congregation, "I notice some of you call this your church. This is not YOUR church! It is not MY church! It is not OUR church! This is GOD's church!

The people remembered sacrificing for many years to pay for the large building. They remembered the last payment, the burning of the mortgage, and the feeling: "It is all ours now!" "We are out from under! With God's help, we made it." They held a special prayer meeting, thanking God for the edifice and dedicating it to His glory and their worship. Now they were told, "This is not your church!"

A former pastor once said, "I am going to say something this morning that may shock some of you who think this is God's church. This is not God's church! When we leave, we leave an empty building. God won't be in it! God lives in the hearts of His people. When we leave, God goes with us."

The words of the people in the Bible seem contradictory if you take only one quote from each one, as was done here. The first minister was speaking against pride and boasting. The second minister was emphasizing the true church which would be received into heaven, people, not buildings.

A Sunday School teacher gave this writer her first (preschool) biology lesson when she said, "My body is a house. My eyes are windows. My heart is an inner room. God wants to live in there and so does the devil. I have to let one of them in. My ears will listen to the one that I choose, and my hands and feet will do his bidding. I chose God. I still do, but I must continually remember that God will not stay where He is disobeyed, and if He moves out, the devil will move in. The devil thrives on disobedience, sin, corruption, and everything that would separate me from God. To be separated from God would be hell."

. . . . . . . . . . . . . . . . . . . . . . . . . . . . . . . . . . . . . . . . .

What are the enduring things in this life?  Certainly not financial security; fortunes can be made and lost overnight, and in the rise and fall of nations, currency can become obsolete, as did the Confederate money of the past in the southern United States.

Love and friendship was once considered durable, but human emotions are not very stable today.  The number of divorces proves that love (the earthly kind) doesn't endure.  The frequency of family members turning against each other, and the long-time friends who have ceased to communicate, show the inconsistency and instability of today's society.

The pen may or may not be "mightier than the sword", but we must acknowledge the durability of WORDS.  Words spoken hundreds and thousands of years ago come to us through history books and the Bible.  The earliest words were handed down by mouth from father to son, from generation to generation, before the use of pen and papyrus.

Whether spoken in anger and hate or in tenderness and love, the kindly cordiality or biting cynicism, words do live on forever and are instantly recalled when memory prompts.

If you have resolved to speak kindly all year, remember it takes a calm mind and kind thought to produce kind words.  If you allow yourself to be hurried and harried, you might find yourself using Rice Krispy language and "snap" heads off as you "crackle and pop" your way into a nervous breakdown.

Here are four different thoughts about these words:

1. "Many a treasure besides Ali Baba's is unlocked with a verbal key." (Henry Van Dyke)
2. "Although words exist for the transmission of ideas, some produce such violent disturbance in our feelings that the role they play in the transmission of ideas is lost in the background." (Albert Einstein)
3. "God wove a web of loveliness, of clouds, and stars and birds, but made not anything at all so beautiful as words." (Anna Hempstead Branch)
4. "Words are the sole expression of the soul and if one interprets them correctly, one knows immediately who owns, guides, and leads that soul into action and knows in advance whether that action will be worthy or unworthy." (Esther B. King)

Why do people work?  Is it because they must eat regularly?  Because they want good health and prestige?  Because they fear public opinion if they don't?  Or is it because they really like working?

Sir James M. Barrie said, "Nothing is really **work** unless you would rather be doing something else."  If you are not doing the kind of work you prefer, because it is not available to you, the work you are doing can be made more enjoyable by learning to like it.

One of our earliest laws (just before the one concerning the Sabbath) says, "Six days shalt thou labor....," not four and a half, not five, but six.  Of course, at that time the population wasn't so great, the machines of the Machine Age were yet to be invented, without electricity, there were no nightshifts or daylight saving time.

It could be that some of those who complain about not having the right kind of work do really not want to work at all.  People who seem to live only for the weekends and holidays may, consciously or subconsciously, want every day to be a holiday.  One CAN work too hard at playing.

People have contradicting thoughts about work.  Of the following quotes, the first seems to be a workaholic; the second, not disposed to work; and the third seems more balanced in his thinking:  "I believe in work, hard work, and long hours of work.  Men do not break down from overwork, but from worry and dissipation." (Charles E. Hughes)  "I like work; it fascinates me.  I can sit and look at it for hours." (Jerome K. Jerome)  "We have too many people who live without working, and we have altogether too many who work without living." (Dean Charles R. Brown)

In our complicated society many irritating things could happen any day while at work.  Don't hate your job because of them.  Use diplomacy!  Think about what Calvin Coolidge said:  "...work is not a curse; it is the prerogative of intelligence, the only means to manhood, and the measure of civilization."

The beginning of wisdom can be found in these four questions: "Who am I? Why am I here? What is my purpose in life? What am I going to do about it?"

There's no excuse for anyone not finding the answers. The Holy Bible reveals them; also the sages, wise men of the ages, have recorded this information. Richard Cecil, English minister who died in 1777 at age 29 said, "There are but two classes of the wise; the men who serve God because they have found Him, and the men who seek Him because they have found Him not." All recorded ideas on the subject of wisdom are similar.

God is the source of all wisdom, and if we would be wise, we must seek Him diligently and earnestly "while He may yet be found" because He tells us through the scriptures: "My spirit shall not always strive with man."

As one grows in knowledge, it doesn't pay to be conceited about it, or as the Bible says, "Be not wise in your own conceit." Quite often it is the one who disclaims wisdom that is the wisest of all. If others think you are wise, you might be, even if you don't think so. The more knowledge that is gained sharpens the feelings of inadequacy and the realization of how much more there is to learn.

The wisdom of one generation may be the ruination of the next or it can be the salvation of it, depending on whether or not the preceding generation had God-given wisdom or were wise in their own conceit. A generation may gain considerable knowledge; however, the ability to learn is not, of itself, wisdom. Wisdom is knowing how to use that knowledge in the right way.

Spurgeon, in the 18th century, wrote: "Many men know a great deal, and all are the greater fools for it. There is no fool so great a fool as a knowing fool. But to know how to use knowledge is wisdom."

Most of the world's governments are in some kind of chaos. They must have knowledge to have won, or taken, such high offices, but do they have the wisdom to put that knowledge into action and use it in the right way? Are they Godly men? Do they go to Him for help and advice?

Having just read in a current newspaper this sentence, "Everyone has problems" my conscious mind was beginning to agree when the subconscious mind pushed through and asked a question: "How can you be sure that this is true?"

"Well," mediated my conscious mind, "the truck drivers are having problems, the farmers are having problems, and the taxpayers are having problems….."

"Wait a minute!" commanded my subconscious mind. "You're repeating what you've heard and read. What do you actually know about it? It could be that the field is overcrowded for truckers; the farmers could be building fine new homes and going into debt for cars, trucks, and elaborate farm machinery instead of saving for the years of crop failures."

There can't be a bountiful harvest every year indefinitely and the very nature of farming requires them to "lay-by" enough to last through one to seven lean years. Some taxpayers aren't patriotic and would rather see the nation fall than to pay hard-earned, or easy-come dollars to help with the economy."

My conscious mind (which is the source of thoughts) is still doubtful. "But what about this statement, 'Everyone has problems'?" The subconscious mind (which is the source of power) asks, "If so, what are your problems today?"

"Plenty!" I thought. The washer is loaded with clothes, and I'm out of soap. The car won't start. With no way to get to the store, dinner will be leftovers plus maybe something out of a tin can. Also, the phone is out of order, and I'm reading this to forget my problems."

"You call those problems? They're only temporary inconveniences! Think about it as you read the next article."

My eyes scanned the next article's heading. The article was about a woman with a terminally ill husband, and she had a son in prison, and she was having money problems. Despite that, she was thanking God for her many blessings.

My problems vanished. Dinner of leftover ham and canned beans was enjoyed and blessed.

Words are the most beautiful things! Words are the most hurtful things! Words, once spoken, are beyond recall, and their durability is forever. Words spoken in anger by friends and loved ones are the hardest to receive and almost impossible to forget.

Words spoken thoughtlessly, heedlessly, and needlessly, in the heat of passion and personal prejudice, especially at town meetings or in civic groups, can cause divisions among people who should be working in unity for the common good. If through unkind or ill-chosen words, the differences become too great; the whole project may have to be dropped and will be of benefit to no one. It will be just a lot of wasted time, energy, passion, and more likely than not, a few friends. No one has so many friends that he can sacrifice a few because of an unbridled tongue and hard words.

Some familiar words are "forgive and forget", and "If you can't forget, you haven't forgiven". These thoughts are taken from the Biblical verses that speak of our sins being forgiven; even though "red as crimson", God will cleanse or wash them "whiter than snow" and remember them against us no more.

This writer is of the opinion that the mind of God doesn't forget anything, and interprets the above scripture to mean that He will not hold them against us anymore if we are truly repentant. When people tell us that they are sorry for their harsh words, it is easy to forgive, but memory is a fickle thing. Who can train their memory to the extent that some passing event, certain words or remarks, witnessing a like circumstance, either in fact or fiction, won't prompt a recollection of words that was thought to be forgotten?

Emerson said, "A man cannot speak (or write) but he judges and reveals himself. With his will, or against his will, he draws his portrait to the eye of others by every word. Every opinion reacts on him who utters it."

There is an old song (my mother used to sing) titled "Kind Words Can Never Die." The words are beautiful. It tells of the beauty and persuasiveness of kind words, and of course, they never die but live on forever, even behind us after we are gone. They are remembered by those we love.

Great leaders must always use kind, gentle and thoughtful words and on occasions when they must speak sternly, their words are not offensive.

How far should a Christian have to go to appease his brothers and sisters?  The Bible says, "If your brother asks you to go with him one mile, go with him two.  And if your brother asks for your cloak, give him your coat also."

Was Jesus speaking here of only those who were in need?  Or did He mean just anyone who asks of you?  Even if they have as much of this world's goods as you have?

Some people are doers; some are manipulators, who get others to do for them.  The manipulator sometimes whines and wheedles and is pessimistic about everything in general, from the high cost of living to the weather and personal health.  Health can be impaired by too much negative and pessimistic thinking.

We have all known people who seem to enjoy "poor health" because of the attention they get from family and friends.  Many years ago a neighbor whom we called "Aunt Polly" had been ill for many years, and in bed most of the time.  Her husband cooked, and was helped by neighbors from time to time, and took her meals to her bed, and waited on her hand and foot when he was not at work.  He died in his early 50's, and Aunt Polly made a miraculous recovery.  She got a full time job and started going out in the evenings.

The elderly, especially, resent the impositions of connivers and manipulators because they have so little time left, and they would rather use it to help the ill, the handicapped, and the underprivileged.

How far should one go to appease and pacify friends and relatives who are as physically and financially able as you are to do the things they ask you to do?  Christ is the Christian's example, and He was always helping people.  However, a closer study of the scriptures reveal that the ones He helped were the ill (both physically and spiritually), the lame and blind and the underprivileged.

The manipulator is very persuasive.  A common approach is: "Won't you do this for me?  You do it so much better than I, and I would so appreciate it."  Or the manipulator might say, "I don't feel very well today, won't you help me?"  The imposed upon usually complies and thinks of the unemployed who would love to have the job he is doing for nothing for someone who could well afford to pay.

The Bible says, "Greater love hath no man than this, that a man lay down his life for his friends" (John 15:13).  But is the constant moocher and deadbeat really a friend?  The Romans had a name for moochers: stoics.  Byron, the English poet, said of stoicism, "To have feelings for no one is the true social art of the world's stoics, men without a heart."

Money has been a "bone of contention" since its inception. Because of it all nations, families and individuals have the problem of balancing their budgets. Money, or the lack of it, is often the direct cause of murders, thefts, poverty, divorces, etc.

The hand of those who are holding the most money, whether it be the Royal Crown, the oil magnates, the dictators, or prosperous democratic governments, have the world's power over the "have-nots". And when those who have the money and the power can fix or set interest rates, their wealth can snowball into almost uncountable riches.

If you are a Bible reader you will recall how Jesus overturned the tables of the Money changers in the Temple at Jerusalem because they were taking too much profit and for using a house that was dedicated to God for the purpose of doing business for profit.

The first two are three years of maintaining a home should prove that there can be no balanced budget until money is handled well and wisely. All of us would, sooner or later, be bankrupt if we gave in to all the requests that come through the mail. Some say, "Please mark the box of the amount you wish to give, $100 or$200 or $500 or a life membership for $1000. Some show pictures of starving children from a country other than the one making the request; others have a Grand Central Station box number for a return address.

Christians believe that God has allowed them to have money (either by giving them the health and strength to earn it or to their parents through inheritance) and that He holds them responsible for how they use it.

We know that unprincipled people will go to great lengths to obtain money. A Roman philosopher, Lucius Annaeus Seneca, who was born four years before Christ, said, "Money does all things for reward. Some are pious and honest as long as they thrive upon it, but if the devil himself gives better wages, they soon change their party."

It is <u>not true</u> that the Bible says, "Money is the root of all evil." Money is the root of our livelihood on earth; God allows us to have it and instructs us about its use. It <u>is</u> true that the Bible says, "The love of money is the root of all evil: which while some coveted after, they have erred from the faith, and pierced themselves through with many sorrows." (First Timothy 6:10)

In the spring everything is new. Just look around, there's new life everywhere. In the great outdoors we see the early flowers, the budding of bushes and trees, and the bright green grass springing up through the brown dead refuse of winter. The birds are singing, the sun is again after the rain, and the whole world seems alive with promise.

What is there about spring that affects us so? It can fill one with wonder when walking through a field of new clover, or driving down the highway and seeing the wild flowers waving in the wind. In Texas, the wildflowers might be bluebonnets, Indian paint brushes, pink primroses, yellow ladies' slippers, field daisies and violets, etc. We don't fully realize what it is that stirs our souls to such joyous jubilation until we view the bed of Easter lilies in all their regal beauty and then the words of the scripture comes to mind, "Consider the lilies of the fields, they toil not- neither do they spin- yet Solomon in all of his glory was not arrayed like one of these."

It is then that we become aware of the fact that all this visible newness of life has meaning. We remember the first human-fruit of the earth who rose to new life and said that because He lives, we shall live also; because He has risen, we shall likewise rise to a new life. With this understanding, spring becomes more than lovely fragrant flowers in a beautiful world. It is an annual reminder of the eternal hope of man to be with God, and that God has not forgotten him. Just look around at the physical evidence!

We awaken from a deep night's sleep every morning to a new earthly day in which we have free choice to do as we wish with the daylight hours. We may choose to work, or not to work; to live and exemplary life, or one of sin and degradation.

The time will come (as surely as time will come for the birth of an unborn baby) when we, each and every one of us, will awaken from sleep to greet an eternal day or eternal darkness. There will be no need of sun where God is because He is the light. The Prince of Darkness is separated from God, so he and his followers, shall dwell in utter darkness and despair.

Behold! He stands at the door and knocks. Today is the day of salvation! But time is limited because God said, "My spirit shall not always strive with man." Seek Him while He may yet be found!

. . . . . . . . . . . . . . . . . . . . . . . . . . . . . . . . . . . . . . . . . .

We have previously discussed how unhealthy negative attitudes, unkind thoughts, and suppressed anger can cause jangled nerves, fierce headaches, emotional stress, and tensions which, if not relieved, can put one in the hospital.

I, slipping in that direction, ask the following question, "Isn't a true child of God supposed to be calm?" What is a Christian to do? A Christian will remember that the reason he is called a Christian is because he has accepted Christ as his example to follow and is committed to obey His teachings. As the song says, "He is Able to Deliver Thee" – from any situation. Think of how He stilled the waters and stopped the raging sea. Also, how He quieted the storms and calmed the winds. Can He not also calm the stress and strain and overwrought emotions in the human heart and mind?

Science has not yet discovered, so we don't really know, the exact connecting link between the heart, the mind, and the soul. But we know it's there. We know that we can train the mind if we put forth the time and effort. Also, that the conscious mind promptly reveals the thoughts of the heart and "as a man thinketh in his heart, so is he." The subconscious mind furnishes the power to control and activate the heart and soul, and give strength of purpose to right desires.

To get acquainted with the subconscious, and in tune with the power of the universe, one must meditate quietly and often. An overactive mind can't relax nor channel its thought without this power. Also an overactive tongue cripples the ears. One must stop and listen for the voice of the subconscious.

The same voice that told the wind and the waves, "Peace, be still", can also calm the turmoil and strife in the human heart. Without the help of the Holy Spirit we "have ears that hear not" and "eyes that see not".

The secret of relaxation lies within the inner self and is not due to outside causes. A sedative may calm for the duration of the sedative and is no longer effective. Help must come from an inward determination.

Most frustrations and vexations are caused by material or trivial things that seem big at the moment. We are all prone to make mountains out of molehills.

One cannot but admire the person who says, "I don't want to be obligated to anyone", but only if he is talking about keeping his honest debts paid. We are prone to over look the fact that there are so many obligations that money cannot pay. Money can't repay gifts of time, talent, and love that we have received.

There are obligations to parents who have nurtured, protected, and loved their children for the first one-fifth or one-sixth of their lives (18 to 20 years). There are obligations to relatives who have been there when needed, through births, deaths, illnesses, through both the tragedies and blessings of life. We also owe a debt to our friends who celebrate with us at weddings, baptisms, birthdays, anniversaries, and gala events. Also, we owe a debt to those who are happy for us at graduation, promotions, inheritances, honors and recognitions received.

So, when a person says proudly, "I am obligated to no one!" It is a statement too broad to accept, because everyone is in moral debt to others. There may be a few loners who do not have the support of friends because they shun people and don't want friends. Perhaps the reason they don't is because they don't want to give of themselves in return, but this is the exception rather than the rule.

The way to repay parents is with respect, love and obedience, (if they are righteous people, regarding this, read Ephesians 6:1) honor and with physical support if necessary. The way to repay friends is to be there for them when needed, as they have (or may not have) been there for you.

(Please note that in the above discussion of people dealing with people, the simple words "committed or commitment" and "relationship", although applicable, were not used. Modern usage of those words seems to have only one meaning which, to this writer, eliminates them for general usage.)

Shakespeare said, "The voice of parents is the voice of Gods, for to their children they are heaven's lieutenants." And Bacon said, "Parents who wish to train up their children in the way they should go, must go in the way in which they would have their children go."

H.W. Beecher spoke of obligations to friends when he said, "It is one of the severest tests of friendship to tell your friend his faults. – so to love a man that you cannot bear to see a stain upon him, and to speak painful truth through loving words, that is friendship."

Modern America has become accustomed to a way of life that can't possibly endure forever; if past histories of other nations tell us anything at all, they reveal this fact.

This column is not taking a "prophet of doom" attitude, but looking at life realistically in the light of past history. Neither are we speaking here of true or false economies, of influence or affluence, of political maneuvering or civilian planning, of international trysts or doubts, of alliances or alienations, but of worldwide change and what causes it.

Years of general crop failures could cause famine that would eliminate fast foods and microwave ovens which seem to be essential to the young, working wife. A disappearance of engine fuel could start us walking again, or riding bicycles. We couldn't go back to the ox-cart, goat-cart, or the horse and buggy; there wouldn't be enough oxen, goats, or horses, not for many years.

It is seldom one big catastrophe causing world change, but a gradual shifting of attitudes, ideas, life styles, inventions, discoveries, and new leadership, etc. It comes about so gradually that we can realize the change only when we think of how different things were 10 or 20 years ago.

There will certainly be race changes in the years to come. With only one race restricting their families to one or two children, while other races are producing prolifically, that one race will soon take a "back seat" as the Indians did when people from other countries came pouring in.

We are not, necessarily, thinking of the rightness or wrongness of situations, but of things that can cause change. Some changes are better in the long run, others are not. If we all practice awareness and are cognizant of where certain changes could lead us, we would be better prepared for the outcome.

Burke, a famous English Statesman and orator, said, "If a great change is to be made in human affairs, the minds of men will be fitted to it; the general opinions and feelings will draw that way. Every fear and hope will forward it; and they who persist in opposing this mighty current will appear rather to resist the decrees of Providence itself, than the mere designs of men. They will not be so much resolute and firm as perverse and obstinate." And Bacon said, "He that will not apply new remedies must expect new evils."

Everything changes except God. "He is the same, yesterday, today, and forever." Our attitudes, our belief in Him, our obedience to His laws, all determine whether future earthly changes will benefit us or not. If God be for us who can be against us? The question is: Are we for Him?

Before we can have a thousand years of peace on this earth someone must bring forth a better prevention for wars.

Remembering eating cornbread for breakfast, as a little girl, during World War I, and eating cereal without sugar during World War II, having a son in the service during the Korean War, and witnessing the lack of patriotism during, and after, the Viet Nam War brings only one conclusion: four wars for one country in one lifetime is four too many!

Shortages of flour, sugar, or any other commodities are of much less concern than the situations on the battlefields. During an alert test on the TV a few days ago, the words of John McRae came to mind, "In Flanders fields the poppies blow between the crosses, row on row, that mark our place; and in the sky the larks, still bravely singing, fly scarce heard amid the guns below."

Memory also returned to the Curtis Grade School in Orange, Texas where a classmate who had chosen the poem "In Flanders Field" for her declamation, and practiced it before the class, brought tears and applause. The war wasn't far enough behind us.

This writer also remembers the words of Woodrow Wilson (president of the United States from 1913 to 1921), "It is a fearful thing to lead this great peaceful people into war, into the most terrible and disastrous of all wars, civilization itself seeming to be in the balance. But the right is more precious than peace, and we shall fight for the things which we have always carried nearest our hearts – for democracy, for the right of those who submit to authority to have a voice in their own governments, for the right and liberties of small nations, for a universal dominion of right by such a concert of free peoples as shall bring peace and safety to all nations and make the world itself at last free."

No nation is ever free to do anything it wants if what it wants to do isn't right in the sight of God.

Anatole France (1844 – 1924), French author, years before atomic energy was discovered wrote, "Universal peace will be realized, not because man will become better, but because a new order of things, a new science, new economic necessities, will impose peace."

But no matter what happens to this old world, the true child of God is promised deliverance! Not necessarily in the flesh because the true child of God is spirit. God is spirit.

• • • • • • • • • • • • • • • • • • • • • • • • • • • • • • • • • • • • • • • • • •

There is a poison much stronger than any chemical compound or liquid. It can destroy families and separate friends. It is more deadly than a snakes' venom. That poison is "hate". Hate is a negative word that we can all do without.

Hate is an attitude of the mind and heart that should never be experienced. It is the enemy of love and everything that is godly. Hate is often the result of suspicions, rumors, jealousies, and more often than not is accompanied by an enormous sense of guilt. Guilt and hate feelings can, and usually do, drastically change one's disposition. The personality cannot thrive and grow with so much evil in the system, so the body begins to suffer. It can make of one a warped and twisted cynic or shrew, or if the inward struggle between good and evil is equal, a nervous breakdown could be the consequence.

Love and hate have always been associated with good and evil. We must disagree with the writer who wrote of love and hate thusly, "There is only a very thin line separating the two." What separates the two is God, and He is certainly more than a very thin line.

Animosity towards another human being denotes a lack of understanding, a failure to put oneself in the other person's place or circumstances or as the old Indian said, "Walk for miles in his moccasins."

Admittedly, it is not always easy to love the unlovely, to be kind to tyrants, to turn the other cheek when slapped, to help the needy who have squandered their substance in riotous living and show no repentance. But those are the Christians tasks! Alone we couldn't do it but with God in us, His yoke is easy and His burdens are light. We can dislike a person's ways but not the person himself whom we must try to win.

Francios Rochefoucauld (1630 – 1680), a French courtier and moralist, said, "When our hatred is violent, it sinks us even beneath those we hate."

Plutarch wrote, "If you hate your enemies, you will contract such a vicious habit of mind as by degrees will break out upon those who are your friends, or those who are indifferent to you."

We should all be able to say as did Booker T. Washington, this simple statement, "I shall never permit myself to stoop so low as to hate any man."

If love indeed makes the world go round, then hate stops it and tears it apart.

The person who is always bubbling over with enthusiasm is the envy of many and nothing is quite so contagious if it is honest and sincere. But care must be taken not to confuse enthusiasm with excitement which to the casual observer sometimes appears the same. But an excess of excitement may hide a deficiency of enthusiasm because enthusiasm runs deep whereas excitement is shallow and on the surface.

John Sterling (1806 – 1844), an English poet, wrote, "Enthusiasm is grave, inward, self-controlled; mere excitement is outward, fantastic, hysterical, and passing in a moment from tears to laughter from one aim to its very opposite."

The Greeks give the word its noblest and truest definition. They say, "Enthusiasm signifies God in us." And Coleridge tells us that if we "enlist the interests of stern morality and religious enthusiasm in the cause of political liberty, as in the time of the old Puritans, it will be irresistible."

We do know that nothing really great has ever been accomplished without incentive and enthusiasm and still greater things could happen if everyone practiced the art of self-control, thus encouraging the growth of brain power. School teachers urge their students to use their full potential. That's another way of saying, "Think! Think! Think!" And that requires enthusiasm for the subject at hand.

Napoleon Bonaparte, emperor and commander of the French legions, was considered a good soldier. He said an army had to have three things: food, weapons, and morale, and the greatest of these was morale. Their moral and mental condition with respect to courage, discipline, confidence, enthusiasm and willingness to endure hardship, was his primary concern. The French have a phrase, "esprit de corps" whose literal meaning in English would be "spirit of body". But that doesn't quite cover the actual meaning which is a sense of union and of common interests and responsibilities, as developed among a body of persons associated together.

We don't need a Napoleon if we practice self-discipline and mind control. Nowhere is esprit de corps more noticeable than in Christianity. An anti-Christian of high rank once said, "Behold, how they love one another!"

As the Greeks have said, "God is within us" and God is love. The Savior of the world said, "This one last commandment I give unto you; love one another as I have loved you."

· · · · · · · · · · · · · · · · · · · · · · · · · · · · · · · · · · · · · · · · ·

Have you read the historical account of the Greek philosopher, Justin, who became a Christian about 132 A.D?

Justin was born in Neapolis, a city of Samaria located in northern Palestine which was then a province of Rome. His family was of Greek origin, so he did not grow up inside the native culture of Samaria and was unfamiliar with the Hebrew's language, religion and laws.

He was highly educated, having several excellent tutors. Then he began to travel extensively while still a young man and he had the yearning to investigate for himself the many different schools of philosophy.

At this time Rome had many religions, all pagan, all believing there was plenty of room in the heavens for as many gods as one wanted to believe. These religions were very tolerant of each other. But Judaism and Christianity were moving in from the East and refusing to offer the customary sacrifices to the images of the deified Caesars and trouble was brewing.

There had been a lull in the persecutions of Christians but when Marcus Aurelius came into power, the ranks of the Christians had so multiplied that "these enemies of our gods" were being executed in Asia Minor, in Africa, and on the Rhone, as well as in Rome. Marcus was considered a humane philosopher but he ignored these persecutions.

While Lucian, the cynic, was writing, "….the Christians, you know, worship to this day the enchanter who was crucified in Palestine for founding their weird sect." Justin was studying with the stoics, the Aristotlians, the Pythagoreans, and the eminent Platonists, to whose ideas he became strongly attached.

Justin was writing, "Without philosophy and right reason, no man can possess practical judgment. Philosophy is the knowledge of reality and the perception of truth; and happiness is the reward of such knowledge and wisdom."

One day in 132 A.D. an elderly Christian dared to talk of Christian philosophy to the learned Justin who always wore his mantel of wisdom (the traditional coarse cloak that protected philosophers from outside interference). After this encounter, Justin wrote that he had "found the oldest, the truest, the most divine of philosophies". Also he wrote, "Think not, O ye Greeks, that I have rashly and without judgment and deliberation departed from the rites of your religion. But I could find in it nothing really sacred and worthy of divine acceptance."

The ancient sages, the early philosophers, modern family counselors and psychiatrists have given a lot of advice about when to talk and when to hold your tongue.

"The tongue is, at the same time, the best part of man, and his worst; with good government, none is more useful; without it, none is more mischievous." This was said by Anarcharsis, a Scythian sage, in the year of 600 B.C.

An unnamed sage wrote, "Beware the tongue that's set on fire of hell, and flames in slander, falsehood, perjury, in malice, idle-talking and thoughtless tales; speak not too much, nor without thought; let truth in all things small or great, dwell on thy lips. Remember, God hath said, 'He that in word offends not, is a perfect man; while he that bridles not his tongue deceives himself and shows his faith in vain'."

In the Bible the tongue is mentioned 26 times. If your Bible has a good concordance, you will find the list of scriptures there. It is fairly obvious that the unknown writer (mentioned above) was inspired by these words from the New Testament, "If any man among you seem to be religious, and bridleth not his tongue, but deceiveth his own heart; this man's religion is vain." (James 1:26)

In the Christian's early teaching, the organ of speech was much discussed. Justin, who was a Greek philosopher – turned Christian, said, "By examining the tongue physicians find out the diseases of the body; and philosophers, the diseases of the mind and heart."

The apostle Paul said in a letter to the Corinthians, "Though I speak with the tongues of men and angels, and have not charity (love), I am become as sounding brass, or a tinkling cymbal."

Some people don't talk very much, others seem to have a tongue that's tied in the middle and loose on both ends. The introverted person may be shy, or find his own thoughts more entertaining, the extrovert is miserable when there's no one around with whom to talk.

A Roman stoic, Marcus Procuis Cato, who lived from 95 to 46 B.C. said, "We cannot control the evil tongues of others; but a good life enables us to disregard them." If our characters are good and we live a circumspect life with our friends and neighbors, we are not a likely target for evil tongues.

"If wisdom's ways you widely seek, five things observe with care: of whom you speak, to whom you speak, and how, and when, and where." – Anonymous.

. . . . . . . . . . . . . . . . . . . . . . . . . . . . . . . . . . . . . .

We do have faith in today's young people. They seem to be seeking more understanding, truer beliefs, with a singleness of purpose that is very gratifying in these troubled and critical times.

An article, in one of Houston's large daily newspapers, reported that many college students were signing for classes in theology. Not that they wanted to make it their life's work but because they though studying religion would help them to better understand their fellowman.

The "flower children", the "hippies", and the "hard rock groups" seem to be going the way of the "flappers" and "jellybeans" of my younger days. They can now be seen for what they really were: a passing fad.

Young people should be taught how to cope at an early age and when they fail at times, as they undoubtedly will, we should give them encouragement instead of disapproval and ridicule. We sometimes perform tasks assigned to them, forgetting that they also learn by trial and error as we do. But, being younger, they feel more inadequate.

Do any of you young readers feel weighed down by your own inadequacies? If so, you are only human because perfection is not for this world. We can only strive toward it.

We must love young people for who they are and as they are, and live a Godly life before them as an example (admitting our mistakes toward them). A good example does more good than all the preaching in the world, and besides, when parents preach to children, the children get the idea that the parent is saying, "Don't do as I do, but as I say for you to do." Believe it or not, our children can see our faults that are hidden from ourselves.

If you can't talk over the heads of children nor talk down to them, if you can't lay down the law and preach to them, how can they be reached? By inspiring them and gaining their confidence. When you do this, they will confide in you, and you can help them to answer their own questions.

H.L. Mencken, American author and editor, said, "Youth, though it may lack knowledge, is certainly not devoid of intelligence, it sees through shams with sharp and terrible eyes."

We can't expect youth to act like adults; they're more active. Their boundless energy caused A. Saywell to say, "Youth is like cordite, quite innocuous in free air but highly explosive in confinement."

. . . . . . . . . . . . . . . . . . . . . . . . . . . . . . . . . . . . . .

One must be friendly to have friends. That is a truism worn thin by emphasis and repetition, but is still true, and it can't be repeated often enough because there are many lonely people in this world.

Anyone can learn to exercise their powers of friendliness. If you are inclined to be a loner and are shy about approaching an acquaintance with conversation, if you find that being friendly is extremely hard to do, then PRETEND! Pretend that is what you want to do, and do it! Pretense helps you gain confidence. If you pretend long enough, you will be sold on the idea and being friendly will, eventually, come naturally. Sure you can! You sold yourself a "bill of goods" when you told yourself that you were timid and shy, didn't you? You weren't born that way.

Quite often we blame our shortcomings on someone else, on parents, teachers, brothers, and sisters or other relatives. This is also pretending, and of the worst kind; but you have told yourself this for so long that it has become a reality and you do not recognize it as pretense. Tell yourself you are friendly until it becomes a reality to you, and you will have friends galore.

Warning: Do not practice pretense as a sham or a vice, but in order to control thought process, to accomplish the better things in life.

What are thoughts? Something flimsy, wispy, or ethereal? No. Thoughts are actual things. A minister once said, "Let any man indulge in lustful thoughts and he finds himself a victim of passion, the man who covets will be tempted to steal and the man who hates is inclined to destroy."

Our thoughts generate wisdom or folly, depending on the discipline we use concerning them. In other words, it depends on the thoughts we admit into our conscious minds because every secret thought has the tendency to become an outward act.

The mind is a human computer and can be programmed as such. Therefore, it is essential that the thoughts being fed into it are those of friendliness, courage, honesty, love, compassion, etc.

If you are not friendly, pretend that you are.

If you don't have courage, pretend that you have.

If you don't feel honest and loving, pretend that you do.

If you persist, it can become a reality. Let's not forget that a thought, if dwelt upon, will eventually become an outward act. Thus, we are what our thoughts and the passing hours make us.

· · · · · · · · · · · · · · · · · · · · · · · · · · · · · · · · · · · · · · · · · · · ·

"Tell me how he spends his leisure, and I'll tell you what kind of man he is." The above quote is worth studying and will invariably cause one to re-evaluate his, or her, own spare time. Time is something of which everybody has inherited exactly the same amount, 24 hours each day. Also, our time is most negotiable; we can spend it in any way we choose.

Arnold Bennett (1867 – 1931), an English author, wrote: "The supply of time is a daily miracle …. You wake up in the morning, and lo, your purse is magically filled with 24 hours of the unmanufactured tissue of the universe of life. It is yours! The most precious of your possessions."

Time well spent is in four parts: working, eating, sleeping, and leisure. Work can be regular office hours plus home chores, such as mowing grass or repair work. It can be cooking, cleaning and caring for children. Sleep should occupy a third or more (depending on age) of those 24 hours.

If we list the number of hours per week spent at work(whether at home or away from home) and add to that the hours spent sleeping, eating and taking care of other physical necessities, then subtract that total from the 168 hours in the week, what is left over is leisure.

We are responsible to God for the way we use all of our time, but leisure seems the most crucial. If a list of all leisure activities was kept, and how much time was devoted to each one, an assessment could be made as to the relative merits of each. Leisure is worthwhile only when it is well planned, with specific goals in mind.

It has been said that the present generation "works too long, plays too hard, eats too much (mostly the wrong things), and sleeps too little." Nervous energy can't last forever. Those who say they can get by on three or four hours of sleep per night are headed for physical disaster.

Sleep and rest are of such importance to our lives that God commanded everyone to work six days and rest one. And the rest is sweeter if six days of work precedes it. Also, leisure is for creating or re-creating joy and happiness. So, please, make sure it's a time of re-creation and not "wreck"-reation!

It's a disquieting reality that there are too many complacent people in today's world.

Borrowing a word from Senator Nancy Kassebaum of Kansas, who is calling for a "revitalized diplomacy" (focusing on human rights), we should try "revitalized" PERSISTENCY for all rights, including our own. It's when we change our stance and consider with approval, or even tolerance, the wrongs that are all around us that we lose our persistency, because persistency and complacency cannot be equally yoked. We may have one or the other, but not both. Persistency has an air of urgent expectancy and visionary accomplishment whereas complacency has the earmarks of a lackadaisical attitude that is uncaring and unfeeling.

Some may say no one can be at their best all of the time. Oh yes, they can! Our best may not always be of the same quality. Our best today may not be as good as our best was yesterday, or as good as it will be tomorrow, result-wise, because persistence requires variable amounts of time to gain its objective.

The story of the unjust judge in Biblical history (Luke 18:1-7) proves the power of persistency. Several times he denied a widow's request to "Avenge me of mine adversary." He refused until by her persistence she wearied him into changing his mind. As the Roman poet, Lucretius (96 – 55 B.C.) said, "The falling drops at last will wear the stone."

Perseverance can also be used by the unrighteous. About this the scripture (Matthew 15:14) says, "Let them alone; they be blind leaders of the blind, both shall fall into the ditch." In contrast to the unrighteous, Job 17:9 said, "The righteous shall hold on his way, and he that hath clean hands shall be stronger and stronger."

Napoleon said of the military, "Victory belongs to the most persevering." This is true of the teams in the sports world, of political parties, of civic groups and most all undertakings, because one can accomplish much with the almost resistless force of perseverance and steadfast effort.

William Gilmore Simms (1806 – 1870), American author, said it best, "The conditions of conquest are always easy. We have but to toil awhile, endure awhile, believe always and never turn back."

We often hear the phrase, yesterday, today and tomorrow. Which of these words are the most appealing? Which is the most important?

Because no one is perfect, and none save the One has lived a life without "spot of blemish", there is always the thought that perhaps we could have done better in our yesterdays. If there were no "sins of commission" that we can remember, and then there may have been "sins of omission" – something we should have done and didn't do. If so, yesterday is probably not our choice, and that leaves us with today and tomorrow.

Tomorrow is unknown to us. What will happen then is still a mystery. Because people like mysteries, and think "the grass in the next pasture is greener", tomorrow has a special appeal. Also, it is one step nearer that fabulous future for which we are always planning. Many precious hours have been wasted in daydreaming, thinking of all the marvelous things that are going to happen to us in the future and the things that are going to belong to us in our tomorrows.

This way of thinking is as vain as the words of Scarlet O'Hara in the movie "Gone With The Wind" in which she often said, "Fiddle-dee-dee! I'll think about that tomorrow!"

Nathaniel Cotton, an English poet who lived from 1707 to 1788 said, "Tomorrow! It is a period nowhere to be found in all the hoary registers of time, unless perchance in the fool's calendar. Wisdom disclaims the word, nor holds society with those that own it. 'Tis fancy's child, and folly is its father: wrought on such stuff as dreams are; and baseless as the fantastic visions of the evening."

Today is the only day that really matters in our lives. What we thought yesterday, and what we think we are going to think tomorrow, is very immaterial. It is the "now" that should concern us and have the most appeal. We should concentrate our attention and our consideration on the present time.

God is a "now" being and the Bible stresses the importance of today: "Behold, now is the acceptable time; behold, now is the day of salvation." (2 Cor. 6:2)

The word "behold", meaning "heed this", is used in the Bible preceding statements of great importance.

No man ever served God by putting things off until tomorrow. If we honor Him and receive His blessing, it is for the things which we do today.

• • • • • • • • • • • • • • • • • • • • • • • • • • • • • • • • • • • • • •

One of the most satisfying experiences in my life is to sit in church on Sunday and listen to a servant of God read and expound on the scriptures, and knowing that you are surrounded on all sides by people who love God as you do. People who also believe that the Bible is the divinely inspired word of God and that He gave His son as redemption for all humanity. Through this sacrifice, we were given the power and knowledge to resume our rightful place in creation as the sons and daughters of God and joint heirs with the One who redeemed us.

The church is not all-powerful. The church cannot save. God is all powerful; He saves! God saves often through churches which are people, the congregations – not the buildings. God, being spirit, is not visible to the physical eye, but He can live inside our human bodies and use our hands and feet, our hearts and tongues for His speech, to deal with those who don't know Him – or refuse to know Him better. He cannot, or will not, use our minds because He saw fit to give us a free spirit at the time of creation so that we have to decide things for ourselves.

We do not have to decide what is right and what is wrong. God made those laws in the beginning and they have been handed down to us. Then, too, there is inherent in everyone that instinctive knowledge of right and wrong. It is as strong as the instinctive knowledge of danger, or of hunger and thirst.

God gave us full control of our minds and thoughts and He wants us to want Him because it's our decision, not His. He had already decided that He wanted us when He created us. Because we were created in His image, we feel lost and alone when we cannot feel His presence.

But, alas and alack, so many lost and lonely people turn the wrong way while searching for spiritual contentment and find only the misery that comes when the soul, or inner spirit, is separated from God.

The church is God's antidote for the poisons of this world. People who truly love God love their fellowman also, and nowhere is this love and understanding felt more than in the buildings where the members of God's church gather each Sunday to worship Him and to sing songs of praise.

Redeemed people are the church and the building is used for a place of prayer and Holy Communion.

. . . . . . . . . . . . . . . . . . . . . . . . . . . . . . . . . . . . . . . . . . . .

An article with no byline appearing in a 1940 magazine, now long out of print, listed a whole page of excuses for not attending church. If you are a "church dodger" see if your favorite excuse or alibi for not going is included. Do any of the following quotes from non-church-goers sound like something you may have said recently?

I had to go enough as a kid to last me the rest of my life!

I worship, but in my own way, when I want to, and not when I'm told!

The minister annoys me by:

His political opinions, giving dull sermons, preaching too much gospel, his style of public speaking.

The church is too cold and the seats too hard.

They're always asking for money.

God's outdoors is my cathedral.

I can hear better sermons on the radio. (There were no TV's in 1940.)

Sunday is the only day I have to: spend time with the kids, get caught up on my rest and sleep, devote to my hobbies, get out into the open, do things around the house, chat with my friends, or catch up with the week's news.

The congregation is too stuffy.

They gang up on me to talk me into joining.

Too many churchgoers sing hymns Sunday and cheat you on Monday.

There's more real religion outside the church than within.

My wife does the churchgoing in our family.

I'm too lazy and I don't want to go anyhow.

All of the above excuses have been used for years, but the last one is the only honest answer on the list. And it is rarely used.

"And they all with one accord began to make excuses." Luke 14:18

"He that is good for making excuses, is seldom good for anything else." Franklin

"Uncalled for excuses are practical confessions." C. Simmons

"Often times excusing a fault, doth make the fault worse by excuse." Shakespeare

There once lived a man in about 600 B.C. by the name of Aesop. He was a Greek and a slave. A slave has very little spare time but what he had he used to write stories called fables. He had a style of writing that gave his stories two meanings: one that was apparent and easy, and one with a hidden meaning.

I became acquainted with Aesop in about the fourth or fifth grade when we studied one of his stories. It went something like this: "There was a man walking across a field wearing a long coat. The wind challenged the sun as to which of them could make the man remove his coat. The wind was to have the first try, so he blew a strong blast against the man, but of course, it made him pull his coat tighter around him. When it was the sun's turn and the warm rays of the sun fell upon him, he quickly removed his coat.

Although the story was a good one, I didn't see its double meaning and my teacher didn't explain it. Maybe she didn't understand it either, or she may have thought it better to wait and maybe someday we would discover it for ourselves.

Years later when my son was in the fourth grade, he brought his homework and this same fable was his assignment. In those days the teachers expected parents to help their children with their studies. As our son finished reading aloud the story, I think I must have felt like Archimedes when he discovered that a floating object displaces its weight in the liquid in which it floats. You remember he ran out into the streets shouting: "Eureka! Eureka! I have found it!"

There, plain as day, was the hidden meaning. Aesop wasn't talking about the wind and the sun at all! He was saying to us that if you want to live a better life and be more successful in this world and have lots of friends, you must treat people with a natural warmth like the sun's rays and not with cool indifference like the cold north wind.

The sun's warm rays and the cold north wind are symbolizing God and the devil. It seems that the devil, or Satan, has been challenging God, over us, since our creation. Knowing that God has given us "free choice", he whispers to us as he did to the first people in the Garden of Eden, trying to get us to choose him. However, a true Christian believer will draw his cloak of righteousness tighter around himself and withstand temptation.

There's an old French proverb which states, "A lie can travel around the world while Truth is putting her boots on." One wonders if the writer of that proverb foresaw the electronic age and the sound waves that encircle the earth bringing our TV programs live from all over the world via satellite.

Watching family shows on TV, it seems to be the "in" thing to do for children to lie to their parents and for their parents to lie to each other.

However, we can't go so far as to say that "lies are in" and "truth is out". That would be too much like saying, "God is dead" which he certainly isn't. But it does seem that Truth is becoming slower and slower "getting her boots on".

What were you taught in childhood about lying? And how were you reprimanded? My mother told me that God hates lies, that mamas and papas hate lies and grandmas and grandpas hate lies and if little girls want to be loved, they must always tell the truth. This may not have been the best psychological approach to the subject (my mother was very young), but it worked!

While tempted to say, "No intentional lies have been told since then", remembrance brings a vivid picture to mind. The picture is of a baffled little first grader who came home from school one day and 'raked his mother over the coals' for telling him there was a Santa Claus. (His mother was quite young too.)

He said, "The boys at school laughed at me when I told them there was too, a Santa Claus because my mother said there was, and my mother doesn't lie!" Needless to say, his younger brother and sister were told about Nicholas the bishop of Myra, and patron saint of Russia, Greece and of young people, and they called him Saint Nick.

Presumably everyone has at sometime in life, forgotten to do something they had said they would do. This is not an intentional lie. This is not a lie against God and does not need His forgiveness. Your apology and request for forgiveness must be extended to the person for whom you promised the deed.

The fifth chapter of the Book of Acts tells of Ananias and his wife, Sapphira, who lied to God; it also tells of their tragic demise. Also, the book of Revelation 21:8 tells us where all liars, who have lied against God and not sought forgiveness, will eventually find themselves.

Do we expect too much from our "men of the cloth", the men (women too, now) who feel that God has called them to spread the Gospel message of the Bible? The widow of a minister said, "People expected too much of my husband because he was a man of the cloth and men of the cloth, however dedicated, are still men and husbands and fathers. Although he is a doctor of divinity, he is not divine and adulation belongs to God."

Seeing the man, robed in the vestment of the church, in the pulpit Sunday after Sunday, we sometimes confuse the sacredness of the office with the man who is merely a human being like ourselves.

This truth was clearly revealed recently when a friend heard her pastor berating a church member who was more than twice his age. She had been reared to respect her elders and was shocked at his lack of understanding and consideration, and especially of his exhibition of anger. She said, "No one should explain a church rule – if indeed it was a church rule – in that manner!" I think the good Lord wanted me to witness that because I had built that man up, high on a pedestal, and that certainly knocked him off of it for me."

When we begin to see our leaders, whether religious or political, as being infallible, we are on dangerous ground. Especially are we in danger of creating dictators and bullies who are not popular with a free people.

People, in any walk of life, who cannot control their anger, are to be pitied. They have not grown up emotionally. They are their own worst enemy and a problem to their families and to their community. The devil fights his battles with anger and unpeaceful means; therefore it is tragic to see his snapping black eyes on the face of a man of the cloth.

It seems that the unruly child needs more attention than the obedient one. Not more love, but more attention. The Prodigal Son's father thought so (Luke 15:11-32). We must pray for and give more attention to God's wayward children. We all need each other's prayers. God tells us, through the scripture, to love and pray for those who berate us, "Who wrongly and spitefully use us." Also, a soft answer will turn away wrath from a humane person, but will not stop the warped and twisted mind that indulges in vindictiveness and revenge for imagined slights or for imaginary intrusions on what they consider their rights only.

If all men and women, of the cloth or not, who have dedicated their lives to God, would think on those things spoken of in Philippians 4:8, there wouldn't be room for anger which is a symptom of hate.

Motivation is one of the more important words in our vocabulary. It is important because it is used in reference to people and people are the most important part of earth. Vocabulary unites them.

Do we fully realize the growth of our vocabulary since the grunting and pointing communication system of the cavemen? The Second College Edition of the New World Dictionary of American Language has over 158,000 entries in its 1,728 pages. And all the words in that multi-thousand word list that refer to mankind are important key words because they teach about life.

Such a word is motivation. What are man's motives? What motivates him to think, speak and act as he does? And from whence comes this motivation? Without it, he is just a dreamer and the difference between a motivated person and a lazy, lackadaisical daydreamer is as great as the difference between black and white, night and day.

The motivated person is one who dreams but in meditative and planning way, with every intention of carrying his plans to fruition. The daydreamer is content merely to dream. He enjoys his fantasy world and never thinks of trying to make his dreams come true unless something or someone can motivate him into action.

Most of us have heard someone say, "I feel so lazy today; I'm just sitting here waiting for the spirit to move me." Although it is said as a jesting and bantering remark, it is literally true. The inner spirit must be inspired or motivated in order to push the body into action. There must be an incentive to work. But how can the inner spirit receive encouragement and the desire to be useful if the thoughts and mind keep it locked up incommunicado in a fantasy world?

Children should be taught, early in life, the difference between the two: Motivation needs meditation, which is a spiritual two way communication (the human spirit in communication with its creator's image); and daydreaming, which is merely the folly of fanciful imagination and a tremendous waste of time.

The greatest motive is love. Love of someone or something – or both. Love for a devoted family, a cherished hobby, a need to be helpful to others. There are also the selfish love motives: driving ambition for worldly goods and personal success. Ambition and success are wrong only when they are given top priority by a selfish motive. Someone has dubbed this the "Me first!" generation which is a good indication of the selfishness in the world today.

There is a Biblical scripture: "Seek ye first the kingdom of God.... And all these things shall be attended unto you." Seek with right motives.

Dr. Merle E. Bonney, a psychologist of the North Texas State College in Denton back in the 1940's gave his 'Formula for Popularity', "Popularity is not the superficial thing it is often assumed to be, but is tied up with the most basic traits of personality and character. Winning friends and achieving popularity is the end result of a good general development, the achievement of many kinds of competence and preparation for all the problems of life."

Winning friends, influencing people, I.Q. tests, social ratings, science in contradiction with religion, popularity polls and tests, made up the bulk of magazine articles back in those days. We were going through a stage of advancement in the scientific world and practically each new discovery was making obsolete that which had formerly been accepted as fact. It seems that new discoveries are brought about by scientific men and women who are always challenging the accurateness of the world's knowledge prior to their time.

The above formula for popularity contradicts the old proverb, "To have friends, you must prove yourself friendly." It says that much more than friendliness is needed to be popular. He said that it takes more than friendly overtures and social gestures. "It takes," he said, "a rounding out of the total individual, his character, personality traits, attitudes and his ability to stand out and make himself count in a group."

He also said, "We must give up the idea that to be a socially useful person, all one needs is to be friendly...." We may not agree with him entirely but must consider that he was writing with foresight while we can look back on his 38 year old article with hindsight. He even went so far as to say, "The reason people have many friends, and are socially successful, is solely because they have such traits as daring, courage, aggressiveness and leadership. And people will ignore you, no matter how kind and friendly you may be, if you lack the aggressive traits."

If we were to make a list of positive and negative words, where would you place the word "aggressiveness"? To be at the very top may take aggressive ambition; but one can be popular without being a president, movie star or famous athlete. It depends on where, and with whom, you wish popularity. Not everyone has world-wide ambitions, but everyone likes to be popular and well thought of where they live. Winning friends, yes, worthwhile friends, is not nearly as difficult as he would have us believe; however, a general development of personality and character traits (without aggression) will help one to be a happier, more well-adjusted person, and a more influential one as well.

Are you a personal question asker (PQA)? If so, don't be offended if others respond in kind and intrude into your private life and thoughts.

In my early married life, an older sister-in-law was always asking me what I paid for things. Whether it was a new dress, hat, shoes, a piece of furniture or just a kitchen gadget, the inevitable question was "How much did you have to pay for that", or "How much did it cost you"?

It never occurred to me not to tell her; and although her nosiness was resented, I did learn to love her for her good qualities, which were many. But all the relatives and friends were subject to her questions; it was her way of making conversation. She never forgot. Five years later she could still tell you what you paid for something, down to the penny. It became a family saying, "If we forget what we paid for it, we can always ask her."

So we can love a person although they are a perpetual PQA. If your particular PQA is not a loveable type, don't let your resentment grow and grow until it changes your personality. Keep your sweet disposition by learning a few pat answers.

One good way is to answer the first question honestly, and then looking them straight in the eye, ask, "Why?" You may ask, why, again and again. They soon refrain from asking questions when they know they will have to answer a lot of nonchalant whys, and the more nonchalant the better. The "whys" will not offend if they are spoken softly and blandly.

If the above method doesn't work, there is a faster way to put an end to personal questions. You could say pointedly, but without malice, "If you will forgive me for not answering that question, I'll forgive you for asking it."

It's important to remember, you're inviting questions when you're guilty of asking them yourself. They always boomerang right back.

Voltaire once said, "Judge a man by his questions rather than by his answers."

Are your feelings easily hurt? Can you take constructive criticism gracefully and thankfully? Does criticism that is given with mal-intent roll off of you like water from a duck's back? The best defense against criticism is self-assurance. If you have enough of it, and always do your best, it will never hurt you. You will be immune.

One would truly have to be isolated to avoid criticism. All active and creative people, whether in a small community, big city, international circles, or law makers and world leaders, and especially politicians receive criticism. The newspapers are full of it.

The more one tries to do, the more one has to train oneself to take the rebuffs and adverse criticism regarding one's efforts to accomplish a set purpose. An honorable purpose may be approved by your critic, but not your method of obtaining it. The critic may think that he knows a better way, or he may just love to find fault, or he may "have an axe to grind."

Those experienced in dealing with the public will not allow themselves to be "rubbed the wrong way"; it will not help their situation to become annoyed. But the beginner, the amateur, may be spiritually crushed by the same sort of criticism. It would seem that people who endure severe criticism would become hardened or callous, but the opposite is true. It takes a kind and gentle person to overcome the natural tendency to fight back. "A soft answer turneth away wrath," and helps the cause. Patience is a wonderful virtue and can be acquired if practiced enough. Next time there is an exasperating or frustrating experience, practice patience and kindness; the reward is great and the aftermath exhilarating.

Yes, the old adage of practice makes perfect says it well. Psychiatrists used to say (and probably still do) that one should not control his rage or anger by bottling it up, but should let off steam by "blowing his top". That has never made sense to me because the more you practice "blowing your top", the more you are going to want to keep doing it. Since practice makes perfect, uncontrollable rages become a habit.

The first hunch, or instinct, is usually right if you let the Holy Spirit guide you, and the main thing to remember about feelings is that the other person has them too.

People who dislike others usually have the feeling that other people don't like them. Believing this to be true, they compensate by strengthening their own dislike. It's a vicious circle, and a debilitating character trait.

It is human nature to like some better than others but it is not natural to actually dislike anyone. Of course, family (blood relatives) and best friends are loved and thought about more often than mere acquaintances and strangers. However, there are exceptions because some not only have favorites within the family circle, but also they intensely dislike the rest of the clan. We are not speaking of mild disapproval (we can disapprove of someone's ways without disliking the person), but of a dislike that disregards the other person entirely.

The person who dislikes all but a few favorite people may be a good manager and have a high position, with co-workers vying for his good graces, or he may be a "down-on-his-luck" individual who gripes and complains about everything and everybody. Whichever, he or she is usually demanding and exacting in his expectancy of those around him, and although he may have favorites, he is never really close to anyone because he doesn't know how to give of himself to be friendly. Others feel this "standoffishness" and are puzzled as to what really makes him tick? They may ask, "Is he really so busy that he doesn't have time for people, or is he just a snob?"

Wrong on both counts! When you dislike others, it's a good sign that you don't like yourself either. If you intensely dislike someone, it's time to take a good long look at yourself, indulge in self-analysis, and put things in the right perspective. One of the Ten Commandments is "Thou shalt love thou neighbor as thyself." Therefore, if you don't like yourself and like your neighbor in the same way, you dislike your neighbor.

Norman Vincent Peale said, "If you want to associate on a good, friendly, normal, creative level with others, you have to do a job on yourself – until you like yourself."

Grief is the most natural thing.  Grief is the most selfish thing.  Those who have waited for and witnessed the death of a loved one (whether it's a sick child dying of some dread disease, a parent or an elderly grandparent deteriorating under the weight of many years) know the terrible pain of grief.  And the person waiting, watching and caring can know, almost to the minute, when it is that the loved one stops fighting to stay here.  When a patient gives up the struggle, death isn't far behind.

Who can blame the frail, hurting bodies for thinking they have suffered enough and that it isn't worth the effort to keep fighting pain and struggling to keep breathing in a pain-filled world?  Yet, with clutching selfish hands, we cling to them and beg them not to leave us.  We think selfishly of how we are going to feel without them, and not of how they will continue to feel if they stay here.

We must not bemoan the fate of the dead because ours is a similar fate.  We shall all cease to breathe and join the ranks of those gone before us.  This is not to say that we shall cease to live!  When my turn comes, may my family and friends remember that "eye hath not seen, and ear hath not heard" of the many beautiful and wonderful things that God has in store for us on the other side of the veil through which we will pass "in the twinkling of an eye" and we shall "know as we are known".

Death of the body is not the ogre some imagine.  Greater to be feared is spiritual death which means separation from God.  Anything, as natural, as necessary and as worldwide as death, could not have been planned unto man for evil.

Bacon said, "It's as natural to man to die, as to be born; and to a little infant, perhaps the one is as painful as the other."

We come to know death better after He has touched someone we love, but the understanding doesn't come until grief is spent.

If you have ever served on a jury, you have no doubt heard the defending attorney say, "The defendant is innocent until proven guilty." The burden of obtaining proof is on the shoulders of the prosecuting attorney. He must prove it "beyond the shadow of a doubt". It is an inalienable right to be considered innocent until so proven.

This is probably the most outstanding idea in our law, yet it is not original with us. It began back in Roman time when Julian was Caesar of Rome (331 – 363 A.D.). The British copied it from the Romans, and we copied it from the British.

The facts in the original case were: a man, charged with embezzlement was being tried before Julian Caesar. The prosecution brought out several points and when each was refuted, he threw up his hands and exclaimed, "Oh mighty Caesar, how can a man ever by found guilty if it be enough to deny the charge?" To which Caesar replied, "How can a man ever be declared innocent if it be enough to have accused him?"

Another of our laws that came by the same route is the one for the protection of women. Augustus Caesar wrote the law which states, "A woman has the right to say 'no' at any time or any place. She may have said 'yes' a hundred times or a thousand times, but if she says 'no' just once, she is inviolable." The literal meaning of the word inviolable is "placing things around." In this particular instance, the rings of protection were being placed there by the law. My new dictionary gives this definition: "Not to be violated, profaned, or injured."

We are not told what Jesus wrote on the ground in the Biblical account of the woman taken in adultery, but it may well have been, Caesar says she's inviolable! We know that He reminded one of His disciples to obey the law when he said, "Render unto Caesar the things that are Caesar's, and unto God the things that are God's." Jesus obeyed both laws. Those of man, by stopping the stoning, and those of God when he told her, "Go and sin no more."

. . . . . . . . . . . . . . . . . . . . . . . . . . . . . . . . . . . . . . . . .

There are many more of us who believe in God, a supreme power and creator, than there are atheists and doubters. However, atheists and doubters shouldn't be placed in the same category because there is hope for the doubter, but none for the atheists. The doubter, more often than not, had no Christian upbringing, or at least, had parents who were lax in their faith and inclined to be doubters themselves; or the doubter like the Biblical prodigal son may have strayed so far from his earlier training that he must return to it and have his faith restored.

A saying, originated during World War I, was to the effect that there are no atheists in foxholes. An atheist is one who has already made his decision against God and does unequivocally deny Him.

There was once a doubter who was beginning to wonder if perhaps he was an atheist and no one seemed interested in trying to increase his faith. He met the small town's clergyman on the street one day and asked, "Brother Jones, who made the earth?"

Brother Jones knew there was more coming, but he smiled and said, "God did."

"How do you know? Did you see him making it?"

"No," said Brother Jones, "but it's written here in this Bible."

The doubter put a hand to his weary brow. "Why should I believe you? Did you see it being written? I just don't know…. I see the evidence of an assembling of nature, but things could have just fallen into place."

Brother Jones looked at the watch on the doubter's wrist. "Who made your watch?" he asked.

"The Elgin Watch company."

"How do you know?" Brother Jones asked.

"It's written on the back, see?" and he handed Brother Jones the watch.

"Why should I believe you? Did you see it being written there? If not, I won't believe it's an Elgin!"

The doubter began to smile as he was beginning to understand the parallelism. The clergyman opened the back of the watch and continued to say, "I don't know…" Then, with a twinkle in his eye, "I think this intricate mechanism, with all these little wheels, just fell into place and started moving."

Sometimes it seems that "For multitudes who call themselves Christians, religion is no more than an agreeable sentiment and Calvary a bit of grim and pleasing pageantry." (Costen J. Harrell)

One of the axioms of a good leader is that if you are wrong you should admit it quickly and emphatically. This is a hard pill to swallow, and one that many people fail to take because they are axiomatically inclined.

On May 7, 1931, New York City witnessed the most sensational manhunt. The search was for "Two-gun Crawley", the killer who didn't smoke or drink. They finally trapped him in his girlfriend's upstairs apartment on West End Avenue. One hundred and fifty policemen and detectives laid siege to his top floor hideaway by chopping holes in the roof to use tear gas, and by mounting their machine guns on the surrounding buildings. They were determined to get the "mild-mannered cop-killer".

For more than an hour that residential district reverberated with gunfire while an estimated ten thousand people watched the battle. Crawley was crouched behind an over-stuffed chair firing at the police. When he was captured, Police Commissioner Mulrooney said, "Two-gun Crawley is one of the most dangerous criminals in the history of New York. He will kill at the drop of a feather."

A blood-stained letter to "Whom it may concern" was written by the desperado during the battle. It said, "Under my coat is a weary heart, but a kind one, one that would harm no one;" yet only a short time before, Crawley was on a country road on Long Island, necking in a parked car, when a policeman asked to see his driver's license. Without saying a word he drew a gun and cut the officer down, grabbed the officer's gun and fired again into the fallen body. Yet this was the man who said he had a kind heart, and would do no wrong. He never admitted his wrongs. At the death house, in the electric chair, his last words were <u>not</u>, "This is what I get for doing wrong", but "This is what I get for trying to defend myself."

We don't have to use two guns, or even one, to hurt people. That old weapon that's sharper than a two-edged sword (the tongue) can "cut" people down too, especially when it's wielded by friends whom you considered to be the salt of the earth variety.

Why is it so terribly hard to say? "I'm so sorry, I really don't want to hurt or offend you; I like you too much for that. And I'm really trying to bridle my tongue and control my temper." It would be good if you could add, "Pray for me, won't you? That I may accomplish this goal?"

"May the words of my mouth and the meditation of my heart be acceptable in thy sight, O God, my strength and my redeemer."

People can be easily hurt, but God has blessed us with a healing process that causes the body to help with its own cure. A healthy mind and body can soon overcome most wounds, of which there are many kinds. There are many weapons and wound causing implements but the hurt that goes the deepest, and causes the most pain, is inflicted by that weapon spoken of in Psalms 52:2 and 57:4. It says that the human tongue is "sharp as a sword", and it never cuts more deeply than when wielded by someone you love. It also takes the longest to heal.

The wound most likely to become infected is received from someone outside the family. It is often infected with germs of anger, bitterness, hatred and retaliation. This type of wound must be thoroughly cleansed before it can heal properly because if the above mentioned germs are allowed to be coated over, the infection will break out again and be harder to deal with. Lives that have been wounded by this fleshy sword can be destroyed, or wrecked and ruined for the remainder of their earthly existence.

We are accustomed to thinking that young people heal quicker than old people. This is not true in this type of hurt. One reason that there is so much conformity among young people is because they fear the ridicule, fun-making, and harassment of their peers if they try to be different.

The older person can best survive this particular type of sword. They have a more mature wisdom and have learned to have tolerance, and most have suffered at least a few nicks or scratches from it over the years. This is not to say that insults and slights don't hurt; they do sting a little, but the mature person considers the source and if the wound needs attention is well-trained in the cleansing process. Just a little sting can be safely ignored.

It is strange how jealousy and worry in the insecure person strives to evoke anger and hatred in others. But God is the great moderator as well as the great physician. To Him and to Him alone, is the power to judge others!

"Let us not therefore judge one another anymore; but judge this rather, that no man put a stumbling block or an occasion to fall in his brother's way."(Romans 14:13)

The meek and lowly have complete humility, the state of being humble with an absence of false pride and self-assertion (not self-assurance nor self-esteem). The character of meekness is kindness and gentle persuasion without anger. Christian humility is forgetting self and seeking the will of God. Those who feel the need to "blow their top" periodically are neither humble nor possessors of Christian humility. Marriage that unites meekness with high temper is pathetic.

There is an old saying that states, "We begin to look like what we look at." It has been said of elderly couples that they look alike. This idea was brought out in a story by Nathaniel Hawthorne when he wrote about the Great Stone Face. The story was about Ernest who lived with his mother near a mountain which had a 100 foot high rocky configuration on its wall which the valley people called The Great Stone Face. The folklore contained a legend with a prophecy that one day a person with a face of exact likeness would come to their valley.

A variety of people came claiming to be the person, but Ernest knew they were wrong because he looked every day at the Great Stone Face, and he could see it even with his eyes closed.

When Ernest became old he taught about life, and preached about God to the valley people. One day while preaching, the setting sun's rays shone upon Ernest's upturned face, and the people shouted, "Look! Ernest, himself, is the likeness of the Great Stone Face!"

One wonders if Hawthorne didn't get his idea for the story from the Bible where it states, "We, who with unveiled faces all reflect the Lord's glory, are being transformed into His likeness with ever increasing glory."

It is true that people and things we are associated with, and look at daily, have a tremendous effect upon our lives. Those who have a daily walk, or meditation with God, seeing Him through His creation and with spiritual eyes, are a Godly people.

Speaking of look-alikes Jesus said, "If you have seen me, you have seen the Father."

We have become a people of customs and traditions. The history of these things is important in order for us to understand the past, and to learn from it. But why do we hang on to them, and refuse to let them remain in history where they belong?

The tradition of Santa Claus has become more of a symbol for Christmas than the nativity or the wise men and the star. Why do we remember and have national holidays for men that no one remembers knowing? Although they were good men who deserve our thanks as well as a permanent place in our history books; why do we think that no one in the past or present can play like the old masters? Why do we think that all of the literary giants of the past have been reduced to a mere few who can write well today?

The original or first meaning of the word holiday was Holy Day, but through the years it has been added to and the latest meaning is, "Any day set aside by law or custom to commemorate one event."

One of the least important days that is still flourishing is Halloween. Why? It began before the year of 200 B.C. and long before Christianity. History shows that Halloween (originally All Saints Day) was purely Druidical. Druidism was the faith of the Celtic inhabitants of Gaul, and also the Celtic inhabitants of the British Isles, until they became Romanized. Druidic paganism existed in parts remote from Roman influence, up to the period of the introduction of Christianity.

We have Diogenes Laertius to thank for our knowledge of the Druids. He found a lost work written by a Greek named Sotion who lived in Alexandria; it was written about 200 B.C. It stated that the greater part of Gaul was Celtic and had observed Druidism for over two centuries. The gods of the Celtic Druids were Mercury, Apollo, Mars, Jupiter, and Minerva. These were also the gods of the Celtic pantheon.

Pliny and Diodorus Sioulus, historians, said the lore of the Druids was a bundle of superstitions and their divinations were achieved by slaughtering human victims. Caesar mentioned the burning alive of men in wicker cages. The Christian era caused the Romans to stop this cruel practice.

These atrocities happened on Halloween. The Druids thought that October 31 was the day when Saman, lord of death, came for the wicked souls and they warded him off with bonfires, human sacrifices and evil rites. Why do we still commemorate this day?

• • • • • • • • • • • • • • • • • • • • • • • • • • • • • • • • • • • • •

What does friendship mean to you?  The Bible tells of many beautiful friendships, perhaps the best known, and the most often told, are those of Ruth and Naomi and Jonathan and David.

The Hebrew word for friend has a slightly different meaning than ours.  One scholar said, "It's comparable to the English word 'fellow' and it means a person with whom one has close fellowship."  The Old Testament Book of Proverbs has more to say about friends than any other book.  The writer of it not only tells about close enduring friendships, but also contrasts them with the false friend.  He says the good friend is characterized by constancy, truthfulness (candor), counsel and encouragement. (Proverbs 17:17, 27:6-9, 27:17)

Naomi and Ruth shared loyalty not seen between in-laws of today.  Earlier in the life of Naomi there was a famine in Israel and Elimelech, his wife, Naomi, and their two sons went into the land of Moab seeking a better life.  The sons married Moabite women.  Later, after all three had died, Naomi decided to go home.  Now that the famine was over she wanted to go back to her people and thought it best that her son's widows stay in Moab with theirs.  One agreed, but the other one, Ruth, said the words quoted in the Biblical Book of Ruth (12:16-17).  Naomi must have been a wonderful woman to have inspired such trusting faith and loyalty, not only in herself, but in her God Jehovah, as well.

The words have become immortal, and show a perfect giving of love, trust, loyalty, friendship and of humble devotion, "Entreat me not to leave thee, or to return from following after thee, for whither thou goest, I will go; and where thou lodgest, I will lodge; thy people shall be my people, and thy God, my God.  Where thou diest, will I die, and there will I be buried, the Lord do so to me and more also, if ought but death part you and me."

The loyal friendship between Jonathan and David is equally amazing.  All the more so because Jonathan was a prince, son of King Saul, and David was a poor shepherd boy and a warrior in King Saul's army.  But the two young men were good friends and they sealed their friendship with a covenant which they renewed several times in the following years.  They vowed to be true to each other under all circumstances, and they were until their death.

When David slew the opposing giant warrior, Jonathan gave him his princely robe, girdle, bow and sword, and let David have his (Jonathon's) rightful kingship and throne.  Was there ever a more unselfish friendship?

True friendship cannot be bought or sold or bribed or neglected.  It is constant and priceless.

We are hearing a lot these days about the inadequacies of our school systems, especially about poor reading and writing.  A recent newscaster (on television) said that from now on there will be more emphasis placed on reading and writing and less on science and math.  Having been a bookworm all my life, it is hard for me to imagine anyone not wanting to read and to read well and often so that knowledge will be increased.

History gives us many examples of things that can be achieved simply by trying.  Think of the poor woodcutter, or rail splitter, who learned the skill or reading and writing, by candlelight.  He became the 16th president of the United States.  Most of our presidents were prolific letter writers, and Abraham Lincoln was no exception.  He wrote this beautiful and popular letter to a Mrs. Bixby in Boston, Massachusetts:

Executive Mansion
Washington, Nov. 21, 1864

Dear Madame:

I have been shown on the file of the war department a statement of the Adjutant General of Massachusetts, that you are the mother of five sons who have died gloriously on the field of battle.  I feel how weak and fruitless must be any word of mine which should attempt to beguile you from the grief of a loss so overwhelming, but I cannot refrain from tendering to you the consolation that may be found in the thanks of the republic they died to save.  I pray that our Heavenly Father may assuage the anguish of your bereavement and leave only the cherished memory of the loved and lost, and the solemn pride that must be yours to have laid so costly a sacrifice upon the altar of freedom.
Yours very sincerely and respectfully,
A.  Lincolnc

There is a copy of this letter hanging in Oxford University, England.  It was placed there to show the beauty of good English.  It is indeed an honor and a rare accomplishment for a man who had attended only three terms of school.

No matter what subject, or subjects, upon which the educators place their emphasis, only the individual application of each student will produce more of that quality.

The Bible says, "Study to show thyself approved unto God, a workman that needeth not to be ashamed, but rightly dividing (handling aright) the word of truth." (2Timothy 2:15)

. . . . . . . . . . . . . . . . . . . . . . . . . . . . . . . . . . . .

Thanksgiving is a time to count our blessings. No matter how raw the deal we think life has dealt us, no matter the condition of the world in general, in war or peace, good environment or bad, each individual in America has much for which to be thankful.

True, all may not be as well with us as at some previous time because time doesn't stand still. Possibly our main problem is that we want life to pass smoothly in the same old rut. Sometimes we can't accept changes when change is inevitable. We grumble, complain, and place the blame on anything except ourselves, yet life is still very much what we make it. We have been fed from a silver spoon for so long that all we can think of is wanting to continue in the manner to which we have become accustomed. That means in many households every member must have a paying job, even those in school may work afterward and on weekends.

This means plenty of food on the table, but not enough togetherness to enjoy it. Problems and strife abound in homes where each goes a separate way. Better a crust of bread and glass of water where love is because food and strife cause indigestion. Continuous indigestion causes illness, organic problems and eventually an inability to work.

If you feel unthankful for your lot, get out the American history book and reread about the first Thanksgiving Day in America. They weren't giving thanks for wealth and luxuries, fine cars or other possessions, they were thanking God for their very existence, for their survival, for the strength that enabled them to work the virgin soil in which they grew their corn and vegetables, and for the wild turkeys and animals they used for meat.

We owe a lot to those pioneers who came over and lived in mud and log houses they built themselves, their endurance of long, hard winters, their back-breaking, manual labor, their blood, sweat and tears and self-sacrifice in order to start a new country, under God, where all could worship Him through the church of their choice. Are we being true to their memory when we allow atheists to own schools and publishing houses to indoctrinate our youth to atheism? What would those early pioneers have done with Madalyn M. O'Hair?

There are parents who would never harbor the thought of punishing their children with physical abuse; yet some of these same parents will administer a tongue lashing that can cause as much damage as bodily bruises. The human psyche is a delicate instrument, and when triggered can cause serious problems of which the nervous breakdown is the most common.

Many parents raise their voices when talking. Angry parents have been known to yell insults at their children. If one yells at a son, "You're just a lazy, good-for-nothing bum!" or to a daughter, "Do you want to be a big fat slob all your life?" What good would it do? None! The harm done could be tremendous. Children subjected to this kind of harassment (it isn't punishment) grow up to feel inferior and insecure, and may never grow up emotionally, and eventually they become emotional cripples.

The Bible teaches that God wants us to think well of others. That would be an extremely hard task, if not an impossibility, if we could not think well of ourselves too. Parents who tyrannically and periodically lash out at their children with such abusive criticism are not thinking well of themselves or their spouse. It is essential for children to think well of themselves in order to have respect for others.

If a parent finds himself, or herself, on the verge of screaming, the following should be repeated, letting all resentment be in the first (very factual) sentence, "Oh, you make me so angry!" Then add, "But I don't want to be angry with you! I love you!" Just saying aloud the words "I love you" has a comforting and soothing effect upon listeners, both young and old.

Love is redeeming and forgiving. Love extends mercy and is kind. If the person who is ranting and raving would stop long enough to say, I don't want to angry with you because I love you" it would be impossible for them to continue because rage and love are not compatible. When love comes in, rage jumps out.

Our hopes for a better tomorrow depend upon the children of today. They should not be verbally or physically abused, not should they be worshipped and spoiled. Their due is to be nurtured and cared for, loved, and taught, and the lessons they remember best are the examples we set before them.

Schools and their teachers and superintendents are still being discussed in the nation's newspapers. These are also topics at many social and civic events. Whether teachers are good or bad, qualified or unqualified, responsible or unreliable are the concern of more and more parents today.

A senior citizen of East Wharton County, Texas was reminiscing about his early schooling. "It has always been a mystery to me that the mind will retain some things and forget others that are equally important. When I went to school, we had what we called assembly. The whole school would assemble and the superintendent, or a guest speaker, would make a short talk to inspire the students. Of all the assemblies I attended, I remember only two."

"Walter Dotson, our superintendent, who years later became District Clerk of Wharton County, told us about one of Solomon's proverbs which says, 'If the tool be blunt and you whet it not, you must do double work.' He compared the human mind to this tool that needed sharpening because if the mind is dull and you stimulate it not, concentration is twice as hard."

"Another time he read the story of Jacob's ladder. 'And he dreamed, and behold a ladder set upon the earth, and the top of it reached to heaven, and behold! The angels of God ascending and descending on.' Genesis 28:12"

"Dotson was a strong believer in education, and he said, 'I like to think of a ladder resting right here on the schoolhouse floor and extending on up through the roof and up into heaven You can climb as high as you want to go on this ladder, but students, this is where you must start! This is where you get on."

The senior citizen paused, looked reflective, and said, "Why, of all the assemblies we had, all of the talks, do I remember only those two stories?" Then he surmised that since prayers were not allowed in school anymore, examples from the Bible probably weren't permitted either.

Teachers could still make the learning process easier, and less forgettable, by teaching with interesting examples from the Holy Book.

Back in 1948 we were planning a trip west, and being a history buff, I remembered that in 1806 the two men that the president of the United States had appointed to explore the western United States had discovered two famous mountain peaks in Colorado which now bear their names. We decided to put Pike's Peak and Long's Peak on our agenda.

Pike's Peak is the best known and the one most visited because of its accessibility; there is a road to its summit. However, not everyone makes it to the top. Our 1947 Packard made it, but we passed other cars with steaming radiators that were still parked there when we came back down.

The approach to Long's Peak, which is taller than Pike's Peak, is difficult and there's no road to the top. At the time we visited it there was a huge felled tree on its slope. The tree was sawed through and the annual rings were exposed. Experts who studied these rings decided that the tree had lived for 400 years. It was a sapling when Columbus landed at San Salvadore, and a half-grown tree when the pilgrims landed at Plymouth Rock. It had withstood the ice storms of 400 winters, but now it was dead.

Do you know what killed it? Forestry experts said that a colony of beetles got under the bark and brought it down. That enormous tree was felled by insects so small they could be crushed between thumb and forefinger.

The fate of that tree is similar to human nature. Humans survive the mighty blows of life: the death of a friend or relative, the loss of wealth or health or jobs. It is the accumulation of all the little troubles of yesterday added to those of today and tomorrow that sap us. We soon become overloaded because the colony of tiny troubles get together and gnaw away at our equilibriums.

When so burdened, give God a second chance. Our bankrupt law has been criticized because it has been used to defraud, but it is still a good law. It is the law of second chance. Paul said, "Let us cast off the weights that dost so easily beset us…." And God says, "Come unto me all ye who are weary and heavy laden, and I will give you rest…."

Trouble can be an enemy or it can be an ally, depending on how you look at it and what you do about it. Every unsolved problem is trouble.

Most people try one of these two ways to solve problems: they either meet it head on and try to solve it alone, and if they fail to do so, will wring their hands in despair, adopt a defeated attitude and give up; or they ask God's help and while waiting on His "fullness of time" learn to cope, as Paul did with his "thorn in the flesh".

Let us list the ways in which trouble is an enemy. It causes worry and weariness, is time-consuming, nerve-racking, is injurious to health, expensive, grievous, hazardous, and unavoidable, to name a few.

If one has never thought of trouble as an ally or friend, descriptive adjectives may not come easily. Some troubles are a help in growing up, others promote emotional stability. With each problem that's solved or overcome, lessons are learned, knowledge is increased, and wisdom is stored for dealing with future troubles.

Trouble befriends people most by drawing them closer to God. Even the most non-praying person will remember to pray if he, or she, is troubled enough.

A man at an A.A. meeting said, "I am an alcoholic. I used to get drunk and cause neighborhood brawls. I was an embarrassment to my family. My wife and children left me. One night in a drunken rage, I seriously hurt a neighbor and he was taken to the hospital and I was thrown in jail. I had never had trouble with the law before and was afraid of losing my job. It was this fear that caused me to stay sober during the week and drink only on Fridays and Saturdays and sleeping it off on Sundays. My real fear was: no paycheck, no money for whiskey."

"I saw only mud and slush through my jail window for two days, then the rain clouds went away, and I saw the moon and stars and began thinking of and talking to God. I asked Him to help me. He did. Friends from work got me out. My boss took me back. The neighbor recovered from his concussion. Best of all, my wife and children are back with me."

"That trouble was the best thing that ever happened to me, and the booze habit was the worst."

Most people try to cover up their shortcomings because they don't want to seem inferior to their fellowman.  They try to accomplish this in different ways, the most common of which is to brag or place emphasis on their weaker points.  Benjamin Franklin is a good example.  Before the Revolutionary War, it was necessary for him to hire a man to row him across the river.  The man said his fee was 50 cents.  Franklin had 75 cents in his pocket which was all the money he owned, yet when he paid the man, he gave him the extra quarter for a tip because he did not want to be thought of a as poor man.

Although Franklin later became wealthy and was our first Ambassador to France, he didn't brag about his higher position.  In fact, when he wrote his own epitaph, he said, "Here lies Ben Franklin – a printer."

A minister once used his anecdote to illustrate a sermon.  He was dining in the home of one of his parishioners and the dinner was delicious, but the pie she served later with coffee left something to be desired.  However, the minster ate the pie and complimented her, telling her several times how good the pie was.

Before he left she said, "Please explain something to me.  I know that my pies tonight were a near failure, yet you praised them extravagantly.  When you dined with us before, my pies were perfect, but you never said a word about them.  Why?"

He replied, "The ones last time spoke for themselves, they didn't need compliments.  The ones tonight did."

The world's finest violin maker made his first one at age 22, and he labeled his instruments: Made by Antonius Stradivarius Cremoonensis Alumnus Nicoli Amati Faciebat Anno – 1666, followed by his personal symbol – a Maltese cross and his initials, A.S., enclosed in a double circle.  When he became known as the best violin maker in the world, he signed himself with proud simplicity "Stradivarious".

No one excels in everything, and we should not be ashamed or embarrassed of minor accomplishments, neither do we need reserve psychology!

Here's hoping that everyone had a good Christmas, also that everyone remembered to leave the first six letters of Christmas in their hearts and that no one over-indulged while observing the last three letters.

It's easy to tell what kind of Christmas a person had if you can observe him or her during the remaining days in December. If mother and grandmother are in house slippers with feet on footstools, you know instinctively that the feast wasn't catered and they have earned their ease.

If children aren't underfoot, but are elsewhere playing, you know they were pleased with their gifts. If dad is relaxed and reading his paper by the fire, you know that he was prepared for Christmas. But if he is at his desk wearing a frown as he manipulates figures, you know that he is worrying about bills coming due in January. If everyone is smiling and happy after Christmas, it's a good sign they were not in a mad rush preparing for the event. A lack of tension and frustration indicates they didn't go overboard in spending, giving, or crowding too much into not enough time. The family that gave "white gifts" (to needy families) has a glow of self-satisfaction, proving that it is indeed "more blessed to give than to receive."

There are those who can't seem to get out of bed the day after Christmas; when they do rise, they wear ice-caps, sip tomato juice, and cringe if the doorbell or telephone rings. The true spirit of Christmas is far removed from a pagan celebration.

The liquor laws of our country are a mystery to me. Even our president, speaking over a television network (Saturday, Dec. 3), asked that you take care of a friend by driving for him or her if you see that the friend is too drunk to drive. Wouldn't it be much easier to simply curtail the sale and drinking of alcohol during the eight days of Christmas? For always would be better!

But Washington, and not the surgeon general, sets the pace. They don't want to be unpopular with their constituents. When Rutherford B. Hayes was president, they called him "granny" and his wife Lucy was dubbed "Lemonade Lucy" because they wouldn't allow wine or strong drink in the White House. The Bible speaks of abominations in high places; abomination means anything hateful, loathsome, and disgusting according to Webster's New World Dictionary.

Last week I heard someone say, "If God doesn't hurry up and relieve the world situation, He is going to have to apologize to Sodom and Gomorrah." (God destroyed them for being wicked.)

This is a very presumptuous remark, and the hint of criticism against the Deity sounds almost sacrilegious; yet it was a very effective and "ear-catching" way of telling what he thought of our existing worldwide conditions.

God made this beautiful world and put men and women (whom he made just a little lower than the angels) here to take care of it. But not without instructions! He gave us a guidebook which is also a textbook of valuable lessons, the Bible. He told us to "study to show thyself the will of God." (2Timothy 2:15) If everyone lived according to the instructions given in this inspired book, evil would be banished from the earth.

Can you imagine a world without crime? There would be no rapes, no murders, no stealing, no cheating, no rioting, no strikes, no prejudices, just brotherly and sisterly love toward all mankind. We could, by following His instructions, make this old world a land of beginning again. Where would be the need for lawyers, courts, juries, judges, peacemakers, or earthly lawmakers, if Gods will reigned supreme? We would definitely have better and cleaner books being published because no editor would send a good love story back to its writer saying to include one murder or one homicide and at least two rapes and the book might sell.

But this, you may say, would be heaven on earth. Hasn't man always had the God-given power within himself to make of his life a heaven or a hell? Love and happiness aren't sought for and found. They are made. They already exist within ourselves. Sometimes they are covered up with wrong attitudes, the chief of which is false pride. But there are others, such as those mentioned in 1 Timothy 6:3 through 5.

A good New Year's resolution, or any time of year resolution, would be to let your love and happiness shine forth towards others, but first remove all pretense and sham so that people can love the real you and not be disappointed.

• • • • • • • • • • • • • • • • • • • • • • • • • • • • • • • • • • • • • • •

Not too many of us are guilty of feeling sorry for ourselves because self-pity is self-degenerating and the instinct of self-preservation is to build yourself up, not down, there are times when most of us wish for something we don't have. The best cure for that is to walk through your home and notice, or make a list, of the things you have that your grandmother (or if you're young, your great-grandmother) didn't have.

My grandparents drove a team of black horses hitched to a black surrey with long black fringe around the top. A Victrola and player piano furnished their music. They had two courts where the young and old gathered on Sunday afternoon to play croquet. If the weather was bad they viewed pictures in the parlor. Not home movies, but beautiful picture cards which became three-dimensional when viewed through the stereoscope.

The utility porch on the shady side of the house was always a busy place. It was there that the clothes hampers were kept, and the scrub boards and the washtubs hanging over the bench. The old black kettle, in which the white clothes were boiled, sat on a brick furnace in the yard near the porch. The firewood for this, also for the indoor fireplaces and the kitchen stove, was stacked in the woodshed not far away.

Other utility items were stored in a closet at one end of the porch; the two most memorable are the old crock churn and the ice cream freezer. The churn, with its hand-propelled dasher, was used every day by whoever was available when the sweet cream was ready, mostly by grandmother, but sometimes her mother or the older children after they walked home from school.

There was a rocker with a side pocket for books built on because grandmother always churned with the dasher in one hand and a book in the other. On Sundays the ice cream freezer was placed on the top step and the men turned the crank while the womenfolk prepared the meal.

Such reminiscing makes us realize how fortunate we are with present day conveniences. Also, it reminds me that "God is still in His heaven and all is right with our world." And "Lo, He is with us always, even unto the end of the world."

In this day of "dog eat dog", "me first" and "myself mostly", it is extremely hard to contemplate every angle of your profession to everyone's advantage. This is especially true of the writing profession, and more so of the freelance writer who chooses his or her own subjects.

No one tries freelancing without previous writing experience. No matter how much training, and background of sales under assigned topics one has, the freelancer is always shocked at the rocks and posies thrown his way. They come in the same mail: unjust accusations of misusing the press, usurping the rights of someone (which are claimed and not factual, or else they would sue) along with the letters of congratulations and encouragement.

No writer worth his salt will accept only the praise and ignore the criticism. These critics have to be dealt with. When the letter states, "all of my friends feel the same way", take it for one person's opinion if the friends aren't given a name. It's best to win the critic over if you can. It's not called a free press for nothing. And any editor worth his salt knows his staff and correspondents well enough to judge their ability, also their loyalty as well as their competence.

Where would we be today if the writers of the Holy Books had let their antagonists, critics, and persecutors stop them from printing what they were inspired to write?

God's message hasn't descended and strengthened through the years by cowards who were afraid to write. Religious writers (not fanatics, but the truly dedicated and inspired) will cling to this thought, "If God be for me, who can be against me?"

Always be kind to your critic, but do not let him browbeat you or rob you of your self-esteem. Above all, never get angry (you're not a qualified religious writer if you do) and have word battles with him. If you can keep your control while he is losing his, you're giving him enough rope to hang himself. While it is not pleasant to see him humiliated before his peers, it is a form of justice that he could easily have avoided.

One of a Christian's duties, and indeed one of his rare accomplishments, is to lift up his fellowman and make him feel worthy of God's love. It's a regrettable fact that most unbelievers wait until life is at its lowest ebb before even considering changing their lifestyle.

Norman Vincent Peale in an article he wrote for "Creative Help for Daily Living" started in this way, and I quote, "There is something that should be of great interest to you. And that something is yourself. Really, you know, you are somebody. You are something! You have far greater potential than you've ever even imagined." Why is Peale saying this? Is he trying to "blow the person up" by giving him a swollen head and making him feel conceited? No, of course not! He realizes that encouragement, and yes even praise of this kind, is the only cure for an interiority complex.

Counselors and spiritual advisers can give good advice; but what Reverend Peale is leading up to is that they are limited to just that – advice, and that you, the individual, must release your best potential. You are the only one who can furnish and release the brain power for your creative thinking. No one can do it for you, and it's plain that a new way of thinking is in order because the old way has gotten you nowhere, but down. Remember that your best friend is the one that brings out the best in you.

People are the most intelligent animals on this earth. If our teeth hurt we know, without being told, we should see a dentist; if we don't know how to fix our car, a mechanic is called; if we need the plumber, the butcher, the baker, or the candlestick maker, we find them. If we break a bone, no one has to tell us to send for, or go to, a physician. So why aren't we intelligent enough to call on God when we have spiritual wounds or a burst ego? Why do we hesitate? The answer, more often than not, is that we won't believe He can, or will, help us.

Don't be afraid to believe what you can't see. You can't see your own spirit when you look in the mirror, so how can you expect to see God who is spirit. You don't see a spirit leave a body that you know it once inhabited. God wants us to ASK! EXPECT! and RECEIVE!

Why is there a lack of religious writing in the newspapers of today?  Are people less inspired, less involved with a personal faith in God than formerly?  Why have the religious pages in the big city papers changed so drastically over the last 15 or 20 years?

Having asked myself the above questions, and recalling to mind some favorite articles and columns of yesteryear, I realized that although life seems to pass swiftly, the wheels of change, even the drastic and radical ones, turn more slowly; so much so that the gradual change is complete before one realizes it.  Then, by comparison, we know that things aren't as they once were.

It seems that the news media, especially in the larger metropolitan areas, have decided to print only what is new about religion, such as "splits" and "mergers" and foreign beliefs, their leasers' activities, and about new sects and "isms" in this country.

Inspirational articles about the Bible and its messages are gradually disappearing.  Billy Graham and a few others still have a small space in the back sections, but I remember when religion, the kind for which America was founded, was on the editorial pages and sometimes the front page.  These were columns entitled: Bible Messages, Thoughts for Today, and Come Let Us Reason Together.  There is always news of what the World Council of Churches is doing, but where are the personal professions of faith that help to make God a reality to the non-believer?

Writers inspire other writers and good writers can inspire everyone by giving their readers a good moral and righteous boost in the right direction.  Some of the writers who have given me the inspiration to write, and whose clippings have filled many pages in my scrapbooks, have gone on to their reward.  My regret of never writing to let know stays with me.

Do you remember Judge Kennerly's column of "Comments on the Sunday School Lessons" that used to be in the Houston Post newspaper?  And there was a farm magazine, now out of print, with a page titled The Country Church.  It was written by a minister who combined poetry with Bible teaching.  Another inspirational writer, Norman Cousins, is still writing today.  He had a one-page editorial in a magazine he edited for years.  His philosophy of life has greatly influenced my thinking and writing.

"Let your light so shine that others will see your good works and glorify our Father in heaven."

There is an old saying; the road to hell is paved with good intentions. The person who coined that phrase must have been feeling guilty about a personal sin of omission, or else had been deceived by a false friend.

Breathes there a man (or woman) with soul so dead, who never to himself (or friend) has said, "Yes, I'll do that for you. I'll do it this week," and then fail to keep the commitment? One may get away with this once or twice provided an apology and reasonable explanation is forthcoming. However, if one makes a habit of agreeing to do something with no intention of carrying through, that one is soon discovered to be a false friend who cannot be trusted.

Whether on New Year's Day or any other time of year, this would be a good resolution; in fact, it would be a good addition to daily prayer: "God, help me to do all of the things that I have agreed to do this year, and if obstacles and stumbling blocks prevent me from fulfilling a promise, revive my sense of loyalty and duty to assuage the feelings of the one to whom the commitment is made."

It has been noted before that we are now living in a "me first" society, which means that it is profitable for a person to disregard promises made to others, this inconsistency, although not a crime, is contemptible.

People are inclined to want a new and better life, but never find the time to turn over the leaf and start. Tillotson said, "… this is as if a man should put off eating, drinking, and sleeping, from one day and night to another, till he is starved and destroyed."

And it was South who said, "God never accepts a good inclination instead of a good action, where that action may be done; nay, so much the contrary, that if a good inclination be not seconded by a good action, the want of that action is made so much the more criminal and inexcusable."

A common cause for a lot of problems is indecision. "A man without decision can never be said to belong to himself; he is as a wave of the sea, or a feather in the air which every breeze blows about as it listeth." (John Foster)

Right inclinations plus forceful decisions are conducive to compatibility, and integrity that's easy to live with.

How can creative writing be so much fun when it's such a chore to write letters? Writing business letters and paying bills is just a time-consuming task. Personal letters to married children, relatives and close friends become a chore too, after you've written the first one.

Because we have been taught that most of our uncomplicated problems can be solved by meditation and reasoning, my conscious mind said to its inner self, "Come let us reason together and find out why so many resolutions to keep up with our correspondence, and promises like 'Let's keep in touch,' go down the drain." After much debate, it seemed very clear that the characteristics in thoughts of a daily writer differed greatly from those who write only a few letters, shopping lists, and recipes.

You sail through like a breeze on the first personal letter. You feel free! You can write whatever pops into your head. There's no restriction on space; so you write on and on and on. There's no taboo on subjects or word usage (as long as they're decent enough to go through the mail).

As you write this friendly letter, enthused over having no restrictions, and because you are trained to put words together to look and sound their best, you've written a small newspaper before you know it.

Now there's no time in your busy schedule to write each of the others. You feel like saying "ditto", but you know that you can't send copies of that letter to everyone because the substance, or subjects, wouldn't suit each recipient. In fact, now that you've looked it over, it looked more like an article than a letter. Also, with a little condensation in a rewrite job, it could be slanted nicely to a certain magazine. Thus, the erstwhile letter goes to a publisher and correspondence is again neglected.

Last Christmas I received cards from people who know me only through my columns. They made me feel so good that I resolved to do likewise and let some of my favorite columnists know how much I appreciate them and enjoy their efforts (and the ones I enjoy are like those described by Leo Tolstoi, "A writer is dear and necessary for us only in the measure in which he reveals to us the inner working of his soul", but I have found that my list of favorite writers is longer than my backlog of correspondence; so what I write daily, and sometime half the night, will have to be considered as letters from me to everybody.

Wise men of old have proven their wisdom to us by the many proverbs they have left behind. Had they written only factual statements, we would probably read them once and forget them, but as conundrums and sayings with hidden meaning they never cease to fascinate us. One of my favorites is under the glass on my desk. Its meaning is clear to me.

## A PERSIAN PROVERB

He who knows not,
And knows not that he knows not,
Is a fool – shun him.

He who knows not
And knows that he knows not
Is a child – teach him.

He who knows,
And knows not that he knows
Is asleep – wake him.

He who knows,
And knows that he knows,
Is wise – follow him.

Although this proverb is written about "he", the real meaning is about "you" (or I) and your own qualification for understanding the ability of your fellow man to make the right judgment or decision. It is a constant reminder to not let anyone mislead you by adopting a commanding attitude.

Just because one takes a brisk and assertive attitude is not sufficient evidence or proof that "he knows that he knows". There are many examples that prove this false. Remember the little house painter who changed his name to Hitler? He stood on his soapbox commanding attention and as Adolf Hitler commanded the army and ruled the nation of Germany until he brought it to its downfall, all because the people of Germany did not realize that Hitler "knew not that he knew not".

A nation "under God" can be fooled too, but need not be. We have been taught not to accept everything and everybody at face value. The Bible says, "By their fruits ye shall know them." In fact, the entire Book of Proverbs, in the Old Testament, is filled with lessons about life. It tells how to live a good and rewarding life, and also tells about the evils that will try to overtake us.

The Book of Proverbs depicts wisdom as crying out in the chief places to the people of Earth, saying, "How long, ye simple ones, will ye love simplicity? And the scorners delight in their scorning, and fools hate knowledge?" (Proverbs 1:22)

. . . . . . . . . . . . . . . . . . . . . . . . . . . . . . . . . . . . . . . . . . . . .

Having been asked to write about today's morality gives me hope that perhaps people are getting weary of this "Sodom and Gomorrah" society.

Immorality was the subject of a sermon, heard recently in a rural church, in which the speaker said, "Things we once didn't dare think about, much less talk about, are now acted out on the TV screens for everyone to see and hear."

Modern morality seems to me to be of the instant variety. We also have instant coffee, instant tea, instant hot cocoa mix, instant lemonade and even instant hot soup. If the water is boiling, whatever suits the mood of the moment is instantly available.

Yet, there are those who think the flavor is better, and longer lasting, if instant desire is controlled and the pot is allowed to brew.

Besides being an unpopular subject, what is morality? Webster's New World Dictionary gives seven definitions. The second is the best, "The character of being in accord with the principles or standards of right conduct." One from the New Century Dictionary is similar, "Conforming to or not deviating from the principles of right conduct." The Reader's Digest Great Encyclopedia Dictionary gave the only clue to right conduct with its third definition, "virtuous conduct."

John Sergeant (1710 – 1749), American missionary and author, said, "The only morality that is clear in its source, pure in its precepts, and efficacious in its influence, is the morality of the Gospel. All else, at last, is but idolatry – the worship of something of man's own creation, and that, imperfect and feeble like himself, and wholly insufficient."

A few years ago someone made the erroneous statement, "God is dead!" The religious and God-fearing people of the world were so stunned by this saying that they roused from their lethargy to regroup and refute, also to emphasize their personal belief and faith in Almighty God.

Perhaps someone should now make the statement, morality is dead! A statement like this may be necessary for all good moral people to take a staunch stand to help change the existing immorality that's corrupting our world today. (Yes, I know its God's world, not ours, but He put us in charge of it, didn't He?)

To one who has grown up in a Christian home, and has been taught that church and Sunday School are even more important than public school, it is hard to realize that there are children in our country who have never heard of Jesus.

This was suddenly brought to my attention recently while reading the international, interdenominational and interracial magazine, The Upper Room. A lady was telling of a new friend's daughter who had been going to Sunday School for several weeks when she decided that she didn't want to go anymore. "Why don't you want to go again?" she was asked. "Because," the little girl replied, "they never talk about anything but Jesus Christ, and I don't even know Him."

The story was emphasizing the fact that "hearing about Jesus", and really knowing Him are not necessarily the same thing.

An imaginative person could carry the dialogue a little further, and hear the lady ask, "so you don't know who Jesus is…. Well, do you know who God is?"

"No, but my mother does because she says, 'My God'! My daddy knows Him too, but he doesn't like Him very much; he's always damning Him."

Some years ago when missionaries and Bible societies were taking the translated scriptures and the Gospel message to every country in the world, we remembered the prophecy of Jesus concerning the end of the world, "And this Gospel of the kingdom shall be preached in all the world for a witness unto all nations; and then shall the end come." (Matthew 24:14)

If God's people in America aren't living and teaching the Gospel message, we may soon have a generation that knows not God. If parents who have heard of God in their childhood have lost interest in Him, they're not likely to teach their children; and unless new laws are made, or an old one revoked, the children will not learn of God in the public schools.

The inactivity and unconcern of Christians could cause America's downfall as surely as cold atomic weapons, because another prophecy (Matthew 24:43) says, "Therefore say I unto you, the kingdom of God shall be taken from you, and given to a nation bringing forth the fruits thereof." The future generations are a part of the nation's fruit.

A parent, leaving a supermarket was heard to exclaim to a meddlesome son, "As God is my witness, I'm going to beat the hell out of you if you don't come here this minute!" Can that small boy love God who can be called to witness his being beaten? A modern prophet would probably say, "Keep the faith, or perish"!

Do you require logical proof of God? Are you a church member who still has doubts because you can't feel God's presence? Do you have communication with Him?

Some ask too much of God, others not enough; some don't recognize God because they know not who He is, or how to accept Him. Man cannot define God nor explain His presence with intellect, because he can't see God, he can't hear God, neither can he feel God.

"How then", you may ask, "can we know that there really is a God?"

We have to know spiritually! God is spirit, and man, being made in His image, can communicate with Him only as one spirit to another. The Bible says that we must worship (communicate) in (the) spirit and (with) truth.

What is spirit? It is the essence of God. This we must believe through faith. What is faith? The dictionary says: loyalty, belief and reliance, but the Bible says, "Faith is the substance (assurance) of things hoped for, the evidence (a conviction) of things not seen." (Hebrews 11:1)

With superior wisdom, God took a part of His spiritual self, built a complicated wall of flesh around it, to withstand earth's environment, breathed the breath of life into it (Genesis 2:;7) and it became a living soul.

This is no greater mystery than man who can also create, from his own flesh and blood, a small human being. The miracle is that only God can give it the breath of life that sustains the soul and causes it to grow.

Don't doubt sane and sincere Christians who say, "God speaks to me", or "I feel God's presence." They are not unbalanced; they're merely using the wrong terminology to describe their relationship to God. Seeing, hearing and feeling are common to all, and there are those who doubt if they can't experience Him through these physical senses too.

Those who love and obey God see Him with spiritual vision; hear Him, not aloud, but with the subconscious which informs the conscious mind. The conscious mind has two root sources: the subconscious mind and the world. Man can listen to one, but not to both; life struggles between spirit and flesh.

We feel God, not by touching, but by awareness. We should disregard the three senses and use the term, awareness of God. Some have an emotional awareness, others a calm methodical awareness (the Bible's Mary and Martha are good examples of this). A few, such as Paul (in the Bible), have an exhilarating, mountaintop-experience awareness.

There is absolutely no substitution for an acute awareness of God.

These questions were asked in an adult Sunday School class. "Just how far should a Christian go in trying to save unsavory characters? The Bible says that we must try to win them, but how? How without being condemned ourselves? Because people say birds of a feather flock together."

The answers to these questions are simple. Many questions seem complicated until we get our minds and thoughts in perspective with two revealing questions:

Why do we call ourselves Christians?

What would Jesus have done?

We are Christians because we have accepted the teaching of Jesus Christ and want to be like Him. (Christians prefer to think that He was, and is, the Son of God, but even if they didn't they would do well to emulate Him and follow His example because a more perfect life has never been lived.)

One day Jesus was dining at the same table with publicans and sinners. The Pharisees criticized Him for being in the same "flock". Jesus heard them, and said, "They that be whole need not a physician, but they that are sick…. I am not come to call the righteous, but sinners to repentance." When the publicans and sinners came and sat down with Jesus and His disciples to eat (in a public eating place, no doubt – Matthew 9:10), He talked with them, causing disapproval among the so-called good people of that day. He missed no opportunity to tell the uninformed about God.

At the tender age of 12, He said to His parents, "Know ye not that I must be about my Father's business"? And He continued to teach about God and about life and of the purpose of His being here until He was crucified at age 33.

He didn't become pals or best friends with unlovable characters, yet He loved them enough to tell them about their wrong-doings, and to give His life for them. He lived such an exemplary life that people sought Him. One ill woman wanted only to touch the hem of His garment thinking it would heal her, and it did. Another asked, "Jesus, remember me when thou comest into thou Kingdom."

Daily good deeds and a life with no bad habits that is unashamed to worship God, has more appeal than all the sermons ever preached. Jesus didn't "preach at" He "talked to", and "did for" the sinners.

We are living in a complicated, opinionated and many-sided world, and at a time when optimism and pessimism take turns in throwing out the headlines. It's also a time in which men's hearts fail them for a fear that's well-founded. It's a time of contradiction, of non-cooperation, inconsistencies, and of moral relaxation among all age groups.

One cannot live the good life that God expects of us without moral character. If one is observing, one will notice that morality and truthfulness are closely wedded while immorality and lying go hand in hand. Immorality is referring not only to the unchaste but to anyone not in conformity with accepted principles of right and wrong behavior.

A wise man once said, "Show me a company president that steals lumber, and I'll show you an office boy that steals postage stamps." We are, all of us, by our daily actions, setting examples that others will imitate.

There are two kinds of people, leaders and followers; and according to Solomon Gabirol, there are only four mental types: 1) "The man who knows, and is aware that he knows.

2) The man who knows, but is unaware that he knows.

3) The man who is ignorant, and knows that he is ignorant.

4) The man who is ignorant, but he pretends to know."

The leaders (that last) of this world are of the first type only; the followers are of the last three. But, beware the paradox! Not all knowledgeable people are truthful, and the presidents of countries, as well as companies, set the trend for the citizens.

When the American people learned that one of our not-so-long-ago presidents had not paid a large sum of money that was overdue to the I.R.S., they began to holdout too. During the next few years many tried to avoid paying their income tax.

Some are saying the world is going to get a lot worse before it gets better; others are saying every day, in every way the world is getting better and better. The same contradicting statements are being made about war and peace, love and hate, inflation and deflation, etc.

It is truly a mind-boggling time for the worrier. Not so for the true child of God who can relax with a song in his heart, knowing that he or she has the best insurance and security there is. Also, that he is never alone because he has the promise made by Jesus, "Lo, I am with you always, even to the end of the world."

The best way to ensure happiness is to never allow yourself to feel disappointment.

"How is it possible", you may ask, "not to feel it, if you're really and truly disappointed?"

It isn't easy, but you can train yourself not to be. In the language of the street, "You must learn to roll with the punches." This is especially true if your expectations are too great.

Not everyone can say as Paul did, "I have learned, in whatever state I am, therein to be content." (Phillippians 4:11) Paul did not engage in self-pity, even when hungry or in jail. He knew that the best medicine for discontent was to count his blessings.

Self-love (selfishness) causes disappointments. Often this mood is brought on by comparison. Why must we love in others what we lack in ourselves? Why do we want to be anything other than what we are?

Everyone has a goal or plan for their life. But if the goal is not reached and the plans don't materialize, there are many and varied reactions. Some get bogged down in disappointment, others become bitter and hate the world and all in it, another will pick himself up, brush himself off, and start all over again, never showing or admitting disappointment. He realizes that failure to reach the first goal made a better chance for success on the second try because hindsight reveals previous mistakes.

Although some set goals too high for their capabilities, this is not always the case. Sudden and drastic changes can occur overnight. Everything can be coming up roses one morning and the next day may wipe the slate clean.

Reading about people who rob and steal makes one wonder. Did they set an unobtainable goal and degenerate into desperation? Were their parents over-indulgent causing them to expect things for nothing?

A young man (or woman) already has two strikes against him if he has gone through college with everything handed him on a silver platter and then is told, you're on your own now. Go out and show us what you can do! He is comparable to pushing a two-year-old toddler into the kitchen, saying, cook you own dinner!

Children should not be overburdened, but have enough responsibilities to learn about life. Suitable chores accompanied by the following advice: Duty before pleasure; a stitch in time saves nine; nothing tried, nothing gained; haste makes waste; and if at first you don't succeed, try , try again.

Most of my life has been spent living next door to a church. I still do, but now there is a parsonage in between. Living next door to your church has its advantages, and also a few drawbacks.

So close to all of the activities, you find yourself a hub of so many things. It was never a problem keeping an extra set of church keys, and the appointment book for the fellowship hall and church kitchen because I was so close. Only once, in the many years, was the hall let out to two separate parties for the same night. A definite drawback! However, the mistake was caught in time, and a satisfactory solution found that pleased both individuals.

Decorating the church for weddings, for young people whom I had taught as youngsters in the various Sunday School classes was pure fun and pleasure, combined with a lot of hard work. When asked to direct wedding rehearsals, I considered it a distinct honor.

The trick of backing out the car into the yard and letting the soon-to-be bride and groom put their getaway car in our garage behind closed doors, hidden from the pranksters with their tin cans and old shoes, was never discovered to my knowledge.

During the last depression the parsonage was over on the next street. Only our house and the church were on the edge of a small town facing the highway. Most all pilgrims and wayfarers thought our home was the parsonage.

Answering the back doorbell one morning I found a slender young man who drew my attention to his shoes by looking down at them and wiggling his toes out the sides. He had literally walked the soles off of them.

"Ma'am," he said "does the Reverend have a pair of old shoes that he doesn't want?"

Looking again at his small feet, I replied, "I'm sorry, my husband is a large man, six feet three with large feet, and his extra shoes would be much too big for you."

Nevertheless he wanted to try them; he needed shoes so badly. He put on the pair I handed him, took a few steps in the yard, almost losing one at each step. He handed them back saying, "You're right. I can't walk in them."

He wanted neither food nor money, just a pair of shoes to get him to the next town where he had been promised a job. (Today's youth need cars and gasoline, not shoes.)

How I have regretted that I didn't remember, until much later, a pair of old but good tennis shoes of mine in an upstairs closet that might have fit him. Regrets are like unsolved puzzles, we often think of them.

. . . . . . . . . . . . . . . . . . . . . . . . . . . . . . . . . . . . . . . . . . . .

People have different ideas about everything, and that is good as long as they don't differ too greatly over the essentials in life. What are the essentials in life? Back in the early school grades we learned that they were food, clothing and shelter. In the higher grades we learned that water, air and fire were essential; in marriage we know that love, trust and dependability are essentials; in friendships, it's reliability, caring, and understanding; the essentials for success in business are honor, integrity and perseverance.

After reading the above list of essentials you may think them quite adequate for a good life, or you may have a different opinion and think them too much to expect. Neither is correct. There are three more essentials: faith, devotion and obedience. They are vital necessities for a right relationship with God.

God has always been for us and if He be for us, who can be against us? No one but ourselves! It is not enough for God to be for us; our whole life depends on whether or not we are for Him.

To be a member of the early Christian church one had to make a commitment for belief before witnesses. In Romans 10:9 Paul told how this faith, devotion and obedience was to be accomplished: "That if thou shalt confess with thou mouth the Lord Jesus, and shalt believe in thine heart that God hath raised Him from the dead, thou shalt be saved."

If we have faith, we will believe; if we are devoted to Him, we will worship, obey and acknowledge Him as did the early Christians. It was, and still is, the one absolutely necessary condition or requirement for admission in the Christian church.

Some people take the attitude that God loves all His children and no matter what they do, He will take care of everyone in the end. Where do they get that idea? Not from Jesus, Paul or the apostles; they based salvation upon definite faith and obedience.

One commentator said, "They think Christ will come in judgment like a silly Santa Claus, handing out gifts of eternal life to all regardless of the way they have conducted themselves through life."

The Gospel is in the hearts and mouths of all Christians. But God pity them if it stays there, and dies there.

Recently while listening to a TV program which included several of our lawmaking officials (senators or congressmen or both), I was surprised to find so many varying opinions on the subject of prayer. They were discussing the bill that would again permit prayers in the schools, if passed.

Most of the arguments I had heard before, and I was beginning to lose interest when this amazing statement fell upon my ear, "The people don't really want to pray as much as they want the right to pray."

I don't remember the name of the man who said it; don't remember which newsman was the MC of the program; but I do remember the shock I felt at that statement. Can it be true? Are we not a praying people anymore? Will people really argue and fight (on TV and the Senate and House floors) for a right that they have no intention of using? I had to sit down and think on this thing for awhile.

How about the public prayers in the church? Will almost every member pray? Is it only the same few who will pray aloud? Do the timid ones pray privately in their homes, or is it their unfamiliarity with prayer that keeps them from praying in church?

By what authority did the man make this statement? (Now we're getting somewhere.) There had been no poll taken of this nature, not to my knowledge. Besides, to be anywhere near accurate, each individual in the nation would have to be contacted.

Finally, I reached the following conclusion. A classroom teacher, seated at her desk looking at her students who are all looking down at open textbooks, could not possibly tell whether they are praying or studying; neither could the politician know whether the all the people supporting that bill were praying people or not.

It has been my observation that people like what they fight for and dislike what they fight against. Honestly, doesn't it sound a little far-fetched that a man would give as his reason for not supporting a bill that "The people don't really want to pray as much as they want the right to pray."

The man may have been speaking for himself and his friends in Washington, but there's no way that he can know about the rest of the nation's citizenry!

People will sometimes be stubborn and determined about things they want to do, but who is so stubborn they will fight for the right to do something they don't want to do? It simply doesn't make sense.

There is much in the news these days about our country's government, including the Supreme Court, being against religion. Some have gone so far as to say that they are trying to suppress religious belief. Others think reporters are enlarging small facts, trying to make headlines and receive more recognition.

Whoever or whatever, we know that religion and morals are playing a big part in this 1984 presidential campaign. And why not? Washington C.D. and the law-makers there need religion and morals as much as anyone else. Maybe more, since they are the ones who run the country.

However, there is one disconcerting thought. Will their type of morals and religion be of the same caliber as that upon which America was founded? Will the religion of un-American activities come to power and Christians again be persecuted for their faith in God?

We now have so many foreign cults and "isms" in our country, and also one of devil worshipers and one of body worshipers whose "church rites" are immoral orgies.

The press discovered the Joneites, before they were slaughtered, and now they are exposing the Terrellites and wondering if they will have the same fate.

We need an exposure of some other groups too. Pornographic entertainment, music with a wild beat that stirs the senses, accompanied by alcohol and drugs, is becoming a way of life for too many young people.

We must never forget what Joseph Stalin said in 1935, "If we can corrupt the morals of any one generation, communism can take that nation." When asked how he would corrupt a generation, he replied, "With three things: immorality, music, and dope." Dope and drug smugglers are one of the largest problems facing the United States today.

Also we must remember that when the Russian premier Nikita Khrushchev was here in the United States, he pounded the table with his fist and said, "We'll bury you! Without firing a shot!" The meaning is probably the same in the statements of both Stalin and Khrushchev.

But the righteous need not fear. They have the source of courage. They can sing as did David the psalmist, "The Lord is my light and my salvation, whom shall I fear?" (Psalms 27:1)

Christians do not fear physical death because "to be absent from the body is to be present with the Lord." Willful sinners should fear those who can corrupt and kill their spirit, and forever separate them from God.

How good is your church?  Can its members truthfully say, "My church does things for me, my church does things in me, and my church does things through me!"  If so, your church is alive and well and can make an impact upon the world around it.

Henarik Kraemer said, "The church does not primarily exist on behalf of itself but on behalf of the world."  And the world is ever changing.  With the long, drawn-out rural revolution, the communities are being affected as more and more city dwellers move to the suburbs and beyond.

The country church is very much a part of the community, and is highly susceptible to the revolution when it comes.  In fact, it is nearly always the country church that determines what the new social order of the community will be.

America is full of country churches.  It would be difficult to find a rural community where no Christian services are conducted.  Many of these churches are quite small and most are Protestant.

It's time that the non-believers, and especially those who teach atheism, took into account the number of these little churches and the number of people they represent.

It is the primary task of these little churches, and indeed all churches to bring men, women and children into a saving relationship with God through Christ.  This is done by the teaching of the Word and by spirit.  Christian education with redemptive impact is unparalleled in most rural churches.  They enlighten and encourage decisions for the betterment of all concerned.

These small rural churches are also so much a part of our not-too-distant past.  It is a revelation to leave the highways and drive through the small towns and villages that are scattered over the countryside. Often one can see the church spire before the buildings come into view.

It has been my observation that most of these places have white painted cottages and houses, well-kept lawns and streets, two or three stores, a cotton gin or grain storage, as well as a good church and parsonage.

There are exceptions of course.  Occasionally there's one with a "dinky" little run –down church, ill-kept streets and houses, grocery and liquor stores, and cars parked around the gambling halls.  These communities are in the minority and are visible proof that God and the devil are not compatible.

All of God's creation would be helpless without Him.

A little girl said at the end of her prayer, " ….and please God, look after yourself because if anything happens to you, we're all sunk!" That is a very accurate summation of the absolute necessity of God.

Out of the mouth of babes! Small wonder that the scriptures say, "Except ye be converted (turn) and become as little children, ye shall not enter into the kingdom of heaven." (Matthew 18:3) This praying child was unknowingly quoting the wisdom of David, the Psalmist. He, too, was aware of the absolute necessity of God, and the futility of a life without Him.

When we leave God out of our lives, goodness departs from us. The natural or worldly man, or woman, takes over and for them God may as well be dead if they are going to stay separated from Him and His sustaining love.

A minister once said, "An atheist is a man with no invisible means of support." When God is left out, it is as though He were eliminated because the invisible support is gone.

It is that invisible support that tides the believers over the crises in this life. Through prayer and meditation the Christian is fully aware of "The Everlasting Arms" that are around and underneath upholding him or her with the invisible means of support while guiding them over or piloting them around the pitfalls and stumbling blocks that so easily beset us in this life.

We must use all of the means at our disposal to make God more visible to the nonbeliever if we want to survive this world because God is the enduring power, not ourselves. Only He can create righteousness which gives our lives purpose. Without God and without purpose, our life would begin in darkness without hope, and end in a great big nothingness of darkness and defeat.

In our weaker moments in this life it is often hard to see any purpose, especially when things happen that we cannot understand. But as long as we believe in God we know there is a purpose, even though we don't see or understand it because that which is purposeless is intolerable to the human spirit.

Within every human mind, whether it be religious or not, whether it ever goes to church or not, and even if it remains half-buried most of the time, consciousness of a creator does exist and comes to the surface at one time or another. However, they need to accept and acknowledge God to receive His goodness.

The devil seeks totalitarian authority. God gives us a free spirit, endowed with love and compassion.

Robert Louis Stevenson, who wrote the ever popular storybook, <u>A Child's Garden of Verses</u>, suffered poor health all of his life. He was such a frail and sickly child that he was often confined to his room for long periods of rest.

The man who lighted the street lamps would often see his pale little face pressed against the bedroom windowpane because Robert was always fascinated by the lamplighter's work. So much so that he later wrote a poem called "The Lamplighter". It's in the above mentioned book.

One night while Robert was watching the lamplighter, his nurse asked him,"What are you doing?"

"I'm watching the man knocking holes in the darkness," he replied.

How many people do we know that are living in a darkness that needs a few holes knocked into it? There is a darkness of grief, there is the darkness of loneliness, and there is the greater darkness of sin. To all of this darkness the Bible speaks (John 8:12) "Then spake Jesus unto them saying, 'I am the light of the world; he that followeth me shall not walk in darkness, but shall have the light of life.'" In the 24th verse, He told them that if they refused to believe, they would die in their sins.

Darkness and doom are bleak negative words; light and life are bright positive ones. The Book of Acts tells of the apostles being sent to the light (and life) and from the power of Satan unto God, that they may receive forgiveness of sins and be sanctified by faith." (Acts 26:18)

St. Paul, later reminding Gentiles of their past, said, "Ye were once darkness, but now are ye light in the Lord: walk as children of light for the fruit of the spirit (light) is in all goodness and righteousness and truth."

How can anyone refuse to believe when we have so great a salvation?

The controversy between the darkness and the light is a real one, and the seemingly never-ending struggle goes on and on and on. Yet we know that we can knock holes in that darkness by turning a switch, by lighting the lamps, and by accepting the spirit of light. When the spirit of light is accepted, don't hide it under a bushel, but use it to knock holes in the darkness that surrounds.

"Let your light so shine before men, that they may see your good works, and glorify your Father which is in heaven." (St. Matthew 5:16)

· · · · · · · · · · · · · · · · · · · · · · · · · · · · · · · · ·

We are all alike in many ways. Everyone wants lots of friends, yet we often forget that we have to prove our own worth as a friend and be friendly. Everyone wants to be loved, but not everyone practices being more loving and lovable. Granted, it is extremely hard to love the unlovely and cantankerous (troublemaker) person; but if we only love those who love us, what reward have we?

Loving is giving, but we are not givers only, we are receivers also. There is a common bond or kinship among humans that in the presence of need and compassion exerts itself.

You don't have to like someone to love them in this way. Luke (10:27) spoke of this type of love when he quoted, "Love thy neighbor as thyself," and illustrated with the story of the good Samaritan who helped the man that had fallen by the roadside. He didn't know the man so how could he have liked him? However, he did show spiritual love and compassion.

Associations, corporations, and federations are formed by men who recognize the gain in grouping together for solidarity. Wouldn't it be wonderful if the love that is the motive for service could become worldwide?

The ways in which we differ are not always apparent. Some people are more farsighted than others. A man, on his way up the corporate ladder, gave his wife a fur coat. She lifted it from the box, saying irreverently, "Thank God! At last, a fur coat!" Her husband sarcastically replied, "Why thank God? I'm the one who bought it and gave it to you!" Neither spouse being farsighted enough to realize that it was God's gift of health, wealth and position that enabled him to buy the coat and other luxuries.

There was the shortsighted man whose pastor told him to go home and pray day and night for God to help him solve a seemingly insurmountable problem. A week later he said, "I did as you suggested and have prayed constantly, but God wouldn't help me, so I finally figured it out for myself." It never occurred to him to wonder why he hadn't thought of it during all those weeks of trying before consulting the pastor and praying.

Yes, all we humans are of the same family. We are members one of another, sharing the common good as well as the common human sins "because all have sinned and fallen short of the glory of God" (Romans 3:23) and however much we may differ, we are alike in the essentials because we all live by God's bounty, and we all stand in need of God's forgiveness.

"All we like sheep have gone astray; we have turned everyone to his own way; and the Lord hath laid on Him (Christ) the iniquity of us all." (Isaiah 53:6)

Some of the things that make life so fascinating, so very worthwhile, are our daily revelations. Our own personalities and character traits, our interests and our hobbies, all have a bearing on the things that are revealed to us.

Psychology, philosophy and writing are my interests, and I am especially eager to hear or read anything pertaining to these subjects. It's interesting to know why two people can read the same article and each see it differently, how two people can have the same vocation, be in the same line of work and react with no similarity.

Yesterday brought an exceptional revelation about the thoughts, and a contrast of opinions, of two newspaper reporters who write for the religious pages of their papers: The Houston Post and The New York Daily News. One (two years with The Houston Post) thought his personal opinions about religion should not even be considered or thought of in connection with his job; the other one, 20 years with the New York Daily News, believed in living and practicing his faith while he worked.

The Post reporter's article was well-written but shallow in religious substance. He said that most of the members of the Religious News-writer's Association said they would talk about their religion with the people they were interviewing, but he would not. His last two paragraphs seemed unrealistic for religious reporting, and I quote from the newspaper, "The greatest strength of the American press is in its diversity, not its occasional efforts to impose 'professional standards' on all its practitioners."

"This means there's more than one way to cover religion. And a good job can be done by a Christian, Jew, Buddhist, pagan, agnostic or atheist – thank God!"

The thought of how a pagan, agnostic or atheist would be a religious reporter stayed with me until the noon mail arrived and with it the New York reporter's article of how he, a former agnostic, had changed because of a friend's definite belief in God. The friend's regular church going and exemplary life impressed him so much that he sought God and found Him. He said, "When I really worked at finding God, God led me to Himself. As a professional reporter, I can promise that anyone who makes an honest effort to seek the truth will be successful. The truth cannot be hidden for long from someone who is seeking it."

"Draw night to God and He will draw nigh to you." (James 4:8)

The strong character must limit the exercise of his own freedom in order to show proper Christian regard for the conscience of the weak man.

Why is this so? And how can it be done?

The conscience is only a partially reliable guide to ethics because an abused conscience, one that has been squelched and soothed too many times, is not reliable. The person of good, strong, moral character usually has a clear conscience and a quick thinking mind, while the weak person is more likely to make a fool of himself or herself.

A story was told of a resourceful Navy chaplain who took a movie camera and a recording machine to a party on board a ship one night when a newly promoted officer was celebrating his new stripes. The chaplain made a complete record of the evening, including the bawdy jests, the drunken speeches and the foul language.

One evening of the next week, he invited the young officer over to hear the recording and to view the pictures of the party. Neither the chaplain nor the promoted officer said a word until the whole disgusting performance had ended. Then the officer, now entirely sober, extended his hand in friendship and said, "So help me God, never again! I never knew what a fool it could make of me."

A fundamental Christian principle is that every man must accept some responsibility for his brother's salvation and his safety. This mutual responsibility means that everyone must first assume the responsibility for his own actions and how they affect other people.

The preacher who smokes, drinks or uses profanity is teaching the young people of his congregation by his examples. The church official who imbibes frequently can't complain if his own son or daughter is arrested for drunkenness or driving while intoxicated. The church going woman who cheats at bridge games gives her church a bad name because she is part of that church. There is a fellow who once said, "I wouldn't ever join that man's church because sometimes it is necessary for me to do business with him during the week and he is as crooked as a barrel of snakes."

Yes, when we don't use our conscience it can go astray and make us think that wrong is right and right is wrong.

Drinking is a moral issue because of what it does to people; so is lying and cheating. We cannot help these people by being pious and judgmental, but by being strong and setting a better example for our weaker fellowmen.

Everyone has to judge how best to spend or use their lives. With me, it's singleness of purpose.

That's not to say one shouldn't broaden one's horizons and learn and do all that one can. It is to say that one can spread oneself too thin and be in the midst of multiple purposes, not knowing which way to turn.

One cannot travel north, south, east and west all at the same time, even though high strung people have been known to exclaim, "I'm so nervous, I could fly off in all directions at once!"

Neither can one accomplish four purposes at the same time. You may see your teenager with one leg draped over the arm of an overstuffed chair, telephone nestled on his shoulder, pen in hand and tablet or notebook on the knee, the stereo or hi-fi ear receivers across his head, and occasionally he picks up a dart from those on his chair-side table and throws it at the dartboard on the opposite wall, but he is not doing all of these things at once.

If you want to know which one he is giving his attention to at the moment, ask the simple question, "What are you doing, son?" He may say I'm writing an essay or I'm talking to Bill or I'm playing darts, but if he doesn't answer at all, you will know that he is listening to loud music from the stereo and didn't hear your question.

Singleness of purpose requires solitude and quietness for creative writing, relaxation, preferably with eyes closed, to enjoy good music. Concentration without interruption in game playing and telephone conversations both require a better reason than merely killing time.

Admonitions such as "anything worth doing is worth doing right", and "do only one thing at a time and do it well" are not heard as often as they were years ago. However, the emphasis was on work then whereas the emphasis today seems to be on play and recreation.

Do not misinterpret the meaning of singleness of purpose. It does not mean having a "one track mind". A one track mind means being in a rut and never branching out; whereas, singleness of purpose is motivated to do one thing well before picking up the next.

People create dilemmas for themselves by having too many irons in the fire. Singleness of purpose acknowledges priority and concentrates on the thing that needs to be done first, giving it undivided attention, forgetting, or at least putting aside, all other worries and cares until they can be taken care of and one at a time. This also helps to keep stress, strain and tension to a minimum, and also doctor's visits.

• • • • • • • • • • • • • • • • • • • • • • • • • • • • • • • • • •

How quickly things become obsolete! Time was when only the elderly noticed the fast passing of time and they attributed this to the fact that their remaining years on this earth were few, and that they were being rushed toward the inevitable. Not so in this modern age! Young people are rushing here and there and not finding time for all they want to do.

Time is not to be faulted; it is our fast changing world! It began with the machine age and automation, advancing rapidly through the atomic age and the space age, and now, we hope, into an age of decision as to which of all these things are beneficial to mankind, and which are not.

What we call progress is moving forward so fast that scientists and science teachers have complained of their textbooks being obsolete by the time they come off the press. Each age having so many facets, and more and more inventions, not the least of which are calculators and computers to do our thinking and writing for us.

It isn't always school and homework that's responsible for the hectic pace of our young people. There are too many other things they can do, and too many places where they can go; if they can't do and go, they are bored.

It's not only the young but adults as well who are seeking more recreation and pleasure time. Many people want a four-day work week instead of the present five. The accidents and deaths reported for a two day weekend are alarming. What would they be like with three days?

If a study were made of conditions, and every phase of family living at the turn of the century and compare it with the present time, the knowledge would probably bring the conclusion that people are going to have to learn how to like work again. To feel the satisfaction of a job well done will also bring more satisfaction to pleasure time. You will feel that you have earned it.

Not long ago an object had to be 100 years old to be an antique. Now the antique dealers consider anything over 50 years old an antique. And why not? Fifty year old objects are more unknown to this generation than the 100 year old objects were to mine.

Have you ever observed small children in an antique store? One was gazing at a daisy churn and said, "Mother, look what a funny lid on that cookie jar!"

Nothing ever changes except change, but the changes are coming too fast!

This year, like every other election year, religion and religious differences become a political football to be kicked back and forth among the office seekers.

The righteous person wants to be represented by a religious politician, but the unscrupulous person and the underworld character would choose to vote for the candidate whose viewpoint is similar to their own, or at least one whose viewpoint they think could be changed.

How well do we know our lawmakers? How many outstanding American politicians are there in Washington right now whose politics are religious?

The life of a Christian in politics is not an easy one because it is his duty to measure every political party, every political program, every political technique by the principles set by Jesus Christ and His living example.

It is his duty to denounce and condemn all motives and measures within his political allegiance which are contrary to the ethics and laws of God's kingdom.

Also, he would have the Christian duty of having to acknowledge any good motives and measures from political groups outside of his allegiance with whom he is not in sympathy.

Mahatma Gandhi was a religious man who was called both a saint and a politician. Which was he, one or the other, or both? Louis Fischer, who wrote <u>The Life of Mahatma Gandhi</u> knew and understood Gandhi quite well and he said that the argument was very foolish.

"The argument, was Gandhi a saint or a politician, is endless and barren. Polak quotes Gandhi as having said in South Africa, 'Men say that I am a saint losing myself in politics. The fact is that I am a politician trying my hardest to be a saint'."

"The important fact is that Gandhi, in politics, cleaved to religious and moral considerations, and as a saint he never thought his place was in a cave or cloister but rather in the hurly-burly of the popular struggle for rights and right. Gandhi's religion cannot be divorced from his politics. His religion made him political. His politics were religious."

Every Christian in government, or trying to be in government, should ask himself, or herself, this question, "Could I take a staunch stand for justice, or democracy, or human freedom, even if I had to stand alone?"

Conklin, said, "Unless the habits of service, sympathy and love overcome selfishness, greed and hate; unless the ideals of justice and brotherhood are cultivated and prevail; unless freedom, responsibility and democracy survive, neither armies nor navies nor world power can save our civilization."

Prayer is not a cure-all for everything that ails one. It is not a magic hocus-pocus that immediately obliterates every problem.

It is not a soothing syrup or an aspirin tablet. It is a source of power only if one knows how to pray and does not ask amiss.

Most of us realize the importance of prayer, but too many of us think of the power in prayer as "power to move mountains". Not so! This kind of power comes only through faith. According to the scriptures, if our faith is as large as a mustard seed we may move mountains.

Prayer is communication with God and God's resources are unlimited, but the answer to prayer depends on how much faith we have in Him. If we have faith, we will pray knowing that we will receive an answer.

If we pray wondering whether or not our prayers will be answered, our faith is very small; if we pray wondering if He will even hear us, we have no faith at all. The Bible tells us to ask, expect, receive!

Prayer isn't always asking. Parents want their children to talk with them at times other than when they want something. The Heavenly Father is no exception!

Every prayer should begin by telling God how we feel toward Him. We may sing, or say elaborate praises as did the Psalmist of old, or we may say simply, I love you, Father.

You may ask, "Why? God sees all, and knows all. He already knows how I feel about Him." This is true. We also know that our children love us, but we still want to hear them say it.

Two very important parts of prayer are thanking God for past blessings and answers to previous prayers, and asking for forgiveness for any sins that have not yet been forgiven.

There are sins of commission and sins of omission. Dedicated Christians rarely commit willful sins, but all of us are guilty of omitting things that we should have done.

Did you not find the time to visit the sick or to help the needy in your community? Did you forget the pledge you made to the church for a certain project? Did you forget about the charity that you promised to help? These are sins of omission.

The parts of prayer used most often are the petitions. These are requests for things that we want God to give us, or help us obtain. And if they aren't immediately forthcoming, don't blame God; He knows what is best for us. That's why the Master taught us to say "Not my will, but thine be done".

. . . . . . . . . . . . . . . . . . . . . . . . . . . . . . . . . . . . . . .

To compete with today's TV and computer screens, church pastors and ministers must use a lot of ingenuity to keep their congregations inspired and interested in Bible reading. One ingenious pastor printed the following on the back of a church bulletin:

A Puzzle

Legend has it that a man in Philadelphia offered $1,000 to anyone who could write a puzzle which he could not solve. The following riddle was posed to him by a lady from California. He did not solve it, and she received the money. The answer is one word and it appears only four times in the Bible (three times in the Old Testament and one time in the New Testament).

Adam, God made out of dust
But thought it best to make me first.
So I was made before man
To answer God's most Holy plan.
A living being I became
And Adam gave to me my name.
I from His presence then withdrew
And more of Adam never knew.
I did my maker's law obey
Nor ever went from it astray
Thousands of miles I go in fear
But seldom on earth appear.
For purposes wise which God did see,
He put a living soul in me.
A soul from me God did claim
And took from me the soul again.
So when from me the soul had fled
I was the same as when first made.
And without hands or feet, or soul,
I traveled on from pole to pole.
I labor hard by day, by night
To fallen man I gave great light.
Thousands of people, young and old
Will by my death great light behold.

No right or wrong can I conceive
The scripture I cannot believe.
Although my name therein is found,
They are to me an empty sound.
The fear of Death doth trouble me
Real happiness I'll never see
To Heaven I shall never go,
Or to hell below.
Now when these lines you slowly read,
Go search your Bible with all speed.
For that my name is written there
I do honestly to you declare.

People were searching the scriptures and calling each other, trying to find the answer before the next Sunday. (The answer is a whale.)

The word independence gets much attention and acclaim. It is a word which, at first glance, seems very important and necessary, yet when we think about it, sift it through our thoughts and analyze it, consider it in relation to people, places and things, the word loses much of its power and significance.

Wars are fought and battles won, but one victory does not guarantee continued independence. Children grow up and leave home, but this does not assure them their independence.

It is true of both individuals and nations, that some have more freedom than others. But freedom, like independence, is also a qualified and limited commodity; each depends on so many other things.

We think we have freedom between church and state, but do we really? They are greatly dependent on each other. Without the churches (church people), our government would soon be communism or some other "ism" because the elected government officials would have to be chosen from unchurched people. Because people are not perfect, the church needs the law and the government.

The proposed project of an elected official was bitterly opposed and criticized by one of his constituents who said, "The people won't want that." The official drew himself up haughtily and said, "whose word will carry the most weight, the less knowledgeable and ill-advised people, or the voice of government?"

"My dear sir, have you forgotten your oath of office? The voice of the people is the government!" was the reply.

The Bible quotes Jesus as saying, "I came not to change the law, but to fulfill the law...." He also told the people to "render unto Caesar the things that are Caesar's and unto God, the things that are God's."

We think we have separation of church and state, and the atheists within our boundaries are really working toward that end, and impossible as it may seem, they have our law on their side because mortal men have stated this fact (which really is not a fact) in our constitution.

Life as we have known it will never be the same again if and when the church and state decides that they no longer need each other.

When that day comes, God's name will disappear from coins, patriotic creeds and law books, and church people will be called heretics and be persecuted as in the early days of Christianity.

Yes, independence is a precious commodity, but it is not guaranteed. Only God can preserve it for us, and will He if we don't obey?

Worry will get you nowhere! It clouds the mind, slowing down the thinking process. If you have problems and can't stop thinking about them in terms such as, "Woe is me and why me, and why do bad things always have to happen to me?" you are deliberately placing yourself in life's lowest ebb.

Prolonged thinking in this manner keeps the mind in a rut, paralyzing it so that other stimuli are unnoticed, therefore, ineffective. How can the thinking processes of the brain reach full potential if we only use the worry cells?

Granted, there are small worries and larger ones, but the detriment to health and clear thinking is the same whether the problem is trivial or monumental. But every problem can be solved, even the large ones that won't go away with counseling and psychiatric therapy. Sometimes the best solution is just to forget it. Put it behind you! Pick up your life and go on from there!

The person who says, "But I can't go on from here!" is the person most unwilling to forget and to let go of the unwanted problem. God said, "Behold, I make everything new." Remember there is always One who will carry our burdens and share our sorrows.

Quite often the problem is coincidental to the question, "What will people think?" In other words, "It's not the crime, it's getting caught." This is the "what if" worry that borrows trouble before it happens. Questions like the following come to mind. What if I lose my job before the home is paid for? What if the new car is repossessed before I find another job? Why didn't I keep the old car? Even if it was the oldest one in the neighborhood, it was all mine.

As a young bride, with a limited household budget, my husband gave me some good advice that has helped me through a half century, "Don't worry about things that you can't do anything about, but only about the things you can." Doing the things you can do keeps one too busy to worry at all.

Help from the old Bible, "Cast thy burden upon the Lord, and He will sustain thee; He will never suffer the righteous to be moved." (Psalms 55:22) Help from the New Testament, "Do not worry about tomorrow for tomorrow will take care of itself. Sufficient unto the day is the evil thereof." (Matthew 6:34) Help from a recent church bulletin, "Worry is wasting today's time to clutter up tomorrow's opportunities with yesterday's troubles."

Today is a new day that the Lord has made. Live in it and be glad.

Although the plan of salvation for the human race is perfectly clear and easily understood, unfortunately other parts of the Bible are not, especially the Old Testament, because it happened so long ago in other lands with unfamiliar customs and languages. Also, it has been translated many times, several times before the King James Version, and very many times since. Then, too, some of the ancient words have become obsolete; others have an entirely different meaning now. My key to the problem is a sincere prayer for help in understanding before reading.

The Bible still heads the list of best selling books. It is a part of God's plan to keep us in awe of it. If it were as easy to read as a third grade reader, we would, no doubt, read it once and discard it.

It is not a history book, although it contains history; it is not a geography book, but it tells of many lands; not a songbook, although there are many songs; it's not a poetry book, law book or how-to book, family counseling, advice to lovelorn, psychiatry, theology, world events, or an encyclopedic book of knowledge; yet it is all of these things rolled into one. The antidotes and parables contain allegories for examples, so there is also some fiction. Above all, the Bible is the inspired word of God, tracing mankind and His plan for them from creation to the last days of judgment and eternal life.

The Bible is to be read to acquire knowledge and wisdom, and must be taken in its chronological order. When you take a word here and a verse there to use in an argument, you can prove, or disprove, anything. For instance, an atheist, or even a temporary doubter, may ask you, "Why isn't your God consistent? Why did He tell Jeremiah (33:3) to shout or call out unto Me, and I will answer thee, yet from the Sermon on the Mount (Matthew 6:6) the people were told to go into their closets and pray in secret and God would reward them openly.

This is not a contradiction of how to pray. God does not judge his children as a common herd, but as individuals. The request for secret prayers was given to people who were living among hypocrites who loved to pray standing in churches and on street corners to be heard and seen of men. God wanted His people to be quiet and sincere by comparison.

Jeremiah, at an early age, was called to be a prophet. He said, "I, oh Lord God! Behold, I cannot speak; for I am a child." This young weeping prophet needed to shout and call out to God to help him gain courage to live through the trying years ahead.

The Bible does not contradict itself.

• • • • • • • • • • • • • • • • • • • • • • • • • • • • • • • • • • • •

The following mythical conversation is symbolic of the difference in characteristics of mankind:

"Who are the people you hate most?"

"I hate no one!"

"Oh, come now! Be honest! Whom do you dislike the most? You're always dishing out philosophy, so answer me truthfully."

That question should be answered, "If you'll forgive me for not answering that, I'll forgive you for asking it. But I see you are serious, and if there is a purpose behind that question, please know that I neither hate nor dislike anyone. I don't believe anybody is totally bad, or totally good. At least, I've never met a person that didn't have some likable qualities."

Of course, one can be more at ease with certain types of people. It is uncomfortable to be around social climbers and impertinent, inquisitive people, even though you don't hate or dislike them.

The continuous question askers fall into three categories. They're either harmlessly curious, smart alecks, or sadistically inclined. The smart alecks may ask if you should say the gasoline tank is half empty or half full? They might ask which is correct to say that I have six apples or I have half a dozen apples. The sadist, wanting to twist his verbal knife in you, will ask, when are you going to get a new car, or don't you think you would save money by replacing that old refrigerator?

The social climber seeks for and caters to the elite of society's upper-crust and likes to indulge in name-dropping as a means of identifying with them. He or she wants to keep their pie and eat it too. The truly great people, whether they have made it to the top of the ladder or not, are usually most gracious and realize that it is the lower-crust and the sweet goodness of the filling in between that holds up the upper-crust.

God is no respecter of persons, and when Jesus was asked who on earth would be the greatest in heaven, He replied, "The last shall be first and the first shall be last."

There was a book published in August of 1915, by Katrina Trask, entitled, <u>The Mighty and the Lowly</u>. She wrote, "Two classes exist, alas! The rich and the poor, the mighty and the lowly, the patricians and the plebeians, the proletariat and the aristocracy! There is injustice in the very phraseology of class distinctions, and there's social immorality in the acceptance of such nomenclature. But these two classes, called by different names in different countries and in different ages, have stood marked in history. It's an age-long problem, tragic, staggering, titanic, repeating itself every century. But this problem will be, and it must be, worked out to an ultimate adjustment."

The world is still class-conscious and the problem is yet to be solved, but it will be "in the fullness of time." The process may already have started because we now have that sweet filling in between the mighty and the lowly, the common man. As one of our presidents said, "God must have loved them, He made so many of them." That middle class group of people is increasing. Time may see them inundating the upper and lower crusts.

We can reminisce about the past; we can plan for the future, but we live in the present, this minute. It is how we meet each minute of today, how we act, how we speak, the thoughts we entertain, and the decisions we make now that really affects our lives and the lives of those around us.

The past cannot be changed or re-lived; the future is in God's hands, and He gives it to us one breath at a time.

It is very revealing to try this experiment. At bedtime take pencil and paper and write everything about the day through which you have just lived. Begin with your first thoughts during awakening and record all of your activities and what you were thinking while accomplishing them. If you're honest and can remember almost all of it, you get a better picture of yourself than any type of camera can make. But beware! You're in for a surprise. The idea for this method of self-analysis came to me many years ago while reflecting upon the title "My Day" which was given to articles written by Eleanor Roosevelt and carried by one of the leading women's magazines.

The day's record will prove you to be either a day person or a night person. If you are alert early, and start planning more things to do than six people could do in one day, you are definitely a day or morning person. Before mid afternoon you are probably putting things off until tomorrow. If you get off to a sluggish start, thinking you can't possibly accomplish much, yet gaining momentum and vigor as afternoon and early evening arrive proving you to be a late day or night person. You'll also see where you placed your priorities and wonder why you did. You get a rare view of yourself with unexpected hindsight.

Things that we see and hear when observing the people around us show the evidence of living in the "now". While shopping in one of those narrow supermarket aisles, one shopper was overheard saying, "Isn't it hot today? The radio said 100 degrees! No matter how low the temperature gets this winter, I'll never complain of the cold again."

"Just wait," her friend replied, "You will be saying 'No matter how hot it gets next summer, I won't complain about the heat.'" Yes , we are all more aware of the here and now than the future.

God emphasized the importance of the present when He said, "….behold, now is the accepted time; behold now is the day of salvation." (2 Corinthians 6:2)

Being an avid reader as well as a compulsive writer keeps my mind filled with many and varied ideas. Today I asked myself the age old question, "Is there really anything new under the sun?"

The provocation for this thought was two books received last week. One by Norman Vincent Peale, pastor of a large church in New York City and head of the world-wide organization, Foundation for Christian Living; the other was authored by two women, Dorothy Heller and June Bower, who left their typewriter jobs to enter the world of computers which was considered to be a man's world.

Although the two young women had no real technical or mechanical skills, they did have college degrees and were well trained in office work. Both wanted more pay, so they resisted the pressure put upon them that "men compute, women type" and soon learned that one need not be a mathematician or technician to learn to use computers.

Their book, Computer Confidence – A Woman's Guide, is very informative and written in a simplified way. Their style of writing was almost the same as that of Reverend Peale: humorous, positive thinking, antidotal, and a just you and me talking approach.

"Learning the computer," they said, "is a matter of attitude not aptitude." If I didn't know better, I thought, I would think Peale wrote this book. The next sentence I read really shook me. "You can do anything with a positive attitude and enough motivation. If You Think You Can You Can." I reached for Reverend Peale's book and reread its title, You Can If You Think You Can.

My next thought was who is copying whom? Checking the copyright dates, I found the computer book date was 1983; Reverend Peale's book stated that the copyright was by the Foundation for Christian Living, but gave no date. However, the Foundation for Christian Living always notifies me of his latest books, so it must be 1983 too. When I asked myself if they were simultaneous, I remembered the old adage, "There's nothing new under the sun."

Another thought, not so intriguing, but as an avid reader, how many of the thoughts of Norman Vincent Peale, Fulton J. Sheen, Billy Graham, Charles L. Allen and numerous others, show in my writing? What you read soon becomes a part of your thoughts too, and we are greatly influenced by what we read. Knowing this to be true, why don't we try a little harder to keep pornography and books marked "Explicit Sex" and "Explicit Violence" off the market?

"We can if we think we can!"

The question has been asked, "What is a Christian?" Also the question, "What is it like to be a Christian?"

A Christian is one who believes in Christ, in what He taught, and tries to live by the examples set by Him.

A child, who had learned to read, saw the name Jesus Christ in print and said, "Mother here's a cuss word!" What do you think when you see the name? Profanity or the savior of the world?

Jesus taught that in order to receive eternal life, one had to be born again. One person asked Him, "Can a man re-enter his mother's womb and be born a second time?" Jesus explained that the first birth was physical and the second one was spiritual.

This is still hard for some to understand, yet if a friend said, "I've got to change my way of living, and stop burning the candle at both ends. I am now going to turn over a new leaf." Everyone would surely know what he meant.

The first birth is a personal and usually private affair between parents. The second birth is a personal and private affair between a person and God. Man's spirit can truly commune with the Holy Spirit and be guided by Him. This is the second birth.

What is it like to be a Christian? It is hard to explain. But one thing is sure; it takes one to understand one! Things of the spirit are a mystery to the physical man. The spiritual man accepts things by faith, whereas the unspiritual man seeks proof. A non-Christian can recognize a Christian, but he doesn't understand him.

To know and love God is to be spiritual, because God is spirit and those who worship Him must worship "in spirit and in truth."

The second birth changes character, not overnight because one grows in grace. The first, or physical, birth doesn't develop into a man or woman for 16 to 18 years. Neither does the second birth produce a saint immediately. Neither does it bring perfection, but a seeking and a striving for perfection – as He was, and IS, perfect. It does bring immediate forgiveness of sins which are not held in remembrance anymore.

Our slate is now clean; washed by the cleansing blood of the Lamb of God who died in our place and for our sins so that we may have eternal life and live with Him throughout eternity in that place, not made with hands, that is being prepared for us.

Do we see the mote that is in the eye of our fellowman, but not the beam that is in our own? The faults, failings, misdeeds and short-comings of others are so easily discerned; not so of ourselves.

A telephone call was received by the FBI in Washington from a man who did not give his name. He began by telling them to go to a certain building, giving them floor and room number, and then he said that they would find some very valuable top-secret documents, essential to the welfare of our nation.

"Who's calling?" asked the FBI officer.

"Who am I? I'm merely a burglar. I found these papers in this apartment and thought it my duty to report it to you, but I'm leaving now and won't be here when you come."

It didn't occur to him to deal with his own guilt, or to consider that he and the one who took the documents were in the same line of work, stealing.

America is fast becoming a melting pot of all different types of the human race. People from all walks of life, of many and varied beliefs, people with no beliefs, and people who believe only in themselves. The "motes and beams" are especially hard to detect in an election year listening to keynote speakers. To the observing voters they sometimes seem to be interchangeable as favoritism swings from one side to another of the candidates.

What the nations, as well as individuals of this world, need is a new conscience, a conscience that will readily recognize the rights of others at all times and not just when benefits are gained by so doing. A conscience that is not always offering excuses and justification for what it says and does, but one that will seek for that which will determine the principles under which it will act. In other words, individuals should think before they speak, and nations should have principles that determine their acts before they act.

The writers of the constitution knew exactly what they meant the document to convey to posterity. But as time flies and the generations come and go people are beginning to regard it as they do with the Bible – according to their own interpretation. Unscrupulous persons can interpret it to mean what they want it to mean.

Our founding fathers were seeking relief from heavy taxes and wanting religious freedom. They were Quakers, Catholics and Protestants, so were the ones who came after them. Had the composers of the constitution known the atheists, devil worshippers, and others like them, would move in and start calling their beliefs a religion, they would not have used the term religious freedom. Instead they might have said, "The right to worship the One true God."

God is truth! God is good! He will prevail!

"Laugh and the world laughs with you, weep and you weep alone." The reason we pass from glad to sad and back to glad again is because the human brain, like other objects in the universe, travels in a cycle. If the ellipses (you may prefer to use the space terms apogee and perigee) are of equal distance, the average amount of highs and lows are experienced. In the downward cycle it can have a mild case of "blues", but if it extends further it may cause mental depression and concern. On the upward swing of the cycle it brings exuberance and a zest for living, and if extended may cause over-optimism that could bring defeat.

The brain is the most creative when it starts the upward swing, and is somewhat dulled as it starts downward. Although it is capable of carrying on its regular work during a normal cycle, there is still enough variance to cause one wise man to say, "You can't be at your best all of the time."

Sometimes one can almost tell what cycle a brain is in by what it says and writes. The Biblical Book of Psalms illustrates this. There are many songs of praise and happiness, others are sad and disheartened.

Dare we guess on which side of the cycle is this well known prayer of several decades ago? "Our Father in heaven, we pray that you save us from ourselves. The world you have made for us, in which we live in peace, we have made it into an armed camp. We live in fear of war to come."

"We are afraid of the terror that flies by night, and the arrow that flies by day, the pestilence that walks in darkness and the destruction that wastes at noonday."

"We have turned from You to our own selfish way. We have left your altars to serve the false Gods of money and pleasure and power. Forgive us, and help us!"

"Now darkness gathers around us and we are confused in all our counsels. Losing faith in You, we lose faith in ourselves."

"Inspire us with wisdom, all of us of every color, race and creed, to use our wealth, our strength to help our brother instead of destroying him. Help us to do your will as it is done in heaven and to be worthy of your promise of peace on earth. Fill us with new faith, new strength, and new courage, that we may win the battle for peace. Amen."

We are commanded not to judge the words and deeds of others, and even though we neither criticize nor praise, we can't help but notice the mood of the person.

Let's not forget that right attitudes and positive thinking can increase the brain's activities in any phase of the cycle.

. . . . . . . . . . . . . . . . . . . . . . . . . . . . . . . . . . . . . .

During this last week of August everyone seems to be working in their fall gardens, either planting or administering last minute soil preparation. Some are repotting house plants. I can't find it in my heart to envy them because of the sneezing and weeping that besets me when venturing out this time of year.

I guess my utility room would be a good place to repot plants if there were any to repot. My love for flowers is obvious though; each spring one or two non-allergenic, small, blooming plants are purchased for my studio desk, and my friends admire them. Then, two or three months later, when their foliage is turning yellow or brown from too much or not enough sun, shade, water or air, they are presented to a friend with, "You've admired this, and I want you to have it."

Any sadness at parting with it is prevented by the knowledge that the poor little thing is at last going to have some tender loving care, and a chance at rebirth. I guess my thumb can never be green; it's always covered over with printer's ink.

In recompense for my lack of horticulture and agriculture, and for not growing food for bodily consumption, perhaps a garden could be planted with food for the soul. In my mind this, figuratively, will be accomplished. In my garden there will be six rows of peas: preparedness, promptness, perseverance, politeness, prayer and patience. Next to them, I'll plant four rows of squash: squash gossip, squash criticism, squash grumbling, and squash indifference. Another essential is lettuce. Let's have six rows: let us be faithful; let us be unselfish; let us be loyal; let us love one another; let us be truthful, and let us be fruitful.

Then, no garden is complete without turnips, and mine will have: turn up for church; turn up with a smile; turn up with a new idea and turn up with real determination.

If you liked the peas, squash, lettuce and turnips from my garden, you may like this real cake recipe found in one of my mother's old recipe boxes:

<u>Christmas Bible Cake</u>
4 ½ cups of Kings 4:22
1 cup of Judges (last clause)
2 cups of Jeremiah 6:20
2 cups of 1 Samuel 30:12
2 cups of Nahum 3:12
2 teaspoons of 1 Samuel 12:24
6 oz. of Jeremiah 17:11
½ cup of Judges 4:19 (last clause)
2 teaspoons of Amos 4:5

Season to taste with II Chronicles 9:9. Bake in a moderate oven in your favorite cake pan.

This writer appreciates the recent letters received regarding this newspaper column. They are a soothing balm for writer's cramp, and a real boost to inspiration. With the exception of the first and last paragraph, I will share a letter from a reader in El Campo:

…..IT FIGURES…
Take your calculator
Begin with 66, the number of books in the Bible.

Add 13, the number of Paul's Books in the New Testament.

Add 7, the number of churches in Asia Minor (Revelation 1:4)

Multiply by 3, the Godhead.

Multiply by 12, the number of tribes of Israel

Multiply by 12 again for the apostles.

Now add 666, for the number of the beast of Revelation.

Press the equal sign, turn the calculator around and read the numbers upside down. You will find the solution for every problem you face in life.

I had not seen this before, and I did enjoy it. I tried it first on the calculator and saw the lighted answer, also tried it by hand which is readable if you make the eights boxy instead of rounded.

In one letter I received was the question, "What is a Christian's greatest sin? (because we all sin)" The majority of Christians will probably agree that their besetting sin is prayerlessness. Daily communication with God is very important, yet this greatest of all Christian privileges is the most neglected. God is near, and is as accessible as the phone, radio or television set; so why don't we tune in more often and take advantage of this wonderful gift from a loving God?

We sing, "Take It To The Lord In Prayer," and "Prayer Changes Things". We see prayer mottos and hear pastoral admonitions and questions that ask, why worry when you can pray? But instead of falling on our knees with the disciples' cry of "Lord, teach us (me) how to pray," we just keep on worrying.

Someone wrote, "God fades out of the life that forgets to pray." The way out of every dilemma is the "way up". What this world needs today, more than discussions, organizations, or summit talks, are more Christians who will "pray without ceasing". (I Thess. 5:17)

Can it be that I rose in the morning and took up the work of the day with its cares and grosses so heavy, without kneeling a moment to pray?

Thoughts from the human brain, like electrical impulses from one micro-chip to another inside a computer, govern our every action. Also the brain, like a computer, must be programmed by someone more powerful and intelligent than itself. The most powerful forces in the world are those of good and evil, and each strives to master the individualistic mind.

It is not enough to just have a mind and let it wander aimlessly until a stronger power takes it over. An aimless or idle mind is the devil's workshop and evil forces don't wait for an invitation to come in.

The inventor or creator of the computer, being man with man's limitations, could only endow the machine with man's logic. The machine can do nothing more than what mankind programs it to do, but the all omnipotent creator of the human brain endowed it with the privilege of free choice to choose its programmer. And He endowed man with his own reasoning power which, if used, will furnish stimuli for a healthy and successful life. But who among us uses the full potential of his or her brain power?

Thoughts are eventually followed by actions and our actions speak loudly, revealing to others what we are really thinking. Only by asking God to program our minds with the right kind of thoughts can we be sure of the right kind of actions. The Holy Scriptures tell us, "As a man thinketh in his heart, so is he." Therefore, what we think is of the utmost importance!

Those of us who believe that the Bible is the inspired word of God search the scriptures diligently for information. This is what the Bible tells us to think: "….whatsoever things are true, whatsoever things are honest (honorable), whatsoever things are just, whatsoever things are pure, whatsoever things are lovely, whatsoever things are of good report; if there be any virtue, and if there by any praise, think on these things." (Phil. 4:8)

This is the scripture that inspired the writing of this newspaper column. The ambition and purpose of this writer is to inspire others to realize the importance of right thinking, and to use the power of positive attitudes to make this world a better place in which to live, with God's peace in our hearts and brotherly love for all mankind.

Happy and productive thinking, with the kind of thoughts described above, is my earnest wish for each and every one of you.

One of the worst disappointments in life, one that psychiatrists discuss frequently, is the experience of being let down by a friend. It is not easy to forgive and forget, but it can be done, especially if you go by the following rules. 1) Don't close all the gates behind you. 2) Don't tell others of your quarrel. 3) Be fair in determining who's really at fault. 4) If the fault is not yours, find and try to understand the reason for your friend's behavior.

Psychiatrists say that when a friendship is dissolved, the most common cause is that one of them has violated a confidence. When you tell a friend something in strict confidence you expect him or her to keep it confidential, yet it is an experience of shock, heartbreak and disillusionment when a friend once-loved and trusted has let you down.

The split may ensue with or without a quarrel, but if tempers do flare, and you feel that you never want to see that person again, don't burn all the bridges; leave the gate partly open. People should never do or say anything that would prevent a future reconciliation.

Two elderly men in a retirement home were very close friends. "Have you always been good friends?" asked another resident.

"No," said one, "Forty years ago we hated each other. We were ranchers and my land joined his, and we each though the other's cattle had torn down the dividing fence. We each expected the other to repair it. One day, we started out at the same time, each intending to give the other a piece of his mind, but a strange thing happened. The worst blizzard of the century blew in, and when we met in the freezing wind, rain, and snow, we were very glad to see each other and became good friends again."

"Yes," replied the other friend, "There's nothing like a cold blizzard to cool tempers and warm friendships."

Don't broadcast your trouble, it might boomerang and make you the heavy.

Quarrels often result from one person trying to dominate the other. Friends as well as married couples can be guilty of playing God and laying down the law, which is their will. Why do they act that way? The more we try to understand the motivation behind a person's actions, the easier it is to find patience, tolerance and forgiveness within ourselves. These attitudes are not a weakness; they give us strength.

Every time we forgive and forget the wrongs done against us, and every time we reclaim a friendship that once let us down, we become just a little more like the person whom one of his friends sold out for 30 pieces of silver. (Jesus)

As the old adage says, "Nothing ever changes except change," and we also change with the changes. Mankind's attitude of fear has changed drastically in the last 70 years; then man feared nothing but God, now it seems that people are afraid of everything but God.

Present fears differ from the earlier ones of witchcraft and the super natural; now we fear the nuclear arms race and the untried weapons; we fear food additives that may cause diseases, and we fear the criminal minds on the streets who no longer fear God.

Long before Franklin Delano Roosevelt made his historical statement, "There's nothing to fear except fear itself," religious leaders were theorizing and expounding the subject of fear. One said, "Men once feared ghosts that walked in the night; now they fear ghosts that tramp through the corridors of their minds."

These little ghosts of the mind are of worry and tension and trouble-hunting that cause people to cross bridges before they get to them, to worry about disasters that never happen, about illnesses that may never occur, about hardships in a land of plenty, etc. These ghosts are more real than the old time ones who said "OOOOOH" when the wind blew hard. The mind that has these little ghosts floating around in its corridors cannot be used to its fullest potential. They are the howling winds that destroy man's ambitions, and push him further back in the wrong direction.

The best way to free the mind of these ghosts is to build up a faith in God so strong that they don't frighten us anymore. When peace and calm come into our hearts and lives, the ghosts cease to exist. They CAN disappear, because they were untrue and unreal in the first place. The prophet Isaiah told how this ghost-dissolving peace could be obtained, "I will keep him in perfect peace whose mind is stayed on Thee."

Whether it be legend or fact is not known (it isn't Biblical), but the story is told of how Saint Peter tried to dodge the ghost of fear. It sounds logical because he was frightened when he cut off the high priest's ear, also afraid when he denied Jesus three times, and very frightened when he and the other disciples fled from the crucifixion. Here is the story:

Being persecuted in Rome, Peter ran away. Leaving Rome he met the risen Lord who asked, "Where are you going Peter?"

"I am frightened," said Peter.

"Then I will have to go back and be crucified again," said Jesus.

Peter said "No Lord," and he returned to Rome where he was crucified, but he told them he was not worthy to be crucified as Jesus was, and he wanted them to put him on the cross with his head downward. Because of his insistence, they did so. (History records that Peter died on a cross with his head downward.)

Self-consciousness is an affliction. Those who have it suffer untold tortures of the mind. It is a mental malady and those who accept it are often miserable.

It is exactly what the name implies, a person who is too aware or conscious of himself or herself. There are different degrees or levels of self-consciousness. Some introverts are so wrapped up in themselves that they think other people are continually noticing them too.

The bad thing about this ailment is that most people who have it don't think highly enough of themselves. They are not comfortable in a crowd. If there are two people talking quietly, the self-conscious person feels that he is the derogatory topic of their conversation. People are never laughing with him but always at him, or so he thinks. He or she is the extreme opposite of that person of whom the Bible said "shouldn't think more highly of himself than he ought to think".

Some people tolerate this maladjustment all their lives, others just try to "live it down", but the sensible thing to do is find a cure because it's not a terminal disease. The cure is a series of "don'ts". Don't fail to be friendly, be more outgoing. Don't bury yourself with thoughts of self when you can take cover in your neighbor's problems and help him solve them. Don't dwell on loneliness; self-consciousness promotes loneliness. Develop special interests, preferably that include other people. When you are alone, get absorbed in hobbies. Even though it's your nature to be a loner, you must fight it!

Don't worry about yourself! Although it's better for our health and our peace of mind if we don't worry about anything at all; it's better to worry about your neighbor's little girl's cough than to commiserate with self.

One of the first lady psychiatrists told her patient, "Stop worrying about how you look! Think of several people who are not as fortunate as you and worry about them; then you won't have time to wonder if your slip shows, or if you forgot to powder your nose." One lady at a church school picnic discovered that she had a runner in her nylon hose and it spoiled her whole day.

Don't forget to take in stride the unpreventable incidents in life and don't be self-conscious because they happen to everybody; fate doesn't have a grudge against you. Don't let minor setbacks become major catastrophes.

When you've considered all of these "don'ts", and take the name of the mental misery apart, making it: consciousness of self, you'll wonder why you ever thought yourself so important in the first place.

Readers have asked for more recipes. I'm glad you liked the Christmas Bible Cake. There is only one other recipe in my files that is suitable for this column. An occasional Bible puzzle or recipe adds variety, but we must be careful not to turn this into a "cook's corner" or "entertainment center" because we must also think on other things.

## SCRIPTURE CAKE

| | |
|---|---|
| ¾ cup soft | Genesis 18:8 |
| 1 ½ cups | Jeremiah 6:20 |
| 5 (separated) | Isaiah 10:14 |
| 3 cups sifted (all purpose) | Leviticus 24:5 |
| ¾ teaspoon | 2 Kings 2:20 |
| 3 teaspoons | Amos 4:5 |
| 1 teaspoon | Exodus 30:23 |
| ½ teaspoon of all three | 2 Chronicles 9:9 |
| ½ cup | Judges 4:19 |
| ¾ cup chopped (blanched) | Genesis 43:11 |
| ¾ cup finely cut (dried) | Jeremiah 24:5 |
| ¾ cup | 2 Samuel 16:1 |
| Whole (blanched) | Genesis 43:11 |

Cream Genesis 18:8 with Jeremiah 6:20. Beat in yolks of Isaiah 10:14 one at a time. Sift together Leviticus 24:5 and 2 Kings 2:20, Amos 4:5, Exodus 30:23 and 2 Chronicles 9:9. Blend into creamed mixture alternately with Judges 4:19. Beat whites of Isaiah 10:14 until stiff. Fold in chopped Genesis 43:11, Jeremiah 24:5 and 2 Samuel 16:1. Turn into 10 inch tube pan that has been greased and dusted with Leviticus 24:5. Bake at 325 degrees for one hour and ten minutes or until golden brown and cake tester comes out clean. Cool 15 minutes. Remove from pan and cool completely. Serve drizzled with burnt sugar syrup and decorate with whole Genesis 43:11. Makes one ten inch tube cake.

## BURNT SUGAR SYRUP

| | |
|---|---|
| 1 ½ cups | Jeremiah 6:20 |
| ½ cup | Genesis 24:25 |
| ½ cup | Genesis 18:8 |

Melt Jeremiah 6:20 in heavy skillet over low heat; continue cooking until syrup is a deep amber color, add Genesis 24:25. Cook until syrup is smooth. Remove from heat; add Genesis 18:8 and stir until melted. Cool. Makes approximately 1 ¼ cups of syrup.

The Bible teaches many things about food, but considers spiritual food more important, "Labor not for meat that perisheth, but for that meat which endureth unto everlasting life, which the Son of man shall give you." (John 6:27) Jesus said, "I am the bread of life; he that cometh to me shall never hunger." (John 6:35) Also he said, "Blessed are they which do hunger and thirst after righteousness for they shall be filled." (Matthew 5:6)

"It is not that which goeth into the mouth that defileth a man; but that which cometh out of the mouth, this defileth a man." (Matthew 5:6)

One of our most festive holidays is just around the corner. Much has been said and sung about Thanksgiving Day. Much is done in preparation for the event whether it's to Grandmother's house we go or to Aunt Mabel's or if the whole clan is coming to our house, there's pumpkin pies to be made, a plump turkey of the right size to be selected, vegetables to be chosen, and we hope the stores haven't sold all of their fresh cranberries, and that we have to use canned ones again this year.

Do the "hustle and bustle" and the anticipation of seeing not-often-seen friends and relatives cause us to miss the real meaning of the day? No one is going to forget the name of the day; it's marked on our calendars. There's at least one in each clan who will say grace something like this, "….and bless the hands that prepared this food, and bless the nourishment of this food to our bodies, and our bodies to do thy service, amen." Then the fun begins with the head of the house carving the bird, asking, "Who wants light meat and who wants dark meat?"

Later, does anyone remember that their bodies are to do service for Him whose blessings were requested? Is the day just another holiday and does grace become lip service only, and a mealtime habit? We've more to be thankful for than food.

The Bible speaks of a man who had a "pearl of great price". We have six such pearls for which to be thankful. Our first pearl of great price is Jesus, the redeemer, without whom we could not have this abundant life. Next, we have the pearl of peace. Not as the world has peace, but we have the heavenly peace of God that was sent down as promised with the comforting Holy Spirit which descended on the Day of Pentecost. Our third pearl of great price is the Bible; the inspired word of God of which Paul said, "Study to show thyself approved unto God…."

Angels are said to covet the next pearl, but it is a privilege that God has given only to Christians, and that is the winning of lost souls for Christ and the privilege of taking sick souls to the Great Physician to be spiritually healed. The lost soul that we have won is a very valuable pearl.

Prayer is the next pearl. An army could get lost without its communication system, and so could Christians if they neglect the pearl of prayer too often. Prayer is vital; Jesus prayed many times daily, and so must we.

The sixth pearl is hope. The blessed hope of the return of Christ who told His disciples, "I will come again…." (John 14:3) He did everything else that He said He was going to do, and He'll do this too! There is an added blessing, "Every man that has this hope in him purifieth himself….." (John 3:3)

Let's not forget the words of President Calvin Coolidge, "The foundation of our society and our government rests so much on the teachings of the Bible, that it would be difficult to support them, if faith in these teachings should cease to be practically universal in our country."

In honor of Thanksgiving Day and the early settlers who originated it, let's review the poem by Helen Jackson as a memorial to:

## THE PILGRIM FOREFATHERS

"Neath hoary moss on crumbling stones
Their names are fading day by day;
The fashions of their lives and speech
From sight and sound have passed away.

The shores they found so bleak, so bare,
Shine now with riches gay and proud;
And we, light-hearted, dance on ground
Where they in anguish wept and bowed.

Unto the faith they bought so dear,
We pay each day less reverend heed;
And boast, perhaps, that we outgrow
Narrowness which marked their creed.

A shallow boast of thankless hearts,
In evil generation born;
By the side of those old Pilgrim men
The angels shall hold us in scorn.

Find me the men on earth who care
Enough for faith or creed today
To seek a barren wilderness
For simple liberty to pray:

Men who for simple sake of God
All titles, riches, would refuse,
And in their stead, disgrace and shame
And bitter poverty would choose.

We find them not. Alas! The age,
In all its light, hath blinder grown;
In all its plenty starves, because
It seeks to live by bread alone.

We owe them all we have of good:
Our sunny skies, our fertile fields;
Our freedom, which to all oppressed
A continent of refuge yields.

And what we have of ill, of shame,
Our broken word, our greed for gold,
Our reckless schemes and treacheries,
Where men's souls are bought and sold.

All these have come because we left
The path that the forefathers trod;
The simple, single-hearted ways
In which they feared and worshipped God.

Despise their name and creed who will!
Pity their poverty who dare!
They knew joys, their lives wore crowns
We do not know, we cannot wear.

And if so be that it is saved,
Our poor republic, stained and bruised,
'Twill be because we lay again
Their cornerstones which we refused.

• • • • • • • • • • • • • • • • • • • • • • • • • • • • • • • • • • • • • • • • • •

Have you heard the story of the preacher who wouldn't do?  A church was in need of a pastor.  One of the elders was interested in knowing just what kind of a minister they desired.  He, therefore, wrote a letter as if he had received it from an applicant.  He read this letter before the pulpit committee:

Understanding that your pulpit is vacant, I would like to apply for the position.  I have many qualifications that I think you would appreciate.  I have been blessed to preach with power and have had some success as a writer.  Some say I am a good organizer.  I have been a leader in most places I have gone.

Some folks, however, have some things against me.  I am over 50 years of age.  I have never preached in one place more than three years at a time.  In some places I have left town, after my work caused riots and disturbances.  I have to admit that I have been in jail three or four times, but not because of any real wrongdoing.  My health is not too good, although I still get a good deal done.  I have had to work at my trade to help pay my way.  The churches I have preached in have been small though located in large cities.

I have not gotten on too well with the religious leaders in different towns where I preached.  In fact, some of them have threatened me, taken me to court, and attacked me physically.

I am not good at keeping records.  I have even been known to forget whom I baptized.  However, if you can use me, I shall do my best for you, even if I have to work to help with my support.

The elder read the above letter to the committee and asked them if they were interested in the applicant.  They replied that he would never do for their church.  They were not interested in an unhealthy, contentious, trouble-making, absent-minded, ex-jailbird; in fact they felt insulted that his application had even been presented.

The committee then asked the name of the applicant, whereupon the elder answered, "The Apostle Paul".  The author is unknown, but the story has been used by religious leaders, laymen, and guest speakers for many years.

Many Christians are as short-sighted as the committeemen in the story; they allow their minds to live in a fog.  They allow a cupful of trouble to cloud their vision and dampen their spirit.  Anxiety, turmoil and defeat strangle their thoughts.  Lives are being "choked by the cares of this world". (Luke 8:14)  But "God has not given us a spirit of timidity, but of power and love and discipline". (2 Tim. 1:7)

Let's not let the fog get us down!  Let's live in the SUNSHINE!

Recently people have been asking, "How does one become a Christian?" This is a very good sign that Christianity is "on the mend" and that religion (belief in God) is again taking the lead in overcoming atheism, communism, and all the other "isms" that are contrary to God's laws. It's time for Christianity to awaken and take "The Great Commission" more seriously. The Bible has perfect answers for becoming a Christian. You may condense them to three words: faith, presentation, and revelation.

What is faith? The Apostle Paul said, "Faith is the substance of things hoped for and the evidence of things not seen." Faith is also the way a man, or woman, reacts to the revealed word of God. Because faith begins with a revelation from God showing His will, believers can discern for themselves what the perfect will of God is, and the revelation is never contrary to the word of God that is in our Bibles. Satan wants to force his will on mankind and his presence is easily discerned because his revelations are contrary to the law and will of God.

It takes a special kind of person to discern the will of God. It takes presentation, which means "presenting your bodies a living sacrifice unto God," a total and complete sacrifice which includes abandonment of worldly standards and worldly values. Faith and presentation mean revelation which brings an inner knowing (Col. 3:15 – 16), also an inner calm and peace with God. You have to trust that inner knowing, calm, and peace which you cannot explain.

It takes a special type of person to discern. The Bible says, "Ye must be born again;" therefore, it takes a transformed person. Faith plus presentation equals revelation; and faith plus presentation plus revelation equals transformation because knowing and loving God, presenting and dedicating yourself to His service, receiving His divine will, you feel separate and apart from the worldly ways of the devil and his followers.

Does that mean that a Christian cannot have fun? By no means! It means that you can have the best time of your life! God wants us to be happy. Wholesome fun with the family and Christian friends will make a happy life.

The Bible says, "Ye are in the world, but be not of the world." Recreation that leaves remorse or guilt feelings is not God's will for His people. We have to practice living here the way we plan to live in heaven, and God has given us the brain power to make our own heaven while here on earth, although the devil will use his wiles to try to make it hell.

The Apostle Paul said, "Behold, I show you a mystery. We shall not all die, but we shall be changed."

How many times have we heard the following passages of scripture read at funerals? "For this corruptible must put on incorruptible, and this mortal must put on immortality," and when we have reached this plane of incorruption, then "death is swallowed up in victory. Oh death, where is thy sting? Oh grave (death) where is thy victory?"

Why do people think morbidly of death and sometimes refuse to think about it at all until a loved one passes away and then they have morbid feelings, and make unkind remarks about the "grim reaper" who took him or her away?

Seldom are these scriptures, and related types, chosen for general reading. Why? If we knew of a certainty that we must go out and confront an enemy and perhaps do battle with him, we would certainly want to be prepared and we would study and think about the situation and learn all there was to know about it.

We know without a doubt that what the world knows as death is a certainty for each and every one of us; so why not learn all there is to know about it? Death is the last enemy we all have to meet, and we should remember that all power in heaven and earth was given to Christ when He overcame this corruptible world and sat down on the throne of the Father. (Matthew 28:18) In overcoming the world, He gained the power over him that had the power of death. (Luke 12:15 and Heb. 2:14) "For since by man (Adam) came death, by man (Jesus) came also the resurrection of death." (Cor. 15:21)

Death is a penalty, a penalty of being eternally separated from God; therefore we shall not all die. It's as unnatural to die as it is to be executed. Jesus said that He came to redeem us from death. I believe Him! Those who are corrupt die; those who have been redeemed and cleansed of corruption do NOT die, but are changed "in the twinkling of an eye."

When Jesus was called to the home of Mary and Martha, where he raised their brother, Lazarus from the dead, He was talking to Martha about death and made this statement, "Whosoever liveth and believeth in Me, shall never die. Believeth thou this?" It's not visible to the physical eye that's observing the lifeless form, whether that person has died or been changed (John 11:26), because the change is into a spiritual body. (I Cor. 15:44)

Jesus said, "I am He that liveth and was dead (died a sinner's death for you and me), and behold, I am alive evermore, and have the keys of hell and death." (Rev. 1:18)

It's beginning to smell like Christmas everywhere you go! Whether it's chestnuts roasting in the fire, fruitcake in the pantry, plum pudding from the oven, cookies baking, the syrupy smell of pulled taffy, or wassail heating in the pot, it's definitely the delicious aroma of Christmas. Although not having the sweetness of spring flowers, the evergreens, including the fire, spruce or cedar trees as well as the holly, mistletoe, magnolia leaves and colorful poinsettias, all give of their own "Christmasy" woodland fragrance.

In December, grade school children study about Christmas customs in other lands; college students may search early history hoping to find why December 25 is a Christian festival and observed as the anniversary of the birth of Christ. Although there are several plausible reasons given by historians and theologians, no one can be sure. The New Testament gives no specific date; however, direct references to other things give us the year and the season. The season referred to was the time shepherds watched sheep "in the fields" which is not easy to relate to December 25th, but calendars have been changed and seasons are always changing.

Perhaps the main reason for the lack of exact date of the Nativity is because the early Christian fathers did not approve of celebrating birthdays. History says, "….the church fathers frowned upon the celebrating of birthdays and thought them a heathen custom." In fact, history tells us that Christmas was probably not celebrated until 300 years after the birth of Christ.

The Christmas customs we observe today did not have their origin in church festivals with one exception, the Nativity scene and the wise men who came to worship the Christ child is displayed in many churches. But the Christmas tree, the decorations, the giving (or exchanging) of gifts, the buying and sending of Christmas cards, hanging wreaths, stringing lights over yards and houses, the recognition of Santa Claus as the true spirit of Christmas, instead of the Holy Spirit, has caused theologians to ask that Christ be put back in Christmas and commercialism be taken out.

Why shouldn't we be happy on Christ's (assumed) birthday? People as well as countries celebrate in different ways. And why not? As long as we remember the character of the man whose birthday we celebrate and keep our celebrating within his principles, which should include prayer, praise and singing as well as wholesome fun with family and friends. Have a happy holiday everyone! God bless!

How easy it is to misread people's motives, and to attach a wrong or different meaning from the one intended in what they're saying. Often the reason behind this is a preconceived idea of what we think a person is like.

Preconceived ideas, like all unjust judgments, are based on the individual's likes and dislikes, and more often than not, the individual likes the person who agrees with him or her ideas and disagrees with the person who does not. A proud person, used to having his own way, will rarely ever listen to the other fellow's ideas and opinions, making it impossible to discover any points they may have in common.

In a small town the local PTC (parent teacher club) appointed a young newcomer to its finance committee. Taking her duty seriously she faithfully attended every meeting. The chairman was always there and so was the lady who served as both secretary and treasurer. The 13 member committee worked hard for the money-raising schemes devised by the chairman and secretary, but only a few attended the business meetings. When the newcomer asked some absentees why they were not at the meetings, one responded, "There's really no use going because the chairman and the secretary run the show and will accept no other ideas; no one opposes them."

There was a lot of wasted talent on that committee, and all because two people had preconceived ideas about who was best qualified to take care of everything. The newcomer brought up the fact that a quorum was needed for voting and was told, "We are just a PT club, not affiliated with the National Parent Teacher Association so we can forget about parliamentary procedure." They were good people, not misusing the funds, although often what they bought was not discussed in meetings until afterwards when they asked for a show of hands for approval of the purchase. There were never any objections from the few who were there because the things; library supplies, drinking fountains, playground equipment, etc. were all needed for the new building and all had worked to help earn the funds.

The two leaders didn't like the newcomer (until years later) because she voiced her opinion on correct procedure, insisted that all projects and purchases be voted on, and got the members to attend and vote. When a friend tries to give you his opinion of a right way and a wrong way of doing things, don't ever have the misconception that he or she is trying to rob you of power and get your position. Only a sneaky person would do that.

Persistence does pay and with the Lord's help we can eventually win over the person who is prejudiced against us, but handle them delicately and with patience. Patience means waiting without worrying.

A lady once told another, "You and I can never be friends, we don't see eye-to-eye on anything!" Since when does one have to see eye-to-eye to be friends? If friends can't talk over their differences and remain friends, how can we expect the nations to do so, and have world peace?

Two of our more joyous seasons of the year are behind us; Thanksgiving and Christmas have passed and also the old year of 1984. Are we still joyous? Do you have a case of doldrums as an aftermath of over-spending and now receiving the bills?

What will the New Year bring? We are living in an unpredictable world; nevertheless, life is still very much what we make it. No matter how bleak and dreary the future may seem as we face unpaid bills, overly appraised and assessed taxes, job insecurities, crop failures, etc. We must still be optimistic and commit ourselves to right living, and say as St. Paul did, "....for I know whom I have believed, and that He is able to keep that which I have committed unto Him." (2 Timothy 1:12)

January and February are appropriate times to also think about what the poet said, "If winter comes can spring be far behind?" It isn't too difficult to think of April showers, May flowers, green grass, Easter lilies, and spring turning everything around and making everything new. It's just as easy to conjure up a beautiful picture within the mind's eye as it is an ugly one, besides happiness and ugliness are not compatible. To the happy person, everything is beautiful (in its own way).

Everyone strives for happiness. And the pursuit of happiness is our constitutional right, but if one doesn't know the formula or secret for obtaining it, one only pursues without finding. Here are nine secrets, or pointers, that will help you to find happiness:

1.) Keep skid-chains on your tongue; always say less than you think.

2.) Make promises sparingly, but keep your promise faithfully no matter what it costs you.

3.) Never let an opportunity pass to say a kind and encouraging word to someone. Praise good work, no matter who did it.

4.) Show your interest in others. Let everyone you meet feel that you regard him as a person of importance.

5.) Be cheerful! Keep the corners of your mouth turned upward. Hide your pains, worries, and disappointments under a pleasant smile.

6.) Keep an open mind on all issues. Discuss but don't argue. It is possible to disagree in a friendly way.

7.) Let your virtues speak for themselves and refuse to talk about another person's vices. Discourage gossip. Make it a rule to say nothing unless it is something positive.

8.) Be very careful of other people's feelings.

9.) Pay no attention to cutting or critical remarks about you; live in such a way that nobody will believe them!

The fact that time is our most worthwhile commodity is not stressed often enough. Not only is it worthwhile, but it is often rare and limited. We must ration it and use it wisely because time, as we know it, is fast running out.

How do you spend your time? Is it well planned? Do you make every fleeting minute count? Does anyone, besides preachers and undertakers, really understand how short our earthly span of life is?

A pastor thought to encourage more people in his community to come to church by placing the following paragraph in his church's bulletin, "I wish you folks would come to church, if only for a visit. For someday they will carry you in and the Lord will say, 'Who is it?'"

Everyone of us has a total of 168 hours in our week. Assuming we attend Sunday School, Sunday morning and evening worship services, and the mid-week prayer service (which unfortunately is not true of everyone), we spend four hours a week in church.

What about the other 164? How are you spending those hours? Those four spent in church equal only 2% of your time. Obviously your spiritual character and depth are going to be greatly influenced by what you are doing the other 98% of the time.

It is said that in the average home the television is on at least five hours a day. That alone amounts to 35 hours a week or 20% of the week. If you spend the non-working part of that 98% that you are not in church to watch TV, read cheap novels and scandal magazines, run from store to store bargain hunting, gabbing on the telephone, and spreading your time among various other God-forgetting pursuits, is it any wonder you forget the worth of time?

Although the young people are taught the story of the ant and the grasshopper in school, it is still harder for them to realize the value of time than it is for the senior citizens.

Want to have some fun? Take a glass and an eye-dropper; put in 164 drops of clear water, and then four drops (or three or two or one – depending on how many services a week you attend) of ink or food coloring. The pale color will tell you something about your spiritual life. Spend the greater part of those other 164 hours in prayer, Bible study, and pursuit of God, and your spiritual life will take on new color and have more meaning.

Two things worth remembering: 1.) "To reach new heights, get down on your knees and pray. Meditate and be humble. 2.) If you ever want to find perfection, don't look in the mirror!

I have just read a story from a church's monthly newsletter and have the pastor's permission to pass it on to you. A Chinese person was converted to Christianity, and he gave an account of his salvation like this:

I was in a very deep well; I was sinking deeper and deeper and couldn't find my way out. As I looked upward I saw a face peering down at me. A voice said, "My child, I am Confucius, the father of your country. Had you obeyed my teaching, you would never have landed where you are now." He waved his hand and left saying, "If you ever manage to get out of this well, be careful to follow my teachings."

Then came Buddha, looking down into the well, he shouted, "My child, you have to quit the condition in which you find yourself. Rest down there where you are. Fold your arms and begin to think. You will find nirvana, the peace which all of us desire."

I called back and said, "Father Buddha, if you could help me get out of here I would be so thankful. Then I shall with great ease follow your instructions, but in this horrible place, how can I rest?"

Buddha did not get me out of the well. He left me in despair.

Another man came over to the well and looked down at me, a man whose face seemed full of goodness and interest although there were marks of great sorrow and suffering there too. He wasted no time in offering me words of comfort from up there, but came down where I was and pulled me out of that terrible clay in which I was wallowing and lifted me up to the surface. He didn't forsake me but brought me to a place of safety. He took my dirty clothing and dressed me in clean new clothes. Then He invited me to follow Him, saying, "I will never leave you nor forsake you." The man was Christ, and that is why I became a Christian. Christ was the only One who descended to the depths where I was. He saved me and has never ceased to have fellowship with me and be my companion. This is exactly what Christ did for me.

The above true story is like the Biblical one of The Good Samaritan in which a man, traveling from Jerusalem to Jericho, was robbed and beaten by thieves and left "half dead" on the side of the road. A church leader came by and walked around him, another religious leader did likewise. Then a Samaritan walked by. He saw, stopped, had compassion, gave first aid, took him to an inn and paid the innkeeper to take care of him.

God can also work through our hands when we care enough to try. Let's not walk on the other side of the road when we have an opportunity to help others. What we do for them, we are doing for Him.

One of the consequences of a world gone pleasure-mad is the absence of opportunity for in-depth reflection and meditation.

Home has become an interval between working hours, dining out, mid-week parties, and sporting events. Home is also another name for the launching pad from which we blast off every Friday after work and return to on Sunday night more tired than when we left. One man said that I have to get back to work in the morning so I can rest. When people work hard at play and rest on the job, what does that do for the economy?

Many of the young to middle aged married people, and even some older ones, of my acquaintance are in a state of sheer exhaustion much of the time as they push themselves from one pleasure trip to another, seeking recreation which they think will be a soothing balm for the stress and strain of a four and a half or five day work week.

I am not saying that working hours should be longer, neither am I speaking against pleasure and fun, but against excesses and extremes that drive people from one to the other while seeking a life of contentment, fulfillment, and peace.

These three things which everyone desires so much can never be attained by depending on ourselves to acquire them. Neither can we depend on any other, save One, our Creator. He knows us through and through because He created us in His own image.

He knows how we think, how we feel, knows our heart's desires, our every longing, and any hidden secrets that we don't reveal.

God surely wants His children to be happy, in the same way that we want our children to be happy. Recreation and clean, wholesome fun is very much a part of life, but it is not life's ultimate goal!

Certain types of recreation, such as hunting, fishing, boating, cycling, etc. can be as tiring as a hard day or working. Small wonder that the scripture says, "Be still, and know that I am God." (Psalms 46:10)

What is there to meditate or think about? The horror movie that we saw, or the violence that we read about in the newspapers? The nude bodies that now appear on the stage and screen? No! Not if you really want contentment, fulfillment, and peace.

Think and meditate about things that are true, honest, just, pure, lovely, virtuous, and of good report and praise. Reread Philippians 4:8. Do these things and "the God of peace shall be with you." (Philippians 4:9)

Arguing can become a devastating habit. It's a sure way of "How not to win friends and influence people."

Bickering, whether between parents, siblings, in-laws, business associates, or whomever is down grading and each participant becomes contentious and irritable. When the habit has formed, irritability becomes chronic and must be treated as an ailment until harmony is restored.

Arguments are usually over trivial things, and more often than not, it is the tone of voice instead of the words that sparks the fire. To illustrate this: a husband came down to the kitchen and remarked to his wife, "It's warmer this morning."

"Warmer! How can you say that? I'm cooking over the fire and I'm freezing! It was cold all night and it's still cold!"

He said, "Why do you have to dispute everything I say and get mad?"

She replied, "You make such ridiculous statements! I'm old enough to know when it's warmer and when it's still cold!"

"Oh yeah? Well, I've looked at the outdoor thermometer and it's seven degrees higher than at this same time yesterday!"

She said, "Then why on earth didn't you say so? Did you want to impress me with your superior knowledge? I still think it's colder, and there's definitely a feeling of snow in the air."

"Snow?" He laughed sarcastically, "You know about as much of the weather signs as the cat does about the stock market!"

And so they go, on and on with each retaliatory remark a little sharper and more hurtful than the last one. What had started out as a pleasant attempt at conversation, ended without good-byes as he left for work. Of course, the roles are reversible and the husband may be the short-tempered one.

On the surface the wife appears more at fault; nevertheless, it could have been prevented because everyone should learn how to side-step arguments. If the husband had said, "If you are cold, perhaps I'm being too optimistic," and then the quarrel might not have occurred.

Have you learned how to side-step an argument? Sometimes we have to re-evaluate our priorities. Which is more important, to assert your ego or to yield a point for the sake of harmony, peace and happiness? I'm not advocating "peace at any price, however, most quarrels, perhaps not as simplistic as this one, are usually about little things that don't really matter, or that can't be proved, or like the weather are things over which we have no control.

Most arguments can be side-stepped by either agreeing, changing the subject, or by keeping quiet, but if principle is involved and you are forced to take a stand, do it by proving yourself right, and not that the other person is wrong.

In days of old, back in the third, fourth, and fifth centuries, there were a considerable number of saints named Valentine or Valentinus. Two of these, one a Roman priest and the other a bishop were Christian martyrs. A special day, February 14, was designated as Valentius Festival Day in their honor.

Historians tell us that "the association of the lover's festival with St. Valentine seems to arise from the fact that the feast of the Saint falls in early spring, and is purely accidental." Nevertheless, lover's day through the ages has been known as Saint Valentine's Day and is celebrated on February 14.

So on February 14, whether you are the recipient of expensive heart-shaped pieces of jewelry, candy, flowers, or any gift that says, "I love you," remember that your gift is in no way associated with the solemnity of the saints. Also remember that according to tradition no one is allowed to lose their temper on this day. Even if you get an unattractive card that states, "Roses are red, violets are blue. I wanted a sweetheart, but I only have you!" Just grin and bear it. It's all in fun.

The Valentines and Valentius and Valentinians of the past were a popular people; three of them became Roman emperors. One was a pope for a short while, and one became a leader of the Gnostic movement. Others held lesser though still prominent positions. The Roman emperor, Valentinian I, successfully established a new British province called Valentia, named for his clan.

A romance novel was printed in 1489 and became a best seller. It was so popular that it was printed in five different languages: French, German, Italian, Dutch and English. Whether it is true or legendary is known only to unwritten history because the original book was lost and there were several versions of the story in circulation.

It is the story of two small boys of the Valentine family. They were twin brothers who became lost in the woods while they were still toddlers. They survived and one grew up as a knight in the king's court. The other grew up in a bear's den and became a wild man. His brother found him, overcame and tamed him, and together they found their mother and rescued her from the power of a giant-sized man who treated her cruelly.

The story was the inspiration for an old, old song, "Poor Babes in the Woods." However, in the song the babies were stolen and abandoned in the woods; they died there, and the robins covered them with strawberry leaves.

Everything I've researched, so far, makes me want to change Valentine's Day to Happy Heart's Day, and for senders of crazy cards, it should be on April first.

Happy Valentine's Day everyone! God loves you and I love you too.

• • • • • • • • • • • • • • • • • • • • • • • • • • • • • • • • • • • • • • •

If the reading material to which you subscribe is above average, you probably take at least one small town newspaper, a large city daily newspaper, three or more magazines, plus an additional magazine bought now and then from display and perhaps books from a lending library.

The old saying may be true that we are what we eat, but it is also certainly true that we can tell what a person's likes and dislikes are by what he reads.

A family of four, two parents and two college students, always shared the evening paper. Father read the business section first, then the front page; mother had the family news, social section and recipes. The daughter read the editorial page, including the letters to the editor and all sound-off columns; the son scanned the sports section and car advertisements.

Knowing what they read, it is easy to see the couple as a business man and his wife is a homemaker. The son is one who likes sports and "wheels" and the daughter is surely interested in psychology because she likes to know what other people are thinking and doing. Their preferred reading was evident in their subscriptions too. The father received Forbes and the Wall Street Journal. The mother took Woman's Day and Needlecraft. The son had Popular Mechanics, and the daughter took no magazines, but read everything in both the city and college libraries about people.

It isn't always necessary to have a degree in psychology to understand why people act as they do, talk as they do, and live as they do.

A friend once remarked, "I wish I knew what made him tick." This is really not too difficult to do, but one must develop a keen sense of observation. Notice particularly his lifestyle and habits, and what he likes and dislikes. Don't note what he says as much as how he says it, and the tone of his voice. You can tell if he's shallow or deep by what he reads and the company he keeps. You can tell if he's harsh or kind by the way he treats children and pets and older relatives and friends.

Observation is a better way to understanding than asking direct questions because sometimes people think they are answering truthfully when they really are not. If you ask someone, "How are you this morning?" and get this surprising answer, "I hate everything and everybody! That's how I feel!"

Is he telling the truth? Most people would be inclined to say, "OK, if that's how you feel!" and walk on by. But the observing person may have noticed an unshed tear, a slight catch in the voice, a nervous movement of body language, and reply with a big smile, "Oh, come now, you can't hate everybody; you're just feeling blue. Cheer up! God loves you, and I love you too." This may not get a smile in return, but as you walk on, you'll have the satisfaction of knowing that he or she will have more pleasant thoughts than before. No one can hate a genuinely friendly person.

• • • • • • • • • • • • • • • • • • • • • • • • • • • • • • • • • • • •

One of the most interesting ghost stories that ever crossed my desk was written in the early 1940's by a man with a PH.D. It wasn't a story about supernatural happenings; it was about ghosts from the past that linger on as fears in the mind.

He said, "They haunt us more effectively than any old-time ghost ever pursued or frightened men in the long ago. They make our sick lists grow, fill our state hospitals, set husbands against wives, turn children away from parents, keep countless persons away from moral social relations, and influence countless more to take roads that defeat rather than win the desires of their hearts."

These ghosts that inhabit the mind as fears are usually not things that have already happened because, as things happen, they are met and dealt with. They are the ghosts of the imaginary fears we accumulated in childhood.

Lack of training, of learning about thought processing in young formative years, makes it hard for an adult to escape the fears of his youth. The tendency is to run away and hide just as one did in childhood, but one must learn to face fear and realize that even if it can't be entirely eliminated, it can be dealt with to our benefit.

It also helps to talk about these fears. One lady was saying to her friends, "I have already told you how as a child I developed a fear of the dark. Today, although I have had an extensive psychoanalysis, I still have this fear. It still persists at times although it never keeps me from doing what I must do, and I have learned to live with it. It is a tiny cross to bear. It is something by my side at night to keep me alert, to keep me on my toes. It keeps me agile, and I think basically, it is good."

The fear of having incurable cancer drove one woman from doctor to doctor, all of whom gave her not only a negative response, but also a statement of good health. She was a religious woman, and when she confided in her pastor, he reminded her that in her religion she was taught the secret of life, and anyone who knows the secret of life is not afraid of death. By not running from one doctor to another, trying to evade the ghost of fear, she learned to live with it and it gradually faded away.

One must deal logically and constructively with these metal ghosts because they are to the mind what winter is to the rest of the year, a screen that blocks the view of spring where new life is waiting, ready to pop-out when conditions are favorable for the transformation.

"Behold! The old things pass away and everything becomes new!"

Do you think Sunday School is just for children?  If so, here is some food for thought.

On page 94 of the International Lesson Annual (Sep. – Aug. 1984-85) there are seven questions.  The teacher of a local ladies Bible class brought them before her group saying, "Questions such as the following are answered differently among Christians; I would like to know each of your thoughts on these questions."

1.) Will we know each other in heaven?
2.) Will we come into the presence of Christ immediately after death, or must we wait for a general resurrection of the dead?
3.) Will we have a body in heaven, and if so, what will it be like?
4.) Will we carry over into the next life memories of our life on earth?
5.) Will we find the answers to life's unanswered questions when we get to heaven?
6.) Will there be universal salvation or will only a certain number be saved?
7.) How can a person be happy in heaven if one of his loved ones is not there?

These are questions that many people think about but few want to talk about.  The first decision, of course, is to answer the age old question, "If a man die, shall he live again?" And because God sent His own Son into the world to die as a man, return in the body, resurrected to new life, we have the answer to that question. (St. John 3:16)

Even those who disregard the teachings of ancient history of Bible times and refuse to believe or have faith in Christianity are still concerned about the miracle of birth and death and life and where it is leading them.

The Greek philosopher, Marcus Aurelius (161-180 A.D.), speaking of life and man said, "We are such stuff as dreams are made of.  Awake, then, and see thy dream as it is, in comparison with that erstwhile it seemed to thee."  Marcus also quoted Homer the poet, "Like the race of leaves, the race of man is the wind in autumn strews the earth with old leaves, then in spring the woods with new endows.  All are born indeed in the spring season and soon a wind hath scattered them, and thereafter the wood peopleth itself again with another generation of leaves.  And what is common to all of them is but the littleness of their lives.  And so it will be when thine eyes close, that he upon whom thy leaned, will himself be a burden upon another."

It is my opinion that no other writer has quite so aptly described the passing of the generations.

I have searched some possible answers to use later.  Meanwhile, if the questions are important to you, write me.  Would you like related scripture references?

Did you read the seven questions asked in last week's column? And have you had time to think on these things to see if they're important to you? Let's consider the first one. Will we know one another in heaven?

Before searching the scriptures for information, there are two important things to remember; 1.) We can't take scriptures out of context (when they're referring to another matter), and 2.) that the person entering heaven has been changed. "Flesh and blood cannot enter (inherit) the kingdom of God." (I Cor. 15:50)

We see the person as he or she was in this life; our memories are of the physical person, and they fade with the years until what we remember most are their spiritual attitudes. The Bible confirms this, "That was not first which is spiritual, but that which is natural; and afterward that which is spiritual." (I Cor. 15:46)

Now the question becomes will these spiritual bodies in heaven know each other? Paul said, "Here I see through a glass darkly; but then face to face. Now I know in part; but then shall I know even as I am known." (I Cor 13:12)

When seeking the truth, the best source of knowledge is from one who has experienced that truth. Christ, being the "first fruit of them that slept", is qualified to speak of the next life, or rather the continuing of life after death. He said, "And this is life eternal, that they might know the only true God, and Jesus Christ, whom God has sent." (John 17:3)

Jesus, speaking in the 124 chapter of St. John, tells us a little about heaven. Of first importance is the fact that God is there. Jesus said that He was going there to prepare a place, that He would return and take His loved ones there to be with Him. "Because I live, ye shall live also. At that day ye shall know that I am in my Father, and ye in me, and I in you." (John 14:19-20). If we are to be that close to God and Jesus, wouldn't we know the other joint heirs as well?

Earthlings, never having been to heaven, can't possibly know where it is, what it is like, and especially who or how many will be there. But the fact that our Father "who art in heaven" is there, makes it a very desirable place. It is written, "Eye hath not seen nor ear heard, neither has it entered into the heart of man, the things which God hath prepared for them that love him." (I Cor. 2:9)

From the New Dictionary of Thought, one friend asked another, "Do you think we shall know each other in heaven?"

"Yes," was the friend's reply, "do you think we shall be greater fools there than here?" (Evans)

Bishop Wilson said, "No man will go to heaven when he dies who has not sent his heart there while he lives."

The glory of heaven cannot be imagined, but we can imagine everyone there being of one accord. That means everyone will know what the will of God is. Do we know now? If we don't, we can find out through prayer and spiritual communication!

In the early 1900's, before TV, radio, even before the phonograph, families used to sit around the table or on the porch in the evenings and discuss thought provoking questions. Sometimes the older youth would take part unless they were "keeping company" (dating) in which case they were usually in the kitchen "pulling taffy" or in the parlor looking at the latest double-picture postcards through the stereoscope which gave them a three-dimensional appearance.

The questions they discussed are again being asked in Bible class lessons. Will we come into the presence of Christ immediately after death or must we wait for a general resurrection of the dead?

If the inspired scriptures answered these questions plainly, there would be no point in researching the scriptures or even asking the questions. However, there are related scriptures (on the same subject matter), which if taken into account and used for comparison, will prove to be satisfactory answers to most of us.

Has anyone ever been with Christ after death? Yes, the thief on a nearby cross to whom Jesus said, "Verily I say unto thee, today thou shalt be with me in paradise." (Luke 23:43) This should also prove the validity of deathbed confessions and conversions. When the thief that wanted Jesus to remember him said,    "….when Thou cometh into Thy kingdom," it proved that he believed Christ to be who He said He was.

Paradise may not be the same as heaven where God is because we remember that Jesus, standing outside the empty tomb, said to Mary Magdalene, "Touch me not; for I am not yet ascended unto my Father, but go and tell…." (John 20:17)

I John 3:18-22 is the only scripture that tells where Jesus was, in the spirit, during the three days that He was supposedly dead and entombed. Read that scripture if you want to know!

To those who think that death brings only a long, deep sleep while awaiting the first or second resurrection, remember that Moses and Elijah, who had been dead for centuries, were not sleeping. They were seen, talking to Jesus, by Peter, John, and James when they "went up onto a mountain" with Jesus to pray. They even heard enough of the conversation between Jesus and Moses and Elijah to know that the two "spake of His (Jesus') decease which He should accomplish at Jerusalem." (St. Luke 9:30-31)

Because of the scripture of Lazarus and the rich man, we know there will be no strife between the righteous and the ungodly after death because "There is a great gulf fixed between them." They talked or communed in some way, but could not cross the gulf.

· · · · · · · · · · · · · · · · · · · · · · · · · · · · · · · · · · · · · · · · · · · · · · · ·

This pre-Easter season is a good time for discussing the questions that are now being asked each week. Today we will consider the third one, "Will we have a body in heaven, and if so, what will it be like?"

People should be much more concerned about getting to heaven than how they are going to look when they get there! But vanity does exist, so let's search the scriptures.

Body, the physical man or woman, can be full of light or it can be full of darkness. (Matthew 6: 22-23) The body can also be "cast into hell." (Matthew 5:29) Man adorns and glorifies the physical body, but God glorifies the spiritual body. Our spirit must worship God "in spirit and in truth" because God is spirit, and He made man "in His own image." Man is a living soul!

God said, "Behold, I will make everything new." Everything includes a new spiritual body! It may look like the old one, it may not; it has not been described. It may even be changeable. After Jesus had risen from the dead He "appeared in another form" unto two believers as they walked, and went into the country. (Mark 16:12)

The Bible speaks of a new heaven and a new earth and the people of Christ as new creatures and of having a new name, but the new things are not dwelt upon. They seemed to think it sufficient to say, the things of the flesh are flesh and the things of the spirit are spirit.

Revelation 21:1 and Isaiah 65:17 tell of the new heaven and earth. This verse from Isaiah also answers the next question, "Will we carry over into the next life memories of our life on earth?" Isaiah said, "Behold, I create new heavens and a new earth, and the former shall not be remembered nor come into mind."

The Bible states specifically, "There is a natural body, and there is a spiritual body." (I Cor. 15:44) "As we have borne the image of the earthly, we shall bear the image of the heavenly," (I Cor. 15:49) which means the same thing.

When the dead is raised incorruptible, we shall be changed in a moment…. In the twinkling of an eye… when the Lord calls us because "flesh and blood cannot inherit (live in) the kingdom of God."

Will we find the answers to life's unanswered questions when we get to heaven? If God told Isaiah, the prophet that "the former things shall not be remembered, nor come into mind," we will probably know the answers but not recall asking the questions. (Isaiah 65:17)

"To be absent from the body is to be present with the Lord. "(II Cor. 5:8) Also read II Cor. 12:2-4.

"To be spiritually minded is life and peace; to be carnally (fleshly) minded is death." (Romans 8:6)

These are the last questions that were asked by the theologians and Ph.D.'s who write the material for the International Lesson Annual used by Bible classes. They are on page 94 of the September-August 1984-85 edition.

Not only are these questions answered differently by the many different denominations, but there are also many and varied answers from members within the same denomination. The selected questions do not have direct scriptural answers, but the scriptures do contain other related subject matter which each interprets to their own understanding.

"Will there be universal salvation or will only a certain number be saved?" A hymn title comes to mind, "Whosoever Will May Come." I assume taken no doubt from Revelation 22:17.

Salvation is not limited or restricted to a certain number, but it is passed over by many who don't want to play the game of life by God's rules: the Ten Commandments. Salvation is full and free but is gained only by accepting Jesus. "Neither is there salvation in any other; for there is no other name under heaven given among men, whereby we must be saved." (Acts 4:12)

"Many are called but few are chosen." (Matthew 20:16) This is because "….not everyone shall enter the kingdom, but he that doeth the will of my Father, who art in heaven." (Matthew 7:21) "….broad is the way that leadeth to destruction and many there be that go in thereat ….narrow and straight is the way which leadeth unto life, and few there be that find it." (Matthew 7:13-14)

Nowhere in the Bible is the number of the saved told, but Jesus, the sacrificial Lamb, is keeping a record of them. "And there shall in no wise enter into heaven anything that defileth, neither whatsoever worketh abomination, or maketh a lie, but they which are written in the Lamb's Book of Life." (Rev. 21:27)

"How can a person be happy in heaven if one of his or her loved ones is not there?" If one lets the world and worldly events keep one away from church and God's people, that one is not worthy of the church. To those who love their families more than they love God, Jesus said, "He that loveth father or mother more than me is not worthy of me; and he that loveth son or daughter more than me is not worthy of me. And he that taketh not his cross, and followeth after me, is not worthy of me." (Matt. 10:37-38)

If we can't, while here, persuade our loved ones to love our Lord and Father like we do, they are not worthy of us and our faith. Isaiah said, "He who blesseth himself in the earth shall bless himself in the God of truth….because the former troubles are forgotten, and because they are hid from mine eyes." (Isaiah 65:16)

It is surprising how many people there are on this earth who think the world owes them a living. Nowhere is this more evident than in the junk mail that seems to be increasing every day. It's a time-consuming task to sift through it, searching for the wanted mail that must not be mistakenly thrown out.

I am not speaking of the 15 or 20 catalogs from novelty houses, the subscription seekers, the informative letters from politicians and insurance companies, book clubs, etc. These things are bothersome, but not exactly junk mail.

Some requests for money for charitable causes seem reasonable, others seem fraudulent, especially when they ask you to send $25, $50, or $100 to a box number in Grand Central Station, New York City. Many of the requests have no signatures and contain pictures of undernourished children, both the letters and the pictures being the product of a copy machine. My real junk mail is from con-artists or gyp-artists.

Have you noticed the ads of recipes for sale in papers like the Capper's Weekly? It seemed incredible to me that there would be that many people trying to sell simple recipes for $2 to $5 each. To satisfy my curiosity, as well as confirming my suspicions, I sent them an ad for "Grandma's Old-Fashioned Biscuit recipe for sale for $1. I received two legitimate orders for the recipe and over 200 pieces of mail resembling chain letters.

It was definitely a racket! Some of them even assured me that everything was legal and according to Post Office regulations, and that it was considered selling by mail. The first part of the letters explained that they were a recipe club or organization; the end of the letters always listed four to seven names. By each name was the name of a recipe and its price from $2 to $3 and an address. The letter asked that each be sent the price of his or her recipe, then to leave off the last name and write my name and address. I was asked to make copies of that letter and send to an unlimited number of people. If I mailed 100 copies, it would net me $60,000.00 in three weeks.

I selected three of the more obvious "scams" and mailed them to the Postmaster General. After a long, long while he replied, but it was a "wishy-washy", and unsatisfactory letter. He didn't say that it was legal and he didn't say that it wasn't.

What advantage is there in living in a land of plenty if that plenty can only be had by the revenue from fraudulent mail that deceives the uninformed, and from the sale of tobacco that costs lives and ill health, and from the sale of alcohol that causes alcoholics and impoverished families, and from the sale of drugs that causes addiction, crimes, insanity and death? It is certainly an abomination that will, sooner or later, cause desolation.

Do you have the desire to win souls? Do you have the desire to teach others about the plan of salvation, and to impart to them the gospel message?

Suppose someone asked you the question, "What must I do to be saved?" If you told him to stop being mean and to give up bad habits, it would do about as much good as whitewashing a dirty house. If you told him to move from that neighborhood to a better one, it would be like trying to improve your car by taking it out of the garage and putting it in the living room. If you car isn't running right, you have it overhauled to see if it needs a new part. If a man or woman isn't doing right, they need a new heart.

You may think you have the perfect answer and tell him to go and join a church, but going to church doesn't make a man a Christian anymore than going to an insane asylum would make him a lunatic.

The only answer for that question is the one Paul gave to the Philippian jailer, "Believe in the Lord Jesus Christ, and thou shalt be saved." He told the jailer where to put his confidence, his trust, and his faith.

Why are so many professing Christians unhappy, discontented, and frustrated? When Jesus was on earth He spoke of a different way of life, a life full of purpose and interest, with happiness, contentment, accomplishment and success. In fact He called His way of life an "abundant life" and said that all who believed in Him would "have life, and have it more abundantly." (John 10:10)

Christianity is practiced in different ways. Some people are astonished when they learn that the Bible speaks of two kinds of Christianity. Of course, one is real and the other is faked. That is what Paul was talking about when he told Timothy of the evil and wicked people "who have a form of Godliness, but deny the power of it." (II Tim. 3:15) They have a form of religion, but know nothing of the power of Christ that is available to a true Christian. The Holy Spirit is not only a spirit of love, but a spirit of power as well.

The Bible says that a true Christian, without exception, must have the Holy Spirit. (Romans 8:9) Nevertheless, many people who have gone to church all their lives have never realized the purpose and power of the Holy Ghost (spirit). The Bible tells in John 14:16 and 26 who the Holy Ghost really is and why He was sent, "to teach you all things, and that He may abide with you forever."

"And when He is come (the Comforter or Holy Ghost), He will reprove the world of sin, and of righteousness, and of judgment....When He, the spirit of truth, is come, He will guide you into all truth...." (John 16:8-13)

. . . . . . . . . . . . . . . . . . . . . . . . . . . . . . . . . . . . . . . . . . .

Isn't it wonderful to know that God judges us by the content of the heart and teaches us to likewise evaluate (not judge) our fellowman? Otherwise we would always be out on a limb. We would become overly sensitive, wear our feelings on our sleeves, carry a chip on our shoulder, brood over imagined hostilities, and in general, feel more sinned against than sinning.

We don't stop to consider that the slight or imposition, whichever, and whether real or imagined, may indicate the other person's insecurities, and who may be aware of cutting you down to build a more secure foundation for self. None of us wants to take a back seat; we are a selfish and "me first" generation, and we all need to walk in our offender's moccasins for several moons.

Perhaps Plato was right. He said no democracy would work after everyone became educated because everyone would want to run things. Is our country becoming like that? Of course, no one wants to stay at the bottom of the ladder and not everyone is content with middle-ground or small successes. It is the ambitious person who has his eye on the top rung that is the least likely to be benevolent to his fellowman.

Reaching the top is not nearly as important as how it is achieved! If by the blood, sweat and tears of self-effort, the leadership is good. But if one claims the efforts of others, or rides "rough-shod" over everything and everybody that's in the way, or simply betrays the opposition with a "Judas kiss", beware of what that one dishes out when he or she rules the roost.

We all know people of good intentions who, because they have had more than their share of rejections and unfulfilled plans, have developed a hard outer-crust that makes them seem like "tough hombres". But even tough armadillo shells make beautiful flower baskets, and once the tough person's armor has been pierced, revealing the true character underneath, both the person and his shell will seem different.

Motives should be considered too. Some want to get to the top for more money; others are satisfied with their life style, but are gifted with creative ability which they want to expand for the benefit of all mankind. Those who want to succeed merely for success alone are show-offs that don't usually reach the top, or stay there long if they do.

Everyone needs a best friend, one who always loves us, not because of our faults, failings and shortcomings but in spite of them. God is omnipresent and ever-ready to be that best friend.

You may live in a suburban mansion, a brownstone townhouse in the city, or in your ancestral home in a village or small town, in a villa, an apartment complex, or in a rose covered cottage at the end of a country lane, but there is one thing you have in common with all others. All have a neighbor or neighbors. Furthermore, we are a neighbor. Whether we are a desirable one or not depends entirely upon ourselves.

Being a good neighbor doesn't necessarily mean being "bosom buddies" or even best friends, but it does require politeness, and kindness and a willingness to help in times of trouble.

When a country feels threatened and needs more allies, we hear a lot about the good neighbor policy. There are times when the individual could use a staunch ally too. Who would qualify better than a good nearby neighbor?

Good and peaceful neighborhoods are essential to a peaceful and prosperous nation, but like a good marriage, you have to work continually to preserve the tranquility. Let's consider several factors that are beneficial in a local good neighbor policy. The chief factor is consideration and the best way to show it is by remembering and practicing The Golden Rule, "Do unto others as you would have them do unto you."

Don't impose or allow your children and their pets to impose on your neighbor's rights and privileges. Privacy is one of those rights. Make sure your company is wanted and welcomed. Learn to read the signs. If she's not busy, and especially if she's lonely, she's glad you came. But if she has just burned the roast or had a word battle and seems preoccupied, think of something that you forgot to do at home. Make understanding your goal and develop that sixth sense called intuition.

No neighborhood is perfect, even though fairly successful. It takes a lot of give and take and a fair amount of good sportsmanship for everyone to fit into the scheme of things. Here again, the Golden Rule applies!

Each neighbor must learn to accept responsibility toward all neighborhood enterprises, whether the project is cleaning a vacant lot or cemetery, repairing churches or community centers or helping a needy family.

We have obligations, one to another. We cannot be part of a community and live only to ourselves.

Neighborhood peace is broken more by parents taking up their children's quarrels than for any other reason. Wise is the dad who, when his son comes in saying, "Dad, Bobby says his dad says he can whip you," will reply, "We'll never know if that is true or not, son, because you see, Bobby's dad and I are friends, and would like for you boys to be friends too."

Oh, what is so fine as a day in May? The strong March winds that always linger over into the first week in April are entirely gone. Whether we're inside or outside the house, it's neither too hot nor too cold. The slow gentle rains of April have done their duty of watering, fertilizing, pulverizing, and pollinating, and May's myriad wild flowers are in full bloom over hill and dale.

Texas is especially beautiful in May. The highways and roadsides and pastures are ablaze with color, and our national colors of red, white, and blue are the predominant ones. There are the red "paint brushes" also called Indian blankets and our fast spreading state flower, the beautiful blue Texas bluebonnets, and the wild white daisies and poppies.

In less abundance are the yellow ladies slippers, black-eyed Susans and daffodils, the wild blue violets and irises, the dark red wild tulips, the delicate pink of the large petals on primroses, often called buttercups by children who find buttery deposits on their noses after smelling them. There are wild daylilies and colorful hollyhocks, and hedging the fences, intermingled with the prairie flowers, are clumps of Queen Anne's Lace with its delicate greenery and white lacy heads of tiny flowers that appear to be fragile, but really are not.

The sweet fragrance of the honeysuckle is more exotic than all the perfume in Paris, and it is found all over south Texas. Although not as prevalent now as in yesteryears when its vines would quickly cover a vacant house, a tree, windmill, fence-row, or just carpet the ground. It mostly grows wild in the untended rural areas now. It will quickly take over the place if one hasn't the time to prune, trim, and train the vine; but it is a prolific bloomer, and one can smell its heady fragrance for blocks.

I have attended two social events that didn't cost the hostesses a penny for flowers. A local doctor's wife and her friend used wild ladies slippers, whose bushy plants fill the prairies here in Wharton County, to decorate the reception rooms, tables, mantel, etc. They made tiny corsages for each guest by pulling three or four flowers from the stem and adding a narrow yellow ribbon bow. It was a huge success!

The other was the wedding of a local school teacher's daughter. They used a wild plant called "snow on the mountain". It's a large, showy, full-leafed plant with so many branches it makes a round mound. It was given this odd name because snow appears to be on the top of it in the heat of late summer when all other flowers are gone. Just as the upper leaves of a poinsettia turn red, the leaves on this plant turn white, looking like large white flowers and they glisten like snow. The front of the church was filled with baskets of them. They were gorgeous! One of the guests exclaimed, "The flowers must have cost a fortune!" Only we who helped to decorate knew that they came from God and the pasture.

We should thank God every day for our five special blessings: seeing, smelling, feeling, hearing, and speaking! Not everyone has them.

Mother's Day and Father's Day have a special meaning for us because they are the two people who have done more than anyone to shape our lives and make us what we are today.

Not all parents are good mothers and fathers. We read in a city paper where a young mother left her newborn infant in a trash can; another mother in Houston killed her eight-day old son because she and her husband had separated, and she was distraught. But they are the exceptions and not the rule, thank God! Most parents still love their children and want the best for them.

The successful religious writer, Eugenia Price, wrote of her parents, "The quality of love I have always received from Mother and Dad conditioned me for quick, rather natural belief in the love of God. They made it utterly possible for me to believe that God loved me. I admit to some problems with accepting His discipline, but never His love. My parents were, like yours, not perfect. I'm sure I needed more discipline at their hands. But human love at its very highest will always make mistakes in its actions. It is the reaction of love that counts."

"My parents have loved me freely and in the process conditioned me to love. Even at the first moment of conscious faith in God, I felt at home. I had grown up in the very atmosphere of giving love, love that left me free to seek my own fulfillment. Love that did not choke my particular personality. Love that did not bend me to the image of anyone. Love that never put me in competition with my brother, nor my brother with me."

As she spoke of her parent's love, she told how they financed her apartment in Chicago when she was 19 years old because they thought she could become a professional writer quicker in a big city. This type of free or unselfish love is alien to many parents, whether toward each other or to their children. Most want to keep those they love near them. Eugenia Price is now a well-known religious writer and she says of herself, "When I became a follower of Jesus Christ at age 33, I began to like myself a little once I stopped pushing aside obstacles and people in order to protect myself." She also gives her parents the credit for her success.

A story is told of four clergymen discussing the merits of the various translations of the Bible. One liked the King James Version because of its simple beautiful English. Another preferred the American Revised Version because it nearer the original Hebrew and Greek. The third liked Moffat's translation best because of it up-to-date vocabulary.

The fourth clergyman, when asked to express his opinion said, " I like my mother's translation best." The other three expressed surprise, "Your mother translated the Bible?"

"Yes, she did," he replied. "She translated it into life, and it was the most convincing translation I ever saw."

You may be wealthier than you think.

A poor servant of the Lord was summoned for taxation. The auditor began to question him to determine the amount of taxes he would have to pay. "Do you have property?" he asked.

"Yes, quite a lot," answered the Christian.

"Then list your possessions, please," the auditor instructed.

"First, I have everlasting life." (John 3:16)

"Second, I have a mansion in heaven." (John 14:2)

"Third, I have peace that passes understanding." (Phil. 4:7)

"Fourth, I have joy unspeakable." (I Peter 1:8)

"Fifth, I have divine love that never fails." (I Cor. 13:8)

"Sixth, I have a faithful wife." (Proverbs 31:10)

"Seventh, I have healthy, happy obedient children." (Ex. 20:12)

"Eighth, I have true, loyal friends." (Proverbs 18:24)

"Ninth, I have songs in the night." (Psalms 42:18)

"Tenth, I have a crown of life." (Jas. 1:12)

"Eleventh, I have a savior, Jesus Christ, who supplies all my needs." (Phil. 4:19)

The Christian paused and leaned back in his chair. The tax auditor smiled, closed his book and said, "Truly you are a very rich man, but your prosperity is not subject to taxation."

The best things in life are still free! Our most cherished possessions are not even taxable. They are ours by the grace and mercy of God, and of those who love us. Consider the gentle power of grace. It is the most powerful and yet the most elusive factor in all our religious experience; we cannot summon or will it into our lives. It is bestowed upon us by a loving God, and He chooses the time and place. When we need it, not when we deserve it!

Just as a young tender vine grows into the crevice of a rock and eventually gains strength enough to split that rock, so does the power of grace enter and grow and strengthen the believer. The Christian filled with grace is a powerful Christian. He gets things done. He is a dedicated servant not only to God but also to his fellowman. All of God's blessings are given by grace, not purchased by our merit. It is only by the power of the Holy Spirit that we become effective witnesses of His grace, freely given to us when we yield ourselves to His creative power and let Him mold us after His will.

"My grace is sufficient for thee…." (II Cor. 12:9) This grace may bring material wealth and riches to people who can be trusted with them. It ALWAYS brings spiritual gifts and un-taxable riches. The eleven possessions listed herein are greater to be desired than silver and gold and may be obtained by anyone who loves God and keeps His commandments.

You may ask, "Are you sure about the sixth, seventh, and eighth, in this modern age?"

Yes, but only if you have the fifth possession of divine love.

Although I have been writing religious articles since the early 1950's, I am still surprised and happy when I receive a letter from a reader who confides in me. Usually it is about a personal problem or maybe just a decision they have to make, and they always quote something from my column which they say helped them.

To all of those who commented on the articles that were published during Lent, let me say, "Thank you." And if they have helped in any way, I'm thankful to God for answered prayer because every time I sit down at my desk to write, I ask God to take control of my mind and pen and let me write only the things He would have me write. Hopefully things that will be helpful to someone. He alone knows the hearts and needs of His children, not me, unless of course, they confide in me.

Another "Thank you" to the two who said they were making scrapbooks of the columns to keep for their children. Tell your children to give God the glory, and to help Him by writing or telling the gospel message to others. The world needs more people who can show us, by word and example, how to live the better life that God would have us live.

The solution for most problems is action! Any good action that will keep you busy will do because if you just sit around and mope and worry about what to do, your problem gets larger, and your load gets heavier. "Take your burden to the Lord and leave it there," and then get busy with something else. Make it something constructive, and your problem will soon be gone.

This is not to say that your problem will vanish into thin air, but to acknowledge that God works in mysterious ways His wonders to perform. No problem is too tough for Him to handle.

A cluttered mind cannot think of solutions, so put your problems out of your mind, and get busy with something beneficial and unrelated to it. Before you know it, you will either have realized a solution, or you will be made aware that you have grown beyond your problem, and it is no longer a problem.

The secret is to keep on trying to accomplish something worthwhile, and God will reward your effort if you put Him and His righteousness first in your life.

Remember the stonecutter may hit the stone a hundred times with no visible success, and then see it crack on the next try. And it wasn't the hundred-and-first blow that broke the stone; it was the cumulative effect of the hundred blows before it that brought success.

That's the way our lives are. It takes many days of trying, and sometimes longer, with effort and perseverance, to gain a right situation to have a problem solved. Sometimes perseverance helps us to grow beyond the problem. God will open the way for us to pass through all difficulties.

In party games, on TV shows, and jokingly among friends, we have heard the following questions asked. If you were involved in a shipwreck and left all alone on a desert island and could have only one wish granted, what one thing or one person would you rather have with you?

Let's consider a similar question, in all seriousness. If you were heart-sick, mentally confused, and weary to the extent of despair, whom would you rather have with you? What type of being? What kind of characteristics?

If you consider the question at length, seriously and honestly, you'll have to agree that there are few, if any, with all the qualifications you desire.

There is only one who has the power to hear this triple threat to your body. Let me tell you about Him. He puts His own ego and all personal desires far from Him as He wrestles with the problem of your heart and mind and soul. Some think He is a church possession only, but this is not true. He belongs to all who will accept Him

Although He once walked this earth as a man, with captivating and compelling qualities that enthralled His listeners, and a shining personality that fascinated them as He told them that they could live forever with Him. But now some have wrapped Him in a mystical shroud and buried Him with the past.

To all who love Him, His personality is as living, as real and vivid as it was 20 centuries ago when His appearance and charisma held people spellbound. He was of average stature, but utterly fearless. He feared neither man nor beast nor the raging elements. When the tempest tossed the ships around and deep waters almost engulfed them, he was unafraid. Men in high positions sought to entrap Him but they didn't frighten Him. He knew that He was being misunderstood and misjudged, but that didn't keep Him from walking in the way that was ordained for Him.

His eloquence and the power of His truth could sway the multitudes who were astonished at His extraordinary power. He exhibited His power to heal, to raise the dead, to revive broken spirits and hearts. His power was made stronger by refusing to use it against His enemies to save Himself.

He displayed an intense magnetism, a life-giving quality which brought people hope just by looking at Him, as was evident by the woman who was healed by touching Him. As He passed, others cried out to Him, "Lord if thou wilt, Thou canst make me whole!"

The power emanating from Him was measureless, accompanied by a straight forward directness and divine charity that stirs the soul and stimulates the intellect.

After knowing Him, can you trust your welfare to a lesser being?

God has been here! Do we sometimes forget that God once walked upon the face of the earth, in and out among His lovely creations? It was here that He said, "Let's make man in our own image."

It doesn't matter to whom He was speaking; although it could have been His Son because Jesus was with God before the beginning of the world, "….His Son whom He hath appointed heir of all things, by whom He also made the worlds." (Hebrews 1:2)

It could have been some other heavenly being. It really doesn't matter. The important thing is that we are here and were made in God's image. Being made in His image, we should be more fully aware of Him, that He once walked and talked with man right here on earth!

Earth people have heard His voice. He came to earth and spoke to Moses from the burning bush. The Bible also tells of times in the life of Jesus when the people who were with Him heard the voice of God. Once, at His baptism, a dove lighted on Him, and the people heard God say, "This is my beloved Son in whom I am well pleased." On the mount of transfiguration the men with Jesus heard the voice of God saying, "This is my beloved Son; hear ye Him!"

At no time are the footprints of God more visible than in the early mornings. His whole creation seems fresh, birds are singing, the earth and the people have slept and are rested. The daily "grind" is yet ahead, but if one dwells upon that, one misses the glory of the morning. Every morning is a new day, a fresh start, and no two are alike.

There never is an ordinary morning. Each one is a new adventure, a new day not yet touched, in which to explore, to think, to compare and learn. That's any morning, this morning, and tomorrow morning! The Psalmist said, "If I take the wings of the morning (Psalms 139:9) …." And "He shall be as the light of the morning."

"And in the morning, we shall see the glory of the Lord." (Exodus 16:7)

Yes, we are often reminded that God has been here. A story is told, by William Barclay, the great explorer of Mungo Park. He had been traveling for many days and covered miles in the wilds of China, in the most desolate surroundings. Then quite suddenly he saw on the ground at his feet a little flower; and as he saw it, he said gently, "God has been here."

Let's open our eyes to the wondrous things about us and realize anew that indeed God has been here, and that we still have visible assurance of His spiritual presence, and we have spiritual assurance by communication with Him through prayer.

When we in Texas look across the fields of bluebonnets, purple sage and Indian paintbrush, we often exclaim, "This is God's country!" This we ask; may it never become desolate! God may choose to walk on it again someday, in the spirit, early in the morning.

Living in an age when girls are reluctant to sacrifice careers to become mothers, we see Father's Day coming into its own. It no longer has to take a back seat to Mother's Day.

Perhaps it's the high cost of living that's causing so many women to work outside the home; anyway, it's about as common to see a father in an apron cooking supper for the family instead of mother, especially if he gets home from work before she does.

It isn't unusual for today's fathers to bathe the children, tuck them into bed, hear their prayers, and help with any after dinner chores before taking an easy chair or going to bed. It isn't strange that he is getting a lot of acclaim that used to be reserved for mothers.

Fathers are taking their children to church and Sunday School too. Time was when that was mother's job because "Dad works such a hard, long week he has to rest Sunday mornings." Sometimes we find the roles are reversed there too, and it's "the little woman" who has been working overtime at the office and needs her beauty sleep.

A mother who isn't a full-time mother doesn't have a full-time claim to Mother's Day. A lot of the old time verses and songs about mother are now being written to include dad. One unknown author wrote:

### WHEN FATHER PRAYS

"When Father prays he doesn't use the words the preacher does; there's different ways, but mostly it's for us. He prays that we may be good boys, and later on good men. Then we squirm, and think we won't have any quarrels again. You'd never think, to look at Dad, he once had a temper too. I guess if Father needs to pray, we youngsters surely do. Sometimes the prayer gets very long and hard to understand, and then I wiggle up quite close and let him hold my hand."

Another father of an older son received the following letter:
"Dear Dad,
There are so many things I'd like to tell you face-to-face; I either lack the words or fail to find the time or place. But in this special letter, Dad, you'll find at least in part, the feeling that the passing years have left within my heart. The memory of childhood days and all that you have done to make our home a happy place and growing up such fun. I still recall the walks we took, the games we often played; those confidential talks we had while resting in the shade."

This letter comes to thank you, Dad, for needed words of praise; the counsel and the guidance too that shaped my grown-up days. No words of mine can tell you, Dad, the things I really feel; but you must know my love for you is lasting, warm and real. You made my world a better place and through the coming years, I'll keep these memories of you as cherished souvenirs! I love you, Dad!" – Author Unknown

Being neither a humorist nor a comedienne but rather a matter of fact person who takes her faith in God quite seriously (It is the dominant factor in my life.), one may think I'm unaware of the lessons that can be taught, and also learned, through comedy.

Crude jokes have never appealed to me. I have always felt sorry for the one who bore the brunt of them. Every joker must have an object or subject against whom he levies his wit. It doesn't take long for a persistent joker to "get my goat" (as they call it here), much to their delight.

Cartoonists who draw caricatures of prominent people are not favorites of mine, neither are the TV jokers. Often they are just a "cover up" to say something not very nice about someone that couldn't otherwise be said. A recent cartoon was a dreadful looking caricature of the president of the United States. Both the horrible picture and the unjust criticism were repulsive to me. How are we going to keep the respect of the other nations in this world when we, ourselves, show disrespect for the highest office in our land?

Unwanted officials who have proved themselves unworthy can always be voted out of office at the next election, or impeached if absolutely necessary.

I'm old enough to remember that when a president took office he became president of all the people and parties, and he never mentioned the "donkey" or the "elephant" until he was out of office. Likewise the people dropped party talk and rallied around their president, whether they voted for him or not. Also back then, other nations considered us very strong!

Now all parties are rallying for the next election and who is going to do what to whom, making slight, and often crude, remarks about the other political party and making fun of the ones in office. The result of all this is that other nations think that America is being divided against itself and is not so strong anymore. This is not so! Most of the people who are falling down on their jobs in America are Christians. They made America strong! It wasn't the political parties!

A Texas pastor with a sense of humor is credited with the following about inactive Christians. "Did you ever notice that a lot of Christians are like wheelbarrows – no good unless pushed; or like kittens – more content when petted; like instant coffee – 98% of the active ingredients removed; like buzzards – never go near a church unless someone dies; like buttons – always popping off at the wrong time; like kites – if you don't keep a string on them they fly away; like footballs – you never know which way they will bounce; like balloons – full of wind and ready to blow up; like trailers – have to be pulled along; like neon lights- keep going off and on; like canoes – need to be paddled."

"But, he concluded, "There are some for which we thank the Lord, they are like good watches – open, gold, busy, timely, and full of good works."

• • • • • • • • • • • • • • • • • • • • • • • • • • • • • • • • • • • • • •

I have just read Norman Vincent Peale's little book titled, <u>Positive Thinker's Guide to</u> <u>….Handling</u> <u>Tough Problems</u>.   He lists those problems as anger, anxiety, criticism, disappointment, rejection, fatigue, illness, nervousness, rejection, resentment, sorrow, temptation and unhappiness.

Each of the 13 words head a chapter on that subject , and it is written in Rev. Peale's own inimitable style of confidence and inspiration.  It is well worth reading and copies may be obtained from the Foundation for Christian Living, P.O. Box F.C.L., Pawling, New York 12564.

Two writers, whom I admire, have influenced my attitudes and concepts about writing: Norman Vincent Peale, a prolific Christian writer as well as a minister of the gospel of Jesus Christ, and Norman Cousins, an accomplished journalist, editor and author.   I haven't met either of them, but feel that I know them well.  They ARE what they write, and I can agree with both of them.

Over the years my column has dealt with every subject, plus many others, that Rev. Peale has listed as problems.  Although our thoughts on the subjects are very much alike, there is one difference, and it is merely a difference in expression.  He speaks of them as problems and how to solve them; I call them attitudes and say that they can and must be changed, but we are both speaking about the same things.

For many years now, non-fiction writing seems to be the most popular reading material. Much of this is about how to get along in a world that seems foreign and unsympathetic to our needs.  It causes one to wonder if the world is getting tougher or if we, the people are getting softer.

Is all the world about us, with its higher learning and technical skills, becoming less civilized? Are men and women returning to a primitive barbaric state?  Have we gotten so soft and dependent that we can no longer distinguish our needs from our hearts desires?  Can we no longer distinguish between right and wrong?

Modern man, meaning woman too, is always trying TO FIND HIMSELF.  Sometimes like the prodigal son he feels that he has to leave home to accomplish this.  Sooner or later everyone asks themselves, "Who am I?  Why am I here?  And where as I going?"

There is definitely more discontent in the world today!  Beliefs falter and lives are shaken.  We need more faith in God!  He will teach us to have more faith in ourselves.

Every medical doctor has his P.D.R. (Physician's Desk Reference) to guide him.  Christians have our H.B. (Holy Bible) that gives not only all the cures and antidotes for bodily ills, but the solution to all life's problems as well.

Flavel wisely said, "Bad men or devils could not have written the Bible, for it condemns them and their works; good men or angels could not have written it, for in saying it was from God when it was but their own invention, they would have been guilty of falsehood, and thus could not have been good.  The only remaining being who could have written it, is God, its real author!  In it He teaches the best way to live, the noblest way to suffer, and the most comfortable way to die."

The most unearthly sound, to my ears at least, is that made by the mourning dove. It's worse that the sound of crying. One can calm a sobbing and crying child, cure his tummy aches or soothe his hurt feelings; a weeping friends grief can be consoled and lessened, but what can one do about that haunting, repetitious sound that comes wafting in on the breeze from outside? And where is it outside? One can only tell if the sound is near or far. They never seem to show themselves.

It's doubtful that even the experts can tell if birds experience the emotions of gladness and sadness; at any rate, the mourning dove makes its sad utterances because it's the only sound he can make. Each cry or call consists of one sound being repeated three times. It begins with a cooing high note and ends with a muffled, long drawn-out wail that fades into nothingness. He repeats this three times. Then after a couple of minutes, the same three melancholy wails can be heard again. They may sound closer or farther away.

There are dozens of species of doves, which are of the pigeon family, and they all make cooing sounds as do the domesticated carrier pigeons, but none of them sound like the mourning dove; their cooing is a shorter fluttering sound, nothing like the mourning dove's soulful dirge.

The mourning doves have been few in number around here for several years. Now, however, like the swallows to Capistrano, they have returned in larger numbers this spring and summer and seem to be increasing.

Since 1938, the mockingbirds and scrappy little bluejays have claimed the trees and birdfeeders around our house. They have kept the martins from using the houses built for them. Not only do the bluejays quarrel with the dog and cat, but three of them took a stand on the birdfeeder and fussed and filibustered and kept a small army of blackbirds at bay.

How sweet it is to awaken to the various sounds of the little mockingbird my favorite by far. But alas, his sweet happy sounds have been interrupted for several weeks now by the intermittent sad wails of the mourning dove whose habitat is from southern Texas to Guatemala.

The mockingbirds still rule the roosts in our trees because their songs are just outside my window, while the sound of the mourning dove is in the distance, but not too far away. The mockingbird is an imitator and a copycat. Here's hoping they don't learn to make the sound of the mourning doves while singing in the tree near our windows.

God's world is truly wonderful!

Every Christian freely admits that in the cause of Christ, men have been led to the slaughter, to wars, to betrayals and persistent persecutions. His name has been used as a battle cry to lead men on to cruelty and massacre. His words have often been used out of their original context to cause crimes to be committed in the name of Christianity, and for persecutions in the name of duty.

Men have excused their passions, cruelty and selfishness by using His name as an endorsement. They have claimed a religious motive as justification for their meanness and wrongdoing. Soothing their sinful consciences, they called it a virtue that is warranted by the church.

Earlier men have lighted the fires to consume victims at the stake; they have applied the rack of torture and tightened the thumb-screws, all in the name of Jesus Christ. Later, still in the name of Jesus, men have sharpened the axe and the sword to punish those who before had lighted the fires at the stake.

The words of Jesus are still being used out of context today. His name is still being used as a battle cry by organizers, candidates, and all who have no conscientious scruples about using Him for their propaganda which they proclaim is His concept.

Using words of Jesus out of context is not a new thing. Recently while reading a book written prior to 1914, where it dealt with leaders of that day using Jesus' words out of context to promote their side, I found this passage from the opposition. "Out with all former concepts of Jesus!" they shout in the field and marketplace. "Down with the church! Down with the rich! Down with the privileged class! Jesus denounced the mighty and the rich; He condemned the privileged class, and He exalted the poor. He was a carpenter, a leader of the proletariat. His gospel was a social gospel. The world sadly needs a New Order, the world demands a social regeneration!"

This writing of 60 some-odd years ago seems unrealistic. Yet, in a way, it reminds us of F.D.R. and his New Deal, and of L.B.J. and his New Society, and recent elections in which candidates mentioned religion in their campaign speeches. And why not? If religion is used correctly and sincerely! They were Christians before they were politicians. At least, we hope they were.

The world does sadly need a change and social reform, but in so far as they take the words of Jesus out of their original context to make them appear to support their campaign they take His name in vain.

You can't say hello and goodbye to God! I heard this statement made by an evangelist during a summer revival meeting. It was his way of saying, you can't visit with God on Sunday and then forget about Him during the week; you can't be religious during a revival meeting and then live by the world's standards until the next Sunday or the next summer's revival.

Do you want to know God personally, or as a speaking acquaintance only? A mere acquaintance is almost a stranger, not yet a friend, and not enough fellowship together to be proven trustworthy. On the other hand, knowing God personally involves a closer day-to-day communication and fellowship with Him.

One has to be obedient to God to know Him personally, for the simple reason that knowing God personally depends first upon His revelation. One does not have to go searching for God; He finds His children and knows when their hearts are receptive to receive Him. Then, and only then, does He reveal Himself to them.

Before the birth of His Son, God was an unknown power, and it must have been difficult for the B.C. people to feel real love for such an abstract and unknown power. However, Christians believe that God is the Father of the Lord Jesus Christ, and as joint heirs with Christ, also He is our Father. Therefore, it is the most natural thing in the world for the Christian to feel genuine love for the God, our heavenly Father, who sent His only begotten Son to save them. It's sad that God is still an unknown power to some. Time and change have wrought many things, including the right or wrong, black or white moral code of our forefathers which has been changed to a dirty grey.

Today's cynic explains the righteous person's life on the basis of some neurotic compulsion, and at the same time, he will excuse the most hideous sins and crimes because of the perpetrator's unfortunate childhood!

People change. They become liberals or conservatives; they become individualistic or party-minded. They become pessimistic or optimistic. Doubters can change to become stronger believers, but one thing we forget; God doesn't change with us! "He is the same yesterday, today, and forever."

The Bible is full of stern alternatives. Because Christ said, "I came not to destroy the law and the prophets, but that through me the law would be fulfilled," it behooves all of us to review Moses' admonition to the 40 year wanderers at Sinai. "I have set before you life and death, blessing and cursing. Therefore choose life, that both thou and thy seed may live, that thou mayest love the Lord thy God, and that thy mayest obey His voice, and that thou mayest cleave unto Him: for He is thy life, and the length of thy days." (Deuteronomy 30:19-20)

Almost all of us, as parents, have told our children the familiar Bible story about the little man named Zacchaeus who was so short that he had to climb a tree in order to see Jesus who was passing by in the midst of the crowd.

While writing this, my mind's eye envisions the second grandchild, Neil, when he was small, dramatically adding to this story as he retold it, "Zacchaeus, (pointing upward) I see you up there in that tree! You come down out of that sycamore, right now! Because I'm going home with you and eat dinner at your house today."

This and other Bible stories have been taught children in Sunday School and in Vacation Bible Schools, but there's one Bible story that's never selected for small children because they wouldn't understand it. Some adults don't seem to comprehend its meaning. It is the story of Nicodemus, an elderly and somewhat wealthy Pharisee and member of the Jewish Sanhedrin who "came by night to visit Jesus." During their talk, Jesus told Nicodemus, "Except a man be born again (anew), he cannot see the kingdom of God."

The last few years have brought a resurgence of that message. Especially since President Jimmy Carter announced publicly on television and in the press that he was a born-again Christian, a statement that endeared him to some, and brought criticism from others. Some respond as did Nicodemus, "How can a man, when he is old, re-enter his mother's womb and be born again?"

Billy Sunday, the evangelist, told of a man who said to him, "Billy, I would try to be a Christian if I could have an experience like Paul had when he was born again." Billy Sunday replied, "You wouldn't have much confidence in God if He hunted a snowbird with a cannon, would you?" In other words, it wouldn't take a big blast, or to become blind, for everyone to be a Christian. Each individual is different.

Birth means a new life; therefore, rebirth means a renewing of that life, changing that life around, turning over a new leaf. The struggle for rebirth is harder for the unbeliever because old habits are hard to break. But to the person growing up in Sunday School and church, learning the scriptures, singing songs like, "Jesus Loves Me" and "Living For Jesus" and "Just as I Am", they soon make a public profession of their faith, and the transition into new birth requires little changing. But there is one BIG difference. The realization is felt, not of perfection, but of a more acute awareness of God, and how He completely and peacefully fills your life. Hard times are shorter and burdens are lighter, and best of all, you never feel alone again!

We speak of priorities and of giving credit where credit is due and presenting our bouquets to the living, but often our priorities become mixed, credits and debits get turned around, and giving bouquets to the living becomes reversed because of our forgetfulness.

"Life IS real and life IS earnest" and no matter what our ultimate goal, we all know that the end is death as the world sees it. "Let us so live that when our summons come" we can view it in another way through the eyes of the spirit.

It seems that the first half or three fourths of a person's life is spent trying to leave "footprints in the sand of time." Something good, something really worthwhile, something for which to be remembered, so that life here on earth will not have been lived in vain. One last great effort to do some lasting good for the people we leave behind on earth, and for the ones that will follow after them.

We have trod through this life leaving many footprints. Much has been written about them. (Have you read Billy Graham's book about hoof beats?) One unknown writer was inspired to write the following:

## FOOTPRINTS IN THE SAND

One night I had a dream, I was walking along the beach with the Lord and across the skies flashed scenes from my life.

In each scene, I noticed two sets of footprints in the sand. One was mine and one was the Lord's.

When the last scenes of my life appeared before me, I looked back at the footprints in the sand, and to my surprise, I noticed that many times along the path of my life there was only one set of footprints; and I noticed that it was at the lowest and saddest times of my life. I asked the Lord about it, "Lord, you said that once I decided to follow you, you would walk with me all the way. But I notice that during the most troublesome times in my life, there is only one set of footprints. I do not understand why you left my side when I needed you most."

The Lord said, "My precious child, I never left you during your time of trial. Wherever you see only one set of footprints, I was carrying you."

The founding fathers of our great country under girded our democracy with moral and spiritual principles. Those principles are not unlike those of the early prophets, Amos and Isaiah. We should read the Declaration of Independence more often. How long has it been since you've read the Constitution of the United States and the Bill of Rights? The very wording of these reminds us of early Biblical morals and principles.

There is no other nation on earth more firmly rooted in the way of life as outlined by those prophets, as is America. One American pastor said, "Where is the way of life wrought out in political framework for a nation more in accord with the spirit and teaching of Jesus than that established by our forefathers?"

All of those who have in the recent past clamored for attention and permission to change the Constitution should realize that our constitution, as is, is what made America great!

As more and more people fall away from those early Christian morals, we are in grave danger of drifting, gradually, unknowingly, into a way of life that is the extreme opposite of those principles.

What America needs most is the courage to practice these laws, as written, and not try to change them. They are, by far, our best defense against atheism. They were written with that in mind. It was the purpose in coming to a new world: to worship God, and not to deny Him. All of our patriotic actions have been done with a sure knowledge of our duty to God, to humanity and to country.

If we are to continue being an efficient nation, and remain "one nation under God", we must lose all motivation toward selfishness, and return to the old time beliefs that nurture people of faith and of hope and of love. Such persons are truly needed to re-structure and old world into a new one that reflects the glory of God.

Continued and efficient religious actions have been known to change the character of nations. Let's remember that as we contemplate the urgency of world problems that are now demanding the attention of all governments.

Let's not try to reason whether or not God is on our side, but rather let us reason whether or not we are on God's side. If you don't know whether or not you are on His side, believe me, you will! You will know when you are put to the test.

We are all subjected to the "ups" and "downs" of life. Don't let anyone tell you that all of his or her days are just the same. They are not, unless one is a moron, and even that is debatable among psychologists. We all have our highs and lows. It's true that some people have higher highs and lower lows than others, but this, largely, depends on the emotional make-up of each individual.

Happy days, such as those of weddings, births, anniversaries, graduation promotions, etc. are a part of our day-to-day living and may happen on either the high side or the low side of the life cycle.

Nature (God) has provided the correct timing for this cycle and in the normal individual, it is perfectly balanced. But people who take narcotics to maintain a false "up" or "down", throw this delicate system of balance. There are lengthy scientific explanations for this phenomenal life cycle, but long ago, a Sunday School teacher expressed it this way, "Just as we must have an occasional illness in order to appreciate good health, the upside of life prepares us for the down swing which enables us to appreciate the again coming elevation."

People who have damaged this system with dope have extremely high and low feelings. Even highly emotional people will range from being overly optimistic to weeping for no explainable reason. Most people experience a slight optimism on the up cycle and a mild case of blues on the down cycle.

Much has been written about this mystery of life and some of it in a way seemingly unrelated, although it profits many dollars to astrologers, fortune tellers, etc. The planets and stars don't influence our lives any more than the wind and the waves. Animal life, including the human animal, depends on all of the elements for a comfortable existence. That is their natural environment created for them by God. A severe change in the environment could cause illness. A severe change in the spiritual life cycle can, and often does, cause mental illness.

That's why it is so necessary to keep our bodies clean and clear of drugs and alcohol, so that it will be a fit habitat for the mind or indwelling spirit, the true cycle of life that was made in the image of God.

We can live like God or we can live like Satan, and we will be possessed by the one we emulate! It's our choice!

Why are so many people today feeling dissatisfied with themselves? There's no denying that fact. The best selling books are "self-help" books. If there were no truth in the above opening sentence, such book titles as Norman Vincent Peale's books about How To Feel Good About Yourself, and How to Stop Being Tense, and You are too Anxious, etc. would never have been written. Neither would hundreds of other books with similar titles, written by well-adjusted people who recognize a ready market because of the insecurity and disbelief of so many others.

A number of these books are required reading in psychology courses, and it is surprising how many would-be psychologists do not recognize that the contents of these books are Biblical. Oh, not chapter and verse per se, but the thoughts and instructions are lifted from the Bible and expressed in different words.

A man goes into a bookstore. He is thoroughly dissatisfied with his life and would like to make himself over if only he could find the way. At one end of the counter there was a stack of moderately priced Bibles. The new and expensive books were titled, Now is the Time to Live and its sequel, How to Live Now! Sincere in his desire to improve his life style, the man paid the high price for both new books. The sad part of this allegory is not the exorbitant price of the books, nor the unfulfilled life style of the man, but his lack of knowledge and wisdom about where to go for help. Had he chosen one of the Bibles and searched the scriptures for God's will in his life, he would have found the answer in one short verse. "He hath showed thee, oh man, what is good; and what doth the Lord require of thee, but to do justly, and to love mercy (kindness), and to walk humbly with thy God?" (Micah 6:8) This admonition is also found in these Biblical books: Deuteronomy 10:12, I Samuel 15:22, Isaiah 1:17, and Hosea 6:6. These scriptures all express the importance of obedience and the understanding of God's word.

The writer of Deuteronomy (Moses) was speaking directly to the Jews, "And now, Israel, what doth the Lord thy God require of thee, but to fear the Lord thy God, to walk in all His ways, and to love Him, and to serve the Lord thy God with all thy heart and with all thy soul." The minor prophet, Micah, did not address Israel only, but said, "Oh man" which included all of mankind everywhere. (These thoughts are found in the New Testament too.)

God demands, and is worthy of our total love. Anything that competes with Him for our affections become, in fact, a God to us, and we will fail to fulfill in our hearts the profession of love for God which our lips may make.

• • • • • • • • • • • • • • • • • • • • • • • • • • • • • • • •

Two women were discussing the book <u>The Ugly American</u> which led to further discussion about the attitude of other countries toward the United States of America. The conversation went like this:

Mrs. A: "What I can't understand is how these little countries, thousands of miles from the U.S.A. can be hostile towards us when they don't even know us."

Mrs. B: "They believe it because their evil little dictators put out effective propaganda about us. Their news media makes us appear as ugly Americans, and you'll have to admit, sometimes we are. They associate the two words, money and mercenary with the word, American. And if you are a realist, you'll have to agree that more often than not, they are right."

Mrs. A: "But I'm not a realist, I'm an idealist. I'll agree with you that God has richly blessed our country, but the leaders of corrupt nations should not turn their people against us with the lies they call being realistic about the U.S.A. I firmly believe they are jealous of us. They surely know that this country was founded on idealism!

Mrs. B: "Oh? How so?"

Mrs. A: "Surely, you haven't forgotten that history records this nation as being established by hard work and dedication, a lot of courage and hope, and a singleness of mind, to have a good and better life, a life more in tune with their ideals; and they left us a constitution to follow to preserve those ideals. If other nations want to hate us because God has rewarded our forefathers efforts, and ours, then they are not being very realistic."

I don't know if those two ladies parted as friends. Also, if they discovered, through one claiming to be idealistic and the other realistic, that no one is ever 100% anything. If Christians were perfect, there would be no need to pray for forgiveness of sins.

While we can't truthfully say there are no ugly Americans, we can say that there are many more good ones than bad ones. Neither can we say that our nation and its government are flawless, but as long as we are a caring people, especially in regard to those we vote into offices that uphold the constitution, the "good guys" will never be outnumbered – not from within.

The constitution is based on the Ten Commandments. If we continue to uphold these ideals and to base our lives on these commandments, there will never be any terrorist uprising from among our own people.

God may try us and test us, and we may have to prove ourselves worth it, but He still takes care of those who love Him enough to do His will.

What is God's will for us? The answer is found in the Bible Micah 6:8, "He hath shewed thee, O man, what is good; and what doth the Lord require of thee but to do justly, and to love mercy, and to walk humbly with thy God."

. . . . . . . . . . . . . . . . . . . . . . . . . . . . . . . . . . . . .

Seldom does poetry appear in this column, but occasionally a piece is found containing thoughts and word pictures that this columnist tries to pass on to others. Such is the following, and indeed you will be surprised at what one person can do.

## WHAT ONE PERSON CAN DO

Ten little Christians came to church all the time;
One fell out with the preacher, then there were nine.
Nine little Christians stayed up very late,
One overslept on Sunday, and then there were eight.
Eight little Christians on their way to heaven;
One took the low road and then there were seven.
Seven little Christians, chirping like chicks;
One didn't like the music and then there were six.
Six little Christians seemed very much alive;
One got travel-it is, and then there were five.
Five little Christians, pulling for heaven's shore;
One stopped to rest awhile, and then there were four.
Four little Christians, each as busy as a bee;
One got his feelings hurt, and then there were three.
Three little Christians, couldn't decide what to do;
One couldn't have his way, and then there were two.
Two little Christians – the story is almost done;
One of them grew weary, and then there was only one.
One little Christian, can't do much , tis true;
But he did bring a friend last Sunday, now there's two.
Two little Christians, each won one more;
Now don't you see, two and two make four.
Four little Christians, worked early and late;
Each of them brought one, now there are eight.
Eight little Christians, if they double as before-
In just seven Sundays we'd have 1,024.

The author's name, if known, was not given on the old church bulletin where the poem was found. Because of the similarity, the writer must have been inspired by the children's song, "Ten Little Indians." Nevertheless, he seems to have made his point.

It is every writer's ambition to get his or her message across in not only as few words as possible, but also in the simplest words that will convey the right meaning. And it is not a matter of "writing down" to someone, nor is it a matter of not "writing over someone's head." It is merely to save time and space, and above all, not to bore the readers, as every student of journalism knows.

How loyal are you to the things you really believe in?

We don't all believe in the same things, but everybody believes in something and our beliefs are very important to us, or should be. If we believe in good government, we find out all we can about the candidates, make our selections and vote. If we believe in patriotism, we are loyal to our country and those who help to preserve it. If we believe in marriage and the sanctity of the home, we try harder to make everything A-OK. If we believe in peace, we work with the peacemakers and the crime stoppers. If we believe in an all-knowing and all-loving God, we will help to carry out His great commission.

We not only give of our time and our energy to the things we believe in, but we open our purse-strings and help in a financial way. Let us take the loyalty to religion as an example for comparison. The predominant religion in America is Christianity. The prevailing religion in Russia is Communism (atheism). How do Americans give to the cause of spreading the gospel message today as compared to Russia's loyalty to Communism?

A man on the street in Europe asked Billy Graham for money to buy a meal. Billy told him that he didn't give money to strangers, but he would go to a café with him and buy him a meal. The man said that he didn't want to take Billy's time, and if he would just let him have the money, he would be on his way. The man insisted, but Billy was adamant and the man confessed that he did not intend to spend the money for food even though he was very hungry.

He said his Communist Party needed a certain sum of money for propaganda materials and he and a group of young men for the party had promised and taken a vow that they would neither eat nor sleep until they had raised the sum needed for the materials.

Oh, that the people of America, both young and old, could be as fully dedicated to the cause of Christianity as that young man and his co-workers were for the cause of Communism

Living and giving are the traits of a Christian. Living, not just for self and family, but for others – even "the stranger that is within thy gates", and giving not just of time, energy and money, but also of kindness, compassion and love.

If our daily living and our daily giving isn't all that it should be, perhaps it's time to take a new inventory. And when we're through with our self-analysis, let's not compare ourselves to our least favored acquaintance and say, "at least, I do better than that!" Let's compare ourselves to the person that we want to become, and ask, "What lack I yet?"

. . . . . . . . . . . . . . . . . . . . . . . . . . . . . . . . . . . . . . . .

One of the advantages of growing old is that we don't have to be so hurried and worried as so many young parents appear to be when we see them shopping with their small children. Quite often the child is being pulled along faster than his little legs can carry him or her.

At a shopping center in a nearby town, I parked next to a truck that had a two or three-year-old baby girl in the cab. She was all alone and the door glass was more than halfway up. I spoke to her saying, "Don't cry. You're too pretty to cry." The sobs stopped, but she held both arms up to me and smiled through her tears.

Every time I started to leave her she would start crying again, and want me to take her. Not wanting to be accused of kidnapping, I didn't lift her out of the car. Not wanting to be accused of car theft, I didn't get in the car with her (It may have been locked.), but I did resolve to stand there in the hot sun and talk to her until her deserter returned, even if it took all afternoon.

About 30 minutes later a young woman hurriedly pushed a shopping cart to the side of the truck and began unloading it into the back. Her face looked sullen and angry, possibly resenting my presence. I said, "This is a beautiful baby you have here, but the poor little thing was badly frightened at being left alone."

For as long as I live, I shall never forget her answer. "No! She's not scared! She's just mean!" Then the mother got behind the wheel, and the baby leaned to her and put both arms around her, but she was shoved to the other end of the seat and commanded to stay there or she would be whipped.

That is not an isolated case. A small boy was watching some older lads playing the game machines in a supermarket when an irate father jerked him away. The yank on the small arm must have been painful because later he was still crying and rubbing his arm. Also, in public places, I have heard parents berating their children with language most inappropriate for small ears. These are the children who will be in charge of the future.

There's a lot of crime and violence among young adults today. Could they be the product of what they were not taught as children? It's never too early to start thinking about what your children will be like when they're grown.

Every parent should be made to realize that children learn what they live!

If a child lives with hostility, he learns to fight.
If a child lives with criticism, he learns to condemn.
If a child lives with shame, he learns to feel guilty.
If a child lives with tolerance, he learns to be patient.
If a child lives with encouragement, he learns confidence.
If a child lives with praise, he learns to appreciate.
If a child lives with gratitude, he learns to be grateful.
If a child lives with fairness, he learns justice.
If a child lives with security, he learns to have faith.
If a child lives with approval, he learns to like himself.
If a child lives with acceptance and friendship, he learns to find love in the world.

• • • • • • • • • • • • • • • • • • • • • • • • • • • • • • • • • • • • •

One of the best religious articles that I have read lately is in the June 1985 issue of Reader's Digest magazine, Its title, "Why I Must Believe In God", and its subtitle, "An old proof of God's reality has a fresh urgency today."

It was written by Paul Johnson, a British author and professor, and the former editor of the New Statesman. He has also written three books: <u>History of Christianity, The Recovery of Freedom,</u> and <u>Modern Times.</u> If his books are as good as his article, I must find time to read them.

He says of the many reasons why he believes in God, the most important one to him is, "Belief in God makes me a better person than I would be otherwise." He realized that without God, mankind quickly degenerates into a subhuman being.

Religious leaders have been telling us for years that not only are broken homes and strife between family members due to a lack of God in the home, but all of the vice and violence and crime are also a direct result of the conditions caused by leaving God out.

Johnson sums up his four page article with this paragraph.

"Only a belief in God will make society decent, but we do not believe in God for that reason. Purely social religions are the route to idolatry. We must truly believe! It is proof of our struggle to be human. But in the struggle, God Himself will help us."

This lack of belief has been going on for so long now that the only cure may be through the children. It is a well-known fact that a child brought up in Bible School is seldom brought up in court.

The following examples are given to illustrate the truth of this statement.

Judge Fossett of Brooklyn sentenced some 2,700 young people to the reformatory during a five year period. Not one of the entire 2,700 was a member of a Bible class.

Lee Baxton was a businessman who served as city mayor for two years. During this time he presided over mayor's court, hearing some 2,400 cases. He made a standing offer to pay the court costs of any person convicted of a criminal offense IF that person had been regular in Sunday School attendance during that year.

There were many who said they used to attend a long time ago or I plan to go when I am released, but not once in 2,400 cases did he have to pay anyone's fine.

While Sunday School may not be a cure-all, there can be no doubt that the influence of regular church worship and Sunday School attendance is a great factor in keeping down crime.

Those who search incessantly for God will find Him!

This is the time of year when schools and civic organizations are planning Halloween carnivals. The youth are planning scary parties and the beginners are making cut-outs of ghosts and goblins and witches and black cats. Faces are being carved on the pumpkins to be used as jack-o-lanterns. Cookies are baked and candies are made or bought to treat the tricksters.

But, if you believe in a divine creator, there is more to be feared this Halloween than the ghosts of the saints on All Hallow's Eve. This evil spirit, according to Christian belief, is also embodied in people like Madalyn Murray O'Hair. She and two of her three children have worked together in their fortress-like Atheist Center in northwest Austin until the spring of 1984 when she turned her business over to her children and retired. She has trained them well because she says, "This is one Atheist movement that is not going to die with its founder."

She is now 66 years old but age has not softened or mellowed this woman and although she has high blood pressure and diabetes, she says that her reason for resigning is to devote more time to writing. She has. Her new book is titled The X-Rated Bible, published by the family-owned American (?) Atheist Press. It sold out the August 5 printing of 5,000 copies in 2 ½ weeks and a second printing began in September. It is a paperback and sells for $7.95. It was issued with an announcement that it included every lewd, licentious and vile sexual story in the Bible. We can assume, because she doesn't believe in God, that she didn't reveal the outcome or punishment of these ancient people who refused to obey God.

O'Hair is a well-educated lawyer and seems to hold her own with the U.S. Supreme Court. She had prayers and Bible reading removed from our schools and is now working on abolishing Christmas songs and carols. She must have quite a following to have gotten 27,000, yes – twenty-seven THOUSAND – signatures so quickly to back her proposal.

Last year a Houston Post newspaper article said of this family, "With a son who has taken over the reins of her Austin-based organization, and an adopted daughter – actually a granddaughter – coming into her own as a scholar, magazine editor, and non-believer, the future of the American Atheist Center seems to be on solid, if unholy ground."

Come on, Christian soldiers, start marching! "A country divided against itself cannot stand." (a paraphrase of Abraham Lincoln, who said, "A house divided against itself cannot stand." He borrowed this from St. Mark.)

There is nothing worse than talking at the wrong time; and there is nothing better than knowing when to remain silent.

Children's grades have fallen in school because they have talked too much and interrupted others in class. Whether you're at the head or the foot of your class depends not so much on whether you're a genius or a dunce as much as it does on your ability to know when to speak and when to keep quiet.

A professor was introducing his job-seeking friend to the head of his college. When asked for it by the dean, the friend handed him a typed resume, but at the same time he launched into a lengthy oral description of his qualifications. Sensing the dean's displeasure, the professor sought to help his friend by saying, "Sir, Bob is a great linguist. He can speak seven different languages."

"That's great," the dean replied, "but does he know how to keep silent in seven different languages?"

There are definite times when we ought to keep silent. One wise theologian has listed five such times: 1) We ought to keep silent when we are angry. 2) We ought to keep silent when we want to criticize. 3) We ought to keep silent when we are criticized. 4) There is a certain company in which we ought to keep silent. 5) There is a need for silence, if even we are to hear the voice of God.

One reason we hear God's instructions so seldom is because we listen so seldom. Men of Bible times heard God's voice. The manner in which they heard it is not important, be it in the voice of thunder, in a dream or by placing His words in the subconscious mind which feeds our conscious minds.

David, the Psalmist, heard God say, "Be still (keep quiet) and know that I am God."

Do we ever give God a chance to speak to us? A time of quiet meditation in the morning and in the evening, before we begin our day and after we have ended it, would make a world of difference to our over-talkative natures.

Sometimes words are really needed. At times, to remain silent would seem that we are agreeing to something we don't believe. We would fail both God and our fellowman by not talking. But in the long run, it is safe to say that speech does far more harm than keeping silent.

William Barclay said, "It is harder to learn not to speak than it is to learn to speak."

Most of us would do well if we were in the habit of listening more. We must develop listening ears, as did the prophets of old. Because the truth is that we are often so busy talking and arguing that we have no time for listening. Even in our prayers we're often so busy telling God what we want Him to do that we have no time to listen to what He wants us to do.

How can we know the will of God if we don't listen? Martin Luther said, "One thing, and one alone, is necessary for life, for justification and Christian liberty; and that is the most holy word of God, the gospel of Christ."

The gospel message is being taught in churches and Bible schools; it is being preached from pulpits all over the country. When we go to church do we really listen? Do we hear and retain enough of it to better understand God's purpose and His will? Are we like the young lady who said, "No, I don't listen. I deliberately think of something else; because if I listen, it makes me want to cry, and if I cry, my makeup, especially the mascara, comes off and runs down my cheeks."

"Then why do you go?" she was asked.

"Because all of my friends are there, and I like to leave with them after church. We always spend Sunday afternoons together. Sometimes we go to a movie, sometimes to the beach, and sometimes we just ride around town. Oh, don't misunderstand me! I like going to church, but I don't want to get too serious and emotional about it."

A minister gave me a copy of his favorite religious poem. Evidently the person being spoken to in the poem wasn't getting emotionally involved either.

A CHALLENGE TO YOUR FAITH
(from an old cathedral)

Ye call me MASTER, and obey me not!
Ye call me LIGHT, and see me not!
Ye call me WAY, and walk me not!
Ye call me LIFE, and desire me not!
Ye call me WISE, and follow me not!
Ye call me FAIR, and love me not!
Ye call me RICH, and ask me not!
Ye call me ETERNAL, and seek me not!
Ye call me GRACIOUS, and trust me not!
Ye call me NOBLE, and serve me not!
Ye call me JUST, and fear me not!
Ye call me WORD, and hear me not!
If I condemn you, blame me not!

Have you ever wondered why God created man?

The fact that God said, "Let us create man in our own image" is enough to make us think that He needed more spiritual images in heaven like Himself and whoever He was talking to, maybe Christ, who was before the world was, and "was in the beginning with God."

Why, if made for heaven, are we on earth?

Heaven is for heavenly beings, and we were made "a little lower than the angels" and therefore, not ready for heaven until we earn our passage.

How do we earn our passage?

Simple! We must learn to get along with our fellowman. If we cannot live in peace with our earthly brothers, we would certainly cause disharmony in heaven. Surely, earth is a place where we are tested and tried to prove our worth.

God has given us a set of rules, His Ten Commandments. If we keep all of them, our election and calling to heaven is assured. Even if we broke some of these rules (which is called committing sin, or sins), there was one who came and bore our sins for us so that we, through prayer, could be forgiven, and by God's grace have another chance to earn our passage to heaven. We should never forget the One who made this possible.

Can you imagine how many spirits there are in heaven? Besides legions of angels there are innumerable early followers or disciples, prophets, saints and ministers of the Gospel who have gone before us. If transplanted into their midst, would we be a good brother or sister for them?

Before answering that, look around you and see what you're in the midst of right here. Do you love and cooperate with the members of your family and other relatives? How about the neighbors, and the loyalty to your friends? Are you a Christian to the strangers that you meet? It seems that we are tested the most within our immediate families. We are with them more and have less tolerance for their mistakes; and they for our mistakes.

Try this HAPPY HOME RECIPE.

| | |
|---|---|
| 4 cups of love | 1 cup of friendship |
| 2 cups of loyalty | 5 T. of hope |
| 3 cups of forgiveness | 3 T. of tenderness |
| 4 quarts of faith and a barrel of laughter | |

Take love and loyalty and mix it thoroughly with faith. Blend in tenderness and forgiveness. Add friendship and hope. Sprinkle abundantly with laughter. Bake with sunshine. Serve daily in generous helpings.

. . . . . . . . . . . . . . . . . . . . . . . . . . . . . . . . . . . . . . . . . . . . . . . . . .

What has become of that good old fashioned attitude of gratitude? People, especially those trying to live by the Golden Rule, often go out of their way to do something nice for somebody else, and more often than not, that somebody else accepts it as deserved homage. There is never a sign of gratitude from those who think they are getting only their just dues.

Often the person doing the good deed is not aware of the lack of gratitude shown by the recipient. Kind deeds to others are a duty, a way of life that brings peace and happiness and a self-satisfied feeling of well-being in which one would scarcely notice the omission of a "thank you." Few people would be rude to a benefactor, but more than a few forget (?) to say thanks.

There are so many different kinds of attitudes. Two mountain women happen to be in the village store shopping at the same time. One lacked almost a dollar having enough money to pay her bill. When the other tried to give her a dollar, she said, "Oh no, I couldn't be beholding to you."

"But you wouldn't be obligated to me. This is my 'lending dollar' which was loaned to me on the condition that I loan it to somebody else. I want to loan it to you, and sometime in the future you can loan it to someone."

Instead of taking the dollar, she took one item out of the sack and put it back on the counter saying, "Put this back. I'll get it next week."

She did not say, "Thanks anyway for wanting to loan me the dollar, but acted as if she had been insulted as she replied with repetition, "I can't be beholding to anybody!"

One of the best recorded sermons bears this title, "Gratitude – Your Greatest Asset," and its message was "no matter what happens, be grateful!"

In the Biblical book of Luke (17:11-19), we are told that Jesus healed 10 lepers. As the lepers walked away from Him, their leper's spots and blots began to disappear and their skin became clear.

One of the ten lepers, a Samaritan, realizing that he was healed, ran back to Jesus, fell on his face and gave thanks to God. Jesus said, "Were not ten cleansed? Where are the nine?"

Nine out of ten failed to say, "Thank you." Have we improved on that percentage?

Wilford Peterson said of being grateful, "The art of thanksgiving is thanksliving. It is gratitude in action. It is thanking God for the gift of life by living it triumphantly, thanking God for your talents and abilities by accepting them as obligations to be invested for the common good. It is thanking God for what others have done for you by doing things for others. It is adding to your prayers of thanksgiving, acts of thanksliving."

The above is a beautiful thought, and if practiced, what a difference it could make in our lives!

. . . . . . . . . . . . . . . . . . . . . . . . . . . . . . . . . . . . . . . . .

Time once lost can never be regained! But the lesson learned during that lost time can prove to be valuable for future use. The following story, found on an old church bulletin, is a very good example.

## TWO DOORS DOWN

Two doors down, I witnessed a tragedy Saturday. No, not one that we will read of in the newspaper, but nevertheless a tragedy!

A huge moving van opened its cavernous mouth and consumed the furniture and belongings of a young family. Three blond-headed boys got in a station wagon headed east and followed the van with their mother; the father in his sedan went west. It was the tragedy of a freshly broken home.

Two doors down, I never knew of any domestic turmoil. They had smiled and waved as I jogged down the street. He always asked how many miles I was going. Their well-manicured lawn matched all the rest and revealed none of the misery which must have been behind their closed doors.

Just two doors down stands an empty house that will always silently rebuke me. I never reached out to that family. I introduced myself on the day they moved in, but that was it. No invitation into our home; no invitation to worship with us; no meaningful interactions with them at all. Just smiles and waves and talk of how many miles I planned to run.

All of us are busy people. This is a fast paced society in which we live. We run on well-defined tracks. There is little time to venture off our well-beaten tracks and slow our pace to interact with people who are not imperative for our well-being.

But let us remember, we can and must continually extend the healing ministering hand, as would Christ, because there are people hurting ....families shattered ...... lives tormented.....
JUST TWO DOORS DOWN.

Much time has been lost that needed prayer for those in need of our thoughts and care. We shouldn't think so much of success, and especially not consider it as fancy homes, expensive cars and dress. The measure of our real success is one we cannot spend. It's the way our children describe us to their friends.

We must make more time to pray. Do you remember this prayer of the late Reverend Peter Marshall? "Forgive us for thinking that prayer is a waste of time, and help us to see that without prayer, our work is a waste of time."

What tries my patience perhaps the most is "wishy-washy" persons who can't seem to make up their mind about anything. A small and rather insignificant decision appears to be a monumental problem for them. Also, they seem to be always looking for, and finding themselves in, such situations. It is their nature to make mountains out of molehills.

Wishy-washy people also have the harmful trait of being like whatever company they happen to be in. I am reminded of the story about a battle between the animals and the fowls. The animals on one side and the fowls were on the other. There happened to be a bat in the crowd. When the animals rushed upon the fowls, the bat drew in his wings and said, "I am an animal," and when the fowls turned upon the bat, he stretched out his wings and said, "I am a fowl." That's the way it is with some people. They are always just like the crowd they are in at the time. They are all right with good companions, and they are all wrong with bad companions.

They are also like a chameleon, that little lizard-like animal that changes color to match its surroundings, especially its background. When put on a green surface, it turns green; on a brown surface, it turns brown; on a dark surface, it becomes dark. Put it on a piece of Scotch plaid cloth, and it has a problem. Not a big one because all it has to do to solve its trivial problem is to crawl off the cloth. But no, it spends itself trying to do something that it cannot do.

Haven't you known people like that? People who try to play both sides of the fence? They usually, sooner or later, get caught in the cross fire.

Problems, trivial or otherwise, usually do not have to be solved in the next few minutes. Take time to "sleep on them". After a night of meditation and prayer, the dawn of a new day changes the looks of things. Attitudes are brighter, burdens are lighter, if we have asked through prayer for God's help, we find that quite often the problems are dissolved and cease to be a problem. Or again, we may realize a simple answer for solving the matter.

Life was beautiful to the musician who wrote the song, "Ah, sweet mystery of life, at last I've found you." Life was "for others" to the soldier who said, "If I have but one life to give, let it be for my country." Life is phenomenon to a young man or woman leaving home to find themselves, mistaken in thinking that the answer lies out there somewhere in the big wide world. The world is more likely to crucify than to sanctify and satisfy. Life is precious to old people because in spite of their beliefs what lies before them is new and untried.

There is no place in the world, or beyond, where one may go to find happiness. It can only be found inside oneself.

Human sacrifice in war is heroic, but it is also patriotic to work for peace in the world, and peace inside oneself.

Neither earth nor space affords a place where a young person may go to find himself or herself, "Come, let us reason together and settle this matter." And the inner self, the spiritual self that is made in the image of God will help you, and will continue to do so as long as you maintain prayerful meditation.

In the end of our days we tend to feel outmoded or have a sensation of being left behind while the world plunges ahead. Steps grow slow and sometimes the spirit, as well as the back, is bent and warped from feelings of frustration due to lack of ability, and not wanting to be a burden to others.

Having looked upon the face of death many times, I have seen gasping and fighting for breath as though determined, by sheer force of will, to stay here. Also, I have seen others who, as they calmly and peacefully took their last breath, had a seemingly contented and joyful smile on their faces.

These experiences have caused me to firmly believe that when our summons comes there is a happening, phenomenal to earthlings, but natural to the spirit world, in which the dying can see the road ahead. If what is seen is not liked, there is a struggle to stay here; if what is seen is desirable, it is accepted with resignation and serenity, perhaps even joyfully as the smile would indicate.

Life begins with a miracle and ends with a miracle. Miracles wrought only by God. In between, "life is real and life is earnest" and we are not our own. We were bought with a price. Our lives should be aware of that redemptive miracle. The sacrificial miracle that cancelled our debts by paying for all that we owed. Now it's up to us to keep the slate clean and follow his teachings.

My heart is full today, with wonder of the universe, with love for every living thing, that makes me want to reach out and touch everyone and say "Hello, kindred spirit, isn't this a beautiful world that God has made? Isn't this a wonderful life that He has given us?" This is the season when on that first Christmas God set everything right for us to live a more bountiful and joyful life. He said, through His Son, "I have come that ye may have life, and have it more abundantly."

There once lived another whose thoughts of life were very similar to mine. Let his words be my Christmas greeting to all of you.

## GREETING

"I salute you. I am your friend and my love for you goes deep. There is nothing I can give you which you have not got; but there is much, very much, that while I cannot give it, you can take. No heaven can come to us unless our hearts find rest in today. Take heaven! No peace lies in the future which is not hidden in this present little instant. Take peace! The gloom of the world is but a shadow. Behind it, yet within our reach, is joy. Take joy! There is radiance and glory in the darkness, could we but see, and to see we have only to look."

"Life is so generous a giver, but we judging its gifts by their covering, cast them away as ugly or heavy or hard. Remove the covering and you will find beneath it a living splendor, woven of love, by wisdom, with power. Welcome it, grasp it, and you touch the angel's hand that brings it to you. Everything we call a trial, a sorrow, or a duty, believe me, that angel's hand is there, and the wonder of an overshadowing presence."

"Our joys too, be not content with them as joys. They too, conceal diviner gifts. Life is so full of meaning and purpose, so full of beauty, beneath its covering, that you will find earth but cloaks your heaven. Courage then to claim it, that's all! But courage you have, and the knowledge that we are pilgrims together, winding through an unknown country, home. And so, at this time, I greet you. Not quite as the world sends greetings, but with profound esteem and with the prayer that for you, now and forever, the day breaks, and the shadows flee away."

These words, although borrowed, are from my heart too. My wish for you is that you may have a very happy and thoughtful holiday season. "Greeting" is from a letter written by Ira Viovanni in 1513 A.D.

Tis the dawn of a new day! A new Year! A new era! An era that is concentrating on high technology! By the end of the 20th century there will probably be inventions that we would never have imagined, even in our wildest dreams. The mechanical robot workman will seem a mere toy by comparison. We now have electronic devices that, to an "old-timer" like me, seem almost incredible.

Although the machine age is history to the present generation who are evolving from the space age to high tech, my advent into the world was almost simultaneous with the automobile. There were three cars in our little community the year before I started school. One of them belonged to my uncle who had bought a black (all cars were black then) Hamilton touring car. Touring meant having four doors. They weren't called sedans until they had glass windows.

Each car came with its necessary equipment, such as four leather-like curtains that snapped on to the top, bottom and sides of the window space. There was a square of isinglass in the center of each curtain so one could see outside. Plastics and clear vinyl were yet to come. Isinglass is clear, but it cracks easily. After self-starters were invented, most auto makers included a crank because those first attempts to start sometimes failed.

Our family was still using the black surrey with long silk fringe on the top. The best team of horses was reserved for the surrey and the second best for the wagon and shorter buckboard. The three teams of young mules were used for pulling all field implements and clearing the land. One December we went with uncle's family to Houston. On the way a sudden hard rain dampened our holiday attire. The men mostly got wet because they had to fasten the window curtains from the outside.

I also remember when the Neils and Mellie Esperson Building was new. It had thirty-one stories! For awhile it was Houston's only skyscraper. Years later, looking down from New York's Empire State Building, I realized how fast the world changes. Quite different from the length of time it took man to invent a round wheel. Can you imagine a square wheel?

But let's go forward with the new technology. I have just ordered a new electronic typewriter that does just about everything except depress its own keys. If a word is misspelled, its built in dictionary of 35,000 words goes to work to tell you with a beeping sound. Touch a certain key, and it automatically finds the error and after the correction, goes back to where it was before the mistake.

Although we live in an ever changing world, we worship an unchanging God. "He is the same, yesterday, today and forever." But man is learning more and more of His wisdom.

When He calls, do we answer? If so, how do we answer?

Too many Christians answer by saying, "I have no time" or "I want to continue with my present interests."

Once upon a time there was a church whose nominating committee was trying to find teachers for the new Sunday School year. They needed a teacher for the youth group, and also teachers for grade school and kindergarten aged children.

Qualified adults were approached who responded, "I'm really enjoying my class and being with my own age group. I don't want to leave them to work with children." Yet the drug pusher on the street said, "Not even the threat of going to jail will keep me from working with your children."

Others who were asked said, "We are out of town on weekends. We work all week and need a change of scenery to break the monotony. We can't stay in town on weekends merely to go to a children's Sunday School." But the porno book dealer (so the story goes) would say, "We're going to stay in town all weekend to accommodate your children."

Many replied, "I've never taught and I am unsuited to work with children." The movie producer might say, "We'll study, survey and spend millions to produce whatever turns your kids on."

"I have no time to attend teacher's meetings and study sessions," was the reply of many. However, the drug pusher, the porno book dealer and movie producer might say, "We'll spend all the time necessary and stay long hours overtime every night to win the minds of your children."

And so the story concludes, those who might have been teachers continued to do what they wanted to do. When the children came to Sunday School class there was no one to teach them. A committeeman passed out literature and said, "Surely someone will come to teach you next Sunday." But no one ever came, and the children soon quit coming to Sunday School. They went to listen to the people who were eagerly seeking their attention and presuming to care about the things they did and what went on in their minds.

Remember that the scriptures say, "Train up a child in the way he should go, and when he is old, he will not depart from it."

Let's paraphrase the last half of Second Timothy 2:15 to read, "Study to show thyself approved unto God"....a teacher capable and worthy of teaching children the undivided truth of God.

There must be a special place in heaven for all good Sunday School teachers. We know there is a place for all who mistreat or mislead children because the Bible says, "it were better for him that a millstone were hanged about his neck, and that he were drowned in the depth of the sea." (Matthew 18:6)

If you're thinking of going to heaven someday perhaps you need the following:

A Traveler's Guide to Heaven

ACCOMMODATIONS: Arrangements for accommodations must be made in advance.

PASSPORTS: Persons seeking entry will not be permitted past the gates without proper credentials and having their names already registered with the ruling authority. (Rev. 21:17)

TICKETS: Your ticket is a written pledge that guarantees your journey. It should be claimed and its promises kept firmly in hand. (John 5:24)

DEPARTURE TIME: The exact time of departure has not been announced. Travelers are advised to be prepared to leave on very short notice. (I Cor. 15: 51-52)

LUGGAGE: No luggage can be taken (1 Tim. 6:7)

IMMIGRATION: All passengers are classified as immigrants, since they are taking up permanent residence in a new place. The quota is unlimited. (Heb. 11:13-16)

AIR PASSAGE: Travelers going directly by air are advised to watch daily for an indication of departure. (1Thess. 4: 16-17)

VACCINATION AND INNOCULATIONS: Injections are not needed as diseases are unknown at your destination.

CURRENCY: Supplies of currency may be forwarded to await the passenger's arrival. Deposits should be as large as possible. (Matthew 5:19-20)

CLOTHING: Will be provided. (Isa. 61:10)

RESERVATION: Apply at once! (I Cor. 6:1)

Please take the time to read the scripture references. I know it is the busy holiday season, but my answer to "I don't have time" is "make time". We always find the time or make time to do the things we really want to do.

## MAKE TIME

Make time to think….it is the source of power.
Make time to play …..it is the key to freedom and relaxation.
Make time to read…..it is the gateway to knowledge.
Make time to worship ….it washes the dust of the earth from your eyes.
Make time to help and enjoy friends ….no other happiness matches this.
Make time to love ….. if you don't, it will fade away.
Make time to laugh and pray ….these are two things that lighten life's load.
Make time to be alone with God….He is the source of everything.

God has blessed His children with many talents of which some have more than others, and all of us have at least one.

What is talent? Besides being the name of an old coin and a unit of weight? A talent is also "any natural ability or power or natural endowment" (Webster's New World Dictionary). This is the same terminology used in the Parable of the Talents of St. Matthews gospel, 25:14-29, about the wealthy man who called his servants together and gave "to every man according to his several ability...." He gave to all his servants, but only three were used in the example or parable.

Every person's ability is a gift from God. When the ability is learned, or even self-taught, it is still an endowment from God who gave us the intelligence and memory to obtain knowledge. He gave this endowment when He made us in His own spiritual image. Our spirits thrive on enthusiasm and working with God for others; but when our thoughts turn inward, we become self-centered and lazy and forget the things we have learned. We become like the sea gulls in the magazine article I read.

Some time ago in the Reader's Digest, there was a short article about a group of sea gulls that were starving to death in St. Augustine. They were not starving because they had forgotten how to fish but because for years now, they had depended on the shrimp fleet operating out of the harbor to toss them scraps from the nets. When the shrimp fleet moved to Key West, the gulls began to starve. They lost their natural ability to fish because they had not been using it.

This is a rule of nature. If you do not use what you have it will be taken from you. This is the lesson in the Parable of the Talents. The servant who did not use the one talent had it taken from him.

It is a natural thing for men to worship God. But if this desire is suppressed and not exercised, it will become calloused and man will become insensitive. Satan will provide enough scraps to allure you and ease the conscience. But as with the sea gulls there will be a day of reckoning, when the scraps of this world will be taken away.

We must serve and worship God and minister to those who are less fortunate than we are. The opportune time is NOW!

Mankind has learned many lessons from nature and wildlife. Many stories have been written as examples or parables. Even in the lower grades of school, the story of the "Tortoise and the Hare" and "The Ant and the Grasshopper" are two I learned. May the true story of the sea gulls also become well-known.

Does God exist?  Is there really a God?

Have you ever seriously considered this question?  If you have and your answer was, "I suppose so" or "I guess so, I have been taught that there is" or "well, I've never seen Him or heard His voice", then you are a good candidate for atheist material.

A conversation between an atheist and a Christian could be something like this:

Christian: "Why don't you believe in God?"

Atheist: "Because not one of my five senses tells me that he's real.  I can't see him and I can't hear him. I can't touch him, and I can't taste or smell what I cannot see or feel.  I trust my five senses."

Christian: "Do you have a liver and lungs?"

Atheist: "Yes, of course."

Christian: "Your five senses didn't tell you that.  You must have read it in a book."

Atheist: "So you're going to ask about the Bible book next, are you?  Well, your Bible teaches that God is within oneself.  Why is it that surgeons can operate, exposing liver and internal organs, and never find God inside anyone?"

Christian: "God is a spirit and can be seen only by those who can spiritually discern Him. Do you read the Bible?"

Atheist: "Only to prove a point.  The Bible is a collection of fantastic legends without any scientific support.  It is full of dark hints, historical mistakes and contradictions.  It serves as a factor for gaining power and subjugating unknowing nations." (This is the Communist Dictionary's definition.)

Christian: "To read and understand the Bible, we must know what the Bible is and what it is not.  Science, as we know it today, was unknown when the Bible was written.  The Bible does contain great literature, but it was not written for that purpose.  There is history in the Bible, but there are different accounts of some of the happenings (they are non-essential to the Gospel message) because many different men writing in many different ages are sure to get a few dates and names mixed.  Besides, their objective wasn't to write an accurate history, but to show how Israel and the Israelites came under the hand of God."

Dr. Chad Walsh says, "Basically …. The appeal of the Bible is that it has provided millions of men and women with satisfying answers to the questions that every human being must grapple with."  That's exactly right!  God wasn't inspiring the Bible writers to write literature or textbooks on history or science.  The Bible is God's word to man; and through it He is holding out His hand, saying, "Come unto me all ye who are weary and heavy laden and I will give you rest."

God is a spirit and must be worshipped "in spirit and in truth."  He is revealed to the world through all who love Him.  He enters their lives and works through them, as loving, willing hands do His bidding.

"Ye are not your own; you were bought with a price."

We are living in a day that seems to shake the very foundations of the world. The forces of evil threaten to hem us in at every turn. The threat and fear of so many things beset us: unemployment, poor national economy, divided minds in government, thievery and mismanagement, the many millions of alcoholics, the accelerating drug traffic, immoralities, the rising tide of divorce, indiscriminate mating without the sanctity of marriage, and the seemingly ineffectual efforts of the churches to combat this flood of evil. Then there is the eternal question, "What can I, just one person, do to stop the tide?"

The trouble with most of us is thinking like Phillip Brooks who once said, "I am in a hurry, and God isn't." Man needs to borrow a little of the eternal unwearied patience of God.

After all, our world was perfect to begin with and man's judgment has made us what we are today. Man was handed a perfect world and given dominion over it. Snap judgments made without consideration for God's laws and guidelines can be disastrous for individuals, families and governments. The prodigal sons can return home and governments can still apply the Golden Rule, if they can be so persuaded. That is the duty of every true child of God to try and bring this about. It is our Christian duty. In trying times, we have a double devotion to duty.

That word "duty" is abused because we think of it as meaning some dark sinister and mysterious force which is driving us to do tasks which are not only undesirable, but repellent and which we do not want to do. We approach "duty" from the wrong end when we think of it as a compulsion driving us rather than as an opportunity challenging us.

Everyone who loves the Creator (Almighty God) who gave life and promised that it could be everlasting, will try to understand what the will of God is for his life, and for the world. It's true that we have difficulty understanding some of the scriptures; it is also true that we have difficulty making ourselves do and obey the things that we do not understand. As a lady in my Bible class once said, "It's not the things that I don't understand in the Bible that worry me, it's the things that I do understand that bother me."

How one reads the Bible makes a big difference in understanding it. If you're reading with half your mind still fixed on unfinished projects, or chores yet to be done, you do justice to neither. Bible reading requires meditation and prayer for tranquility or peace of mind and for understanding.

People who love God and do the best they can each day, regardless of heritage or environment, will live a good life and be happy in the knowledge that God loves them and will be with them "even unto the end of the world."

. . . . . . . . . . . . . . . . . . . . . . . . . . . . . . . . . . . . . . . . .

We are creatures of destiny. Thoughtful men of all nations feel that these days in which we are living are days of destiny. We are not peculiar in that respect because, no doubt, each generation has felt the same way.

Remember Vietnam? Remember the Bay of Pigs? How about the crossing of the English Channel on D Day? There was Martin Luther shaking the foundations of the religious world in 1517. In 1789 the French Revolutionists seemingly were undermining civilization itself. The American Union fell apart in 1861. These and many other events were fateful days, and so are the present ones.

With the coming of each new year, man(kind) takes inventory, evaluating the past year and making resolutions concerning improvements for the new year. These commitments, whether they be for business, the military, social or religious benefits, whether they are successful or disastrous, will determine our destiny for the year ahead. Perhaps for many years!

God has not predestined our lives, other than giving us laws and guidelines and examples, but we do determine our own future by the choices and decisions we make as we exercise our free will in the gift of choice.

Our days of destiny draw from us the things we put into them, and what we put into them depends on which side we're on, God's or the devil's. Yes, there are devils and angels who stand for either the hurt or the healing of the world. The choice is ours to make, a demonic nature or a divine nature?

Some have asked, "Why try to be good when the evil seems to prosper and have the upper hand in the world today?" Believe me! It is only temporary. The hijackings, the murders, the rapes, the cheating and swindling, the porno, the dope, the child abusers can only exist until the righteous take a firm stand against it. Things may get a lot worse before they get better. That is predicted for the last days, but no one knows when they are, not even the angels in heaven have been told.

Whether the end is thousands of years from now or tomorrow, we are not to worry! The scriptures tell us that "Many are called, but few are chosen." Cast your lot with the few!

Scripture also tells us that evil will prevail in the days before the second coming of Christ, "and because iniquity (evil) shall abound, the love of many (for God) shall wax cold. But he that shall endure to the end, the same shall be saved." (Matthew 24:12 and 13) Also in verse 22, "and except those days should be shortened, there should no flesh be saved but for the elect's sake those days shall be shortened."

When you read Matthew 24 remember that verse 34 applies to verses 1 and 2 and could well have been placed after them. (The destruction of the temple in Jerusalem was in that generation, 70 years later.)

If we are unregenerate renegades, we will indulge in evil; but if we are of the redeemed of Almighty God, we will strive for the redemption of the world as we combat evil.

The story has been told of a small town and a weary traveler who stopped there. "You really have a fine little town here. I'm sure you must be proud of it. I am especially impressed by the number of churches in such a small town. Surely, the people here must love the Lord."

"Well," replied the hotel clerk, scratching his ear as he pondered the thought, "they may love the Lord, but they sure hate each other."

Ten miles east of Wharton, Texas on the Boling highway, is the little town of Iago. Since the first three families settled there in 1903, it has never had more than one church building at a time. One early church burned and was rebuilt. In time, it was remodeled and a two-story annex added on for classrooms; still later a fellowship hall, kitchen and modern facilities were added, but these were sold and moved away when the present large brick plant was built to house the Iago Federated Church and its growing membership.

Many different denominations worship together in this church. There is also a parsonage; it and the church's pulpit have been filled by men of various denominations. This church exists because of the attitude of the people, their love for God and each other. Not to my knowledge has anyone, through the generations since 1903, tried to destroy the fellowship in this community or to wreck the church by dividing its congregation. If they did they found a wall of love that held them back.

With genuine caring and sharing, people can work together for the good of all. The constructive forces in the world are greater than the destructive ones!

## IT CAN BE DONE

I watched them tearing a building down,
A gang of men in a busy town.
With a ho-heave-ho and a lusty yell,
They swung a beam and a side-wall fell.
I asked the foreman, "Are these men skilled,
And the men you'd hire if you had to build?"
He gave a laugh and said, "No, indeed!
Just common labor is all I need.
I can easily wreck in a day or two
What others have taken a year to do."

And I thought to myself as I went away,
Which of these roles have I tried to play?
Am I a builder who works with care,
Measuring life by the rule and the square?
Am I shaping my deeds to a well made plan,
Patiently doing the best that I can?
Or am I a wrecker who walks the town
Content with the labor of tearing down?
-author unknown

Why do some people have to fight monotony and boredom while others have to harness their enthusiasm and hold their exuberance in check? Could it be in the way they reckon time and life? Could Christianity and non-Christianity be involved in it?

Marcus Aurelius, a Roman emperor and philosopher who lived during the time of the transition from paganism to Christianity wrote in his book of meditations, "Time is like a river made up of events that happen, and a violent stream; for as soon as a thing has appeared, it is carried away, and another comes in its place; and this will be carried away too."

One can just imagine this ancient Roman ruler standing in "philosophic serenity" on the bank of the fast moving river watching tree limbs and other debris floating swiftly past. As his eyes followed the debris out of sight, other floating things continually followed and were also carried away. His analogy of the floating objects as events in life, and the river as life itself, is a good one.

Perhaps his maturing years and his responsibilities as emperor made the events (debris) and life (river) seem to go faster. Young people think the opposite because time passes slowly between events they are anticipating. However, the point of Marcus Aurelius' comparison was not the speed of passing time and events, but the sameness of it, the monotony of it happening over and over again.

I remember Franklin D. Roosevelt and his enthusiastic fireside chats. Listening to the radio, the lilt in his voice made one forget that he was sitting in a wheelchair. Religious writers, evangelists, and people with a purpose are nearly always enthused.

We must not think that enthusiasm belongs only to the young and energetic. It is an attitude of the mind. The enthused one has attitudes and attributes equal to that one's exuberance and exultation. I believe the enthused person has a vision to be in love with life and the Giver of it; to practice the presence of God; to forget self, that Christ may be remembered.

To be strong enough to master evil; to be wise enough to let the good master us.

To see in every friend a proof that God is good; to see in those we may dislike, an opportunity to show that love never faileth.

To turn hindrances into helps, to see the light that dims the shadows' to be a living example of the joy deeply rooted in Christian faith.

To be courteous to the aged, gracious to the maturing, and to guide gently the steps of little children.

To profit from the past, to live earnestly in the present, to look hopefully to the future.

"The spectacle of a nation praying is more awe-inspiring than the explosion of an atomic bomb. The force of prayer is greater than any possible combination of man-controlled powers, because prayer is man's greatest means of tapping the resources of God." So said J. Edgar Hoover more than 30 years ago.

When I was a very little girl, we not only went to church on Sundays but during the week as well. I remember gatherings of relatives, friends and neighbors in the various homes on several nights of the week for prayer meetings. Some were routine and some were especially called. The main request at that time was the same as many current ones: prayers for world peace.

You see, many members from our community had gone to Europe with General John J. Pershing to fight the Kaiser. There was a dreadful epidemic of "flu" in this country. Then the combination of pneumonia and German measles spread like wildfire. Indeed, there was much talk of "germ warfare".

My 19 year old cousin's husband of three months, with a ship load of other sick soldiers, was returned to the USA and to Camp Bowie hospital in Fort Worth where he, and thousands of others were to succumb to that illness that plagued World War I (548,000 in the USA alone; 20 million "flu" deaths worldwide).

There was much religious fervor. In trying times, people turn back to God. Then in 1918, when I was 9 years old, it was all over. I remember whistles blowing and church bells ringing and people shouting, "We won! We won!" There was much backslapping and jokes of "chasing Kaiser Bill over the hill," but I don't remember too many people thanking God.

Then came 20 years of fun. Everyone seemed to be making up for lost time. Girls were known as "flappers"; boys as "jelly beans". The Charleston, The Black Bottom, and the Jitterbug replaced the waltzes and "Put Your Little Foot." Honky-tonks became more numerous and more frequented than churches. No one seemed to realize that all the crosses in Flanders Field, and at home, were proof that no one wins in war.

The whole scene changed again as American soldiers, chanting "I like Ike! I like Ike!" went across the ocean to fight Hitler's armies. The "old time religion" again became popular. Do you remember when they came home? There were parades, and the confetti from tall buildings and the pride of winning. Since then there have been the Korean and Viet Nam War.

Now there is great confusion in all our nation because with new technology and having to harness devastating atomic weapons and to contend with suicidal terrorists who want to die for a little piece of God's land for their leaders, our world gets more and more complicated.

Having lived through that many wars, I can honestly say that what surprised me most was that the people who begged God to be on their side in wartime, neglected to be on His side in peace time.

Are any of us really the master of our fate? Are any of us the captain of our soul? If you think so, why?

We should all take or make the time to search for perspectives, priorities, and most of all, motives. What motivates you to do the kind of work that you are doing? If you are a banker, why? Do you enjoy high finance, or are you a banker because the family expects you to follow in Dad's footsteps? Did you major in banking to please your dad and minor in what you really wanted to do? If so, you'll never be the banker your dad was. Your whole heart won't be in it.

Many business people, whether merchant, baker or candlestick maker, go to work each day with heart and/or high blood pressure pills in their briefcase To further avoid the stress and strain of hating what they do, they take indigestion pills after lunch. Many of these people do what they do because they are expected to carry on the family business.

Sometimes the positions we desire are not open to us, and sometimes we are too timid or lack the initiative to step out and try the new when the old routine is making a living for us. If this paragraph applies to you, then you should learn to say as Paul did, "Brethren, I have learned that whatever state I find myself in: therefore to be content."

Ideas and ideals have been known to change. Paul also said, "The things I once loved I now hate, and the things I once hated I now love." That's why it's so necessary that we take inventories of ourselves and especially to re-evaluate our lifestyles by re-examining our motives. The result of this self analysis will show you the best kind of life and the one that will bring the most contentment for you. After all, contentment is the only antidote for stress and strain.

Don't keep on drudging from day to day, automatically putting one foot in front of the other and getting more and more dissatisfied with what you do. Re-examine those motives today! Get that smile back. Also that spring in your step, and find contentment! Then, if you can retain that attitude for a healing length of time, you can throw all of those pills down the drain.

You don't know how to start? Ask questions! What are the things in my life that I do like? Have I been leaving God out? Have I been neglecting to have fun with my family? Or have I been commiserating with myself at their expense?

What motivates me to do the kind of work I do? Why am I a writer? Do I write merely to see my name in print? Am I trying to get public recognition? Am I writing to make a lot of money? Or am I writing because I love to write and because I hope to help people?

Why am I living? What is my life all about, anyway? What am I going to do with the rest of my life?

"For I say, through the grace given unto me, to every man that is among you, not to think of himself more highly than he ought to think; but to think soberly, according as God hath dealt to every man the measure of faith." (Romans 12:3)

"For if a man think himself to be something, when he is nothing, he deceiveth himself." (Galatians 6:3)

The story is told of a very rich and pompous woman who was proud in spirit and overly conceited. She constantly talked about her accomplishments which always brought praise from those who would listen to her; and there are always those who love to listen and "kow-tow" to presumptuous persons.

But all of the lady's money didn't bring her contentment. She finally became so unhappy that she went to a psychiatrist and asked him if he could help her. "Tell me all about yourself," he said. She did. In the same way that she talked to everyone. She talked and talked.

On the second visit the doctor again said, "Tell me more about yourself." She liked that! She talked the full session. Again, on the third visit she was extremely pleased to talk about herself. But after several more visits she grew tired of the repeated request, and said, "Doctor, I want you to cure me!"

"I'm sorry, Madame," he replied, "but you can help yourself if you will follow my advice. Take a trip to Niagara Falls, and take a good look at something bigger than yourself!"

Do you extol the virtues of others, or your own? Can you do things just a little bit bigger and better than anyone else in your group, or on your committee? Do you feel slighted and left out if you aren't the center of attraction?

The self-centered person is also a selfish person. We must think of others. There was a very nice-looking man in Houston looking for employment. He went to the owner of a theater and asked to be hired as an usher. He dressed well, looked alert and capable. The owner was impressed and willing to hire him, but first he asked, "What would you do if the theater caught fire while you were ushering?"

"Oh, you wouldn't have to worry about me sir, I'd get out all right!" Needless to say, he didn't get the job.

There is a Christian motto which reads, "God first, others second, and myself last."

Matthew 24:42-46 describes the difference between a selfish person and a righteous person, and what the end of each shall be. If you haven't read it lately, please make the time.

The most memorized and remembered Bible verse among children, and perhaps among grown-ups as well, is undoubtedly First John 4:8, "He that loveth not knoweth not God; for God is love." Sunday School teachers for the very young have shortened the verse to: "God is love," and that is the way most of us remember it.

Those who reach maturity before realizing the extent of God's love, seem to favor another verse, "For God so loved the world, that He gave His only begotten Son, that whosoever believeth in Him should not perish, but have everlasting life." (John 3:16)

The Biblical book of John is known as the "love book," and he speaks of himself as "that disciple whom Jesus loved." One of the Bible's commandments is "This commandment I leave with you, that you love one another as I have loved you." What kind of love? The kind of love that puts God first ("Thou shalt have no other Gods before me.") and others second. (Greater love hath no man than this: that he lay down his life for his brother.") Thirdly, love yourself ("Love yourself!" and "Love thou neighbor as thyself.")

Much has been sung and written about love. One of my favorite quotes is from Robert Louis Stevenson who said, "So long as we love we serve; so long as we are loved by others I would almost say that we are indispensible; and no one is useless while he has a friend." Just one person to love and from whom to receive love may save one from despair, and may also save some young people from committing suicide.

Just as "A kind word turneth away wrath" so can a loving heart turn away evil. The evil will receive their just reward, "For they have sown the wind, and they shall reap the whirlwind." (Hosea 8:7) Also, "for whatsoever a man soweth, that shall he also reap." (Galatians 6:7) Part of the following is from Galatians the 6th chapter.

If a man love God, he will keep His commandments and obey Him. If a man or woman loves their spouse and family, they will keep circumspect and honorable. "For he that soweth to his flesh shall of the flesh reap corruption; but he that soweth to the Spirit (God) shall of the spirit reap life everlasting."

"Therefore, as we have opportunity, let us do good unto all persons, especially unto them who are of the household of faith. Let us not grow weary of well-doing for in due season we shall reap if we faint not.

Whether our remaining time on this earth is short or long, we should always take the long view of life and choose our priorities accordingly. Because the deeds we do here is the only construction material used to build our heavenly home. Will our deeds build a hut or a mansion?

The flowers that bloom in May make this one of nature's most beautiful months. The countryside of South and central Texas is especially lovely in May. The white, also pink, dogwood blossoms, the flowering wild plum, haw and mayberry peeping through the different shades of fresh greens in the woods, in the edge of the denser forests and along the Texas streams.

The prairie wild flowers show every color there is. The deep red wine-colored tulips, bluebonnets, yellow field daisies, yellow lady's slippers, pink and white primroses, purple violets, and the wild red salvia of the sage family that comes along about the time the Indian paint brush begins to fade away. Blue forget-me-nots, tiny blue violets, pink clover and dainty flowering moss that hug and cover the ground under the tall black-eyed Susans, white daisies, sunflowers and shrubs. The tall stately Queen Ann's Lace loves to grow in the fence rows along the highways.

Texas open fields and prairies have certainly put on their prettiest and most colorful dresses to celebrate their 150th birthday this year. Let us savor it and rejoice in this our sesquicentennial minute, and renew our vows to God and country: to preserve it, "one nation under God, with liberty and justice for all."

There's no greater beauty than God's creations (I prefer the term God's creations to mother nature's handiwork which doesn't exactly give God the glory for it.) However, He may have set up certain laws in the beginning and let mother nature (earth) take it from there. Who can limit their praise to Mother Earth when they know that the creator of the earth, the skies and the whole universe is more worthy of our thanks and praise.

With strife, unrest and often turmoil and terrorism in high places of government in all nations, the peace and beauty of the countryside is especially dear. With new terrorists' threats being beamed every day and TV programs interrupted with warning system tests, it behooves us to remember that we are a nation "under God" so that infiltrating foreign doctrines cannot divide and conquer us.

Neither should we fear war or that bombs might fall (even though they may) because fear can also paralyze and destroy. I remember when once before our country seemed to be at a crossroad of indecision and peoples' hearts were failing them because of fear, and there was a division of opinions in high places in our government and between the different branches of our military forces.

Luckily, however, we had a president at that time who had a very soothing voice which came to us through the radio (no TV then) really often to have a "fireside chat" with us. And everybody believed him when he said, "We have nothing to fear but fear itself." (F.D.R.)

"The fear of man bringeth a snare; but whoso putteth his trust in the Lord shall be safe." (Proverbs 10:27)

"The fear of the Lord is strong confidence and His children shall have a place of refuge. The fear of the Lord is a fountain of life, to depart from the snares of death." (Proverbs 14:26-27)

An adult Sunday School class was discussing Bible scriptures from the Old Testament that tell of how fanatical the Jewish religion became at one time over details in their laws.

The Jews believe, as we do, that the Ten Commandments are God's original laws. But their lawmakers began to write books of explanations, giving details of what each law meant. Soon others were written to explain what the details meant. Each scribe felt he must work at his job and he added more books until the temples were full of law books. As is usually the case when writings and facts are tampered with, the later writings often bear little resemblance to the original ones.

The same thing has happened in the United States. The Library of Congress wouldn't contain so many volumes of old and new amendments to the laws of the United States if people through the ages had lived by God's original ten laws that were given to Moses, and were recorded in the Holy Bible, the inspired word of God.

This poem, by an unknown writer, doesn't change the meaning of God's original laws.

Ten Requirements for Eternal Life

Above all else, love God alone,
Bow down to neither wood nor stone;
God's name refuse to take in vain,
The Sabbath rest with care maintain.

Respect your parents all your days,
Hold sacred human life always.
Be loyal to your chosen mate,
Steal nothing, neither small nor great.
Report with truth your neighbor's deed
And rid your mind of selfish greed.

When and why is it necessary to change old laws and make new ones? One would suppose that the scribes of old felt somewhat like present day lawmakers, that they must keep busy or they might not be re-elected and lose their jobs. Their main job is law-making, so they make laws and then more laws.

A scribe took the original law, "Remember the Sabbath day and keep it holy" and wrote something like "Rest on the Sabbath and do no work." Another scribe thought some work, such as preparing food, was necessary, and he wrote, "Carry no burdens on the Sabbath because that is work." Another wrote, "Burden is weight; carry no weight neither great nor small." Later other writers made lists such as "wear no ornamental metals, carry no books, handkerchiefs, etc."

The original laws should never have been tampered with! No, I am not anti-Jewish. Their present generation is no more responsible for the release of Barrabas and the crucifixion of Christ than ours is guilty of bringing slaves over from Africa. I do hope that all U.S. citizens of foreign extraction are truly citizens in reality and not just sacrificing their lives for their homelands. U.S. dollars should be used in the United States. "Render unto God the things that are God's…." and unto Uncle Sam the things that belong to Uncle Sam.

An unhappy person may be told to find their perspective, and to look for the happy medium. However, living in the extremes and finding mediocrity and boredom in between is the accepted way of life at this point in time.

Unfortunately, a happy medium doesn't exist between all extremes, or even between all contrasts, and if there is one, it may not be desirable.

Our most visible contrasts are night and day and black and white. The medium or midway between night and day is twilight, or as some say, dawn and dusk because we have two twilights. Because twilight is of a short duration and earth related, we do not have a choice. When our earthly existence is over, we will be with our Creator in His kingdom where it is always day because there is no night there.

Being creatures of light, whose eyes cannot penetrate utter darkness, we love light and have discovered artificial lights such as candles, oil lamps, flashlights, and electricity to dispel the darkness for us.

Let's consider the extremes of success versus failure; right versus wrong; truth versus untruth and hot versus cold. Inheritance can bring overnight riches, but personal success comes only through effort and the seemingly endless struggles that precede achievement and recognition. Where is the happy medium in the story of "The Ant and the Grasshopper? There isn't one. Either the grasshopper works hard like the ant, or he will starve.

How can one be happy mid-way between right and wrong? We have heard people say, "What is right for me may not be right for you." Dr. Charles Allen, a minister and religious writer, says, "Wrong is wrong even if everybody is doing it. And right is right even if nobody is doing it." We must choose to do what is right to be happy.

Have you heard this one? It's better to tell a little white lie, if the truth will hurt someone. Do lies come in black or white and in different sizes? The teller of lies thinks he or she won't be found out, but it seldom works that way. Truth is eternal and should be eternally practiced. The devil is the "father of all lies" and by lying he deceives many.

The term happy medium is often a misnomer, and it is NOT always a wise admonition to tell somebody to find one. However, if we find our perspective and choose the right priorities, we can learn to say as did Paul of Tarsus, "I have learned that whatever state I am in, therefore to be content." Contentment brings happiness!

Another thought for contentment is "Better a crust of bread in a house where love is, than a sumptuous feast in a house filled with strife."

To continue our thoughts on extremes and happy mediums, let's consider hot versus cold and love versus hate and birth versus death.

A modern saying, used often in the business world and also in sports, is "If you can't stand the heat, stay out of the kitchen." This means that if you aren't big enough or don't have enough intestinal fortitude to compete with the opposition, then you should stay out of the game or business.

The medium between hot and cold is not a pleasant one. Do you like lukewarm soup or coffee? The Master Teacher, speaking on indecisiveness, said, "I would that ye were either hot or cold because I will spew the lukewarm out of my mouth." We have to choose in our day as they did in theirs, whether to be for Him or against Him and not remain undecided and lukewarm. He also said, "He that is not for me, is against me."

An acquaintance once gave the above phrase a social connotation when he said, "I prefer the heat of some kitchens to the cold formality of some drawing rooms."

Love and hate are the two extremes of which it has been said that only a thin line separates the two. My way of thinking is that a great gulf lies between them. It has also been said that "love looks through a telescope while hate looks through a microscope." Microscopic vision helps the one who wants to see and find fault. Love's vision, through the larger scope, has God inside him because "God is love."

"Love," it has been said, "flows downward. The love of parents for their children has always been far more powerful than that of children for their parents; and who among the sons of men ever loved God with a thousandth part of the love which God has manifested to us?" (A quote from Hare, an early English clergyman)

Hatred is an evil enemy of mankind. Colton said, "We hate some persons because we do not know them; and we will not know them because we hate them."

Birth and death are two extremes out of eternal life. The in-between is a process of growing in stature and gaining in wisdom. Bacon said, "It is as natural for men to die, as to be born, and to a little infant, perhaps the one is as painful as the other." According to H.W. Beecher, "Living is death; dying is life. On this side of the grave we are exiles, on that, citizens, on this side, orphans, on that, children; on this side, captives, on that, free men; on this side, disguised, unknown, on that, disclosed and proclaimed as the sons of God."

We often see death pictured as the "grim reaper", a long white-bearded old man carrying a scythe and coming to destroy, when in reality death is only a transition. Why do we think of death as life's end? It is really a new beginning. When there is a loss, there is a gain; when there is a parting, a meeting follows; when there is a going away, there is an arriving at a destination; and when the death angel calls, we are merely passing "in the twinkling of an eye" into that place that is prepared for us where there is no sighing, no sorrow and no tears.

Once I heard an argument between two women office workers in which one told the other, "I wish I could buy you for what you're <u>really</u> worth and sell you for what you <u>think</u> you're worth! Boy, I would make millions!

What is the human creature worth? To answer that question we must consider the composition of the human body and know the market price of each ingredient. Medical science has discovered that in your body you have enough fat to make seven bars of soap; enough sugar to sweeten 10 cups of tea; enough lime to whitewash a chicken coop; phosphorus to make 2,000 matches; potassium to explode a toy cannon; enough sulfur to rid a small dog of fleas, plus enough water to take a bath in.

An average of the different body sizes show, at today's market prices, we are each worth about eight American dollars. So, whenever you have to deal with a critical or snobbish person whose attitude shows that they think only in terms of BIG I and little u, remember that they are wearing only an $8.00 price tag.

But there is more to life than the body, and with today's morality, this fact cannot be over-emphasized. What makes you important? It is not the physical body which was made of clay and will eventually become dust and ashes again. You are important because somewhere inside that clay body, you have a living soul …. a soul that was created by God and made in His image. That is where your real value lies. That part of a person which we cannot see (and miss so terribly when it is housed in the body of a loved one whose body has returned to clay) is the spirit that dwells within the soul and lives forever.

We should always remember that although we were created with an eternal soul, like God, if we refuse to invite the Holy Spirit into our lives, then Satan, the evil spirit, usually moves into our heart, in order to wage war with our soul without an invitation.

We are not our own. We belong either to God or the devil who is called Satan. God said, "Behold, all souls are mine; as the soul of the father, so also the soul of the son is mine." (Ezekiel 18:4)

"The soul that sinneth, it shall die. The son shall not bear the iniquity of the father, neither shall the father bear the iniquity of the son. The righteousness of the righteous shall be upon him, and the wickedness of the wicked shall be upon him. But if the wicked will turn from all his sins that he hath committed and keep all my statutes, and do that which is lawful and right, he shall surely live, he shall not die." (Ezekiel 18: 20-21)

There is a framed and embroidered picture (a Christmas gift from my daughter-in-law) hanging on my studio wall. The floral design of red roses encircles a motto which fits well with these thoughts on the worth of a person. "What we are is God's gift to us; what we become is our gift to God."

How wide are your thoughts? Just wide enough to encompass your family, your friends and your local interests? Do your thoughts often stray to encircle the entire globe? Going from one small country to another as though on an urgent mysterious quest for some unknown fact that must be brought to light, not only for the benefit of the whole world, but also, to satisfy that inner craving for knowledge?

There must be an inherent instinctive longing in each of us to know more about the world we live in, also its Creator and His creations. I think this is especially true of ourselves and the peoples of other nations because we are all children of God and were made in His image.

We, living in one of the two strongest nations on earth, with 50 free states to roam at will, can't possibly imagine how frightening it must be to live in a small country that is continually being threatened. Think about the countries of Iran and Iraq. Do you remember some years ago when one of them pushed across the other's border? At that time, I made a very stupid remark. I said, "Why don't all of those dumb little countries 'wake-up' and realize that it's the forces from larger nations that cause them to antagonize each other? If they're too small to fend for themselves, why don't they unite and work for their common good?"

This was stupid because of not realizing how grateful a small country of hungry people can be toward those bringing in food, medicine and other needed supplies, even though the givers may have ulterior motives. Also, there are barriers existing between small nations the same as between larger ones: differences in language, race, creed, and religion.

Another thing that we often forget is that even though no individual or nation holds the answer to the world's problems, God still holds the key. Right now there is a master plan being carried out in the east that hasn't even caught the attention of western reporters. The leaders of seven Asian countries have joined to form an organization called the South Asian Association for Regional Cooperation (SAARC) and they held a summit meeting for last December (1985) in Dhaka, Bangladesh. This was the first summit meeting for these seven brave men representing the countries of Bangladesh, Bhutan, India, Maldive Islands, Nepal, Pakistan and Sri Lanka.

Not only was this, in itself, a significant accomplishment, but an event of historical proportions! It should have made worldwide news, but to my knowledge, only a few religious reporters, keeping up with world trends to better interpret Biblical prophecies, reported it. I did find this brief paragraph, May 2, in the Houston Post Newspaper by Kathy Lewis. It was near the end of her article about President and Mrs. Reagan's trip to Bali, Indonesia. It said, "On his final day in Bali, Reagan also conducted business with Indonesia's President Suharto and the six foreign members of the Association of Southeast Asia Nations." (ASAN?) Could she have meant SAARC and seven nations?

Unity, not uniformity, is the Christian's goal. We cannot find in the gospel of Christ that He expects, or has ever provided for, the uniformity of churches, but He does expect, and has provided for, their unity.

There are those who think that before the end of time all of the churches in the world will be united in such a way that each will conform to the same rituals and procedures, with no conflict of thoughts or differing opinions regarding the welfare of the church and its people.

This seems to me to be wishful thinking, or else meant for a period after the end of our time when, and if, celestial beings live and rule on earth. The fact that no two things were made alike discredits the thought of conformity. Just as each leaf on the tree is different, so are the millions of people on the earth different. So doesn't it seem unreasonable to expect that the many churches in the world would suddenly conform to the same pattern?

Conformity? NO. Unity? Yes! United in faith to God and to our God-loving and God-fearing fellow men. "The just shall live by faith." This knowledge can bring universal unity of all the churches.

Habakkuk, in the Old Testament, declared that the just shall live by faith. The Apostle Paul also used this text. He built his doctrine of "justification by faith" with the help of Habakkuk's text. "The righteous man survives if he is faithful." We might say, "if he maintains his integrity." Paul used this thought in his letter to the greatest of the European churches (Romans 1:17) and again in a letter to the greatest of the Asian churches (Gal. 3:11). He also used this text when he wrote to the Jews in his letter to the Hebrews 10:38. He was enthralled and captivated by what Habakkuk had said.

This unity of souls through faith in the most high God has fascinated men of learning throughout the ages. Martin Luther in his quiet cell at Wittenberg, studied the epistle of St. Paul and his quotations from the Old Testament writer, and mused, "For the just, then, there is a life different from that of other men; and this life is the gift of faith!" He felt as though he had indeed found, or that God had unveiled for him, the secret of living the good life of a Christian.

Today this text of Habakkuk, Paul, Luther and others is everybody's text. Every Christian can know and feel the power of it. To have faith in God is to be at peace with Him and oneself. Erasmus said, "To be at peace with God is the fountain of true tranquility of mind."

Although millions of people confess to a belief in God, all but a small minority lack faith enough to receive answers to their prayers, answers that would free their minds from fear and worry.

For "by faith" and "through the grace of God" we are saved and not by any works or good deeds of man. Salvation and redemption from sin are free, a gift from God to all who are not ashamed to confess their love for, and their faith in Him. Daily Bible reading increases a growing faith! Cultivate a mature faith and FEEL the power of it!

There has never been a time in history when the world has been so over-flowing with as many "How to …." And self-help books as we have today. Some are quite good, others were a waste of time and effort. Such a wide range of topics! One would think that all possible titles have now been used.

After publishing two "How to" books, Reader's Digest has now come out with another one titled, "How To Do Just About Anything". That sounds like a title to end all titles, but like World War I was a war to end all wars, it probably won't be.

The "How to" books that deal with mending, building or fixing mechanical and material things around the home have no appeal to me. I'll leave those to the handy-man in the family and browse through How To Improve the Quality of Your Mind, How to Write Better, How To Live Life More Effectively, and How To Have Better Human Relations, etc.

As we read or scan the philosophical books, the realization comes that they are based almost entirely on the teachings of the Bible. As we delve deeper into our thoughts, knowing that humans were on the earth much longer than the Bible, we also realize that the accumulated knowledge and ever increasing comprehension, of mankind was transmitted from generation to generation long before there were ways of writing and recording this information.

Now we have a vast storehouse of knowledge because all of the accumulated wisdom of the ages has been written down, and even the most avid reader could not in one lifetime read all of the books that exist today.

Millions of books are published, but comparatively only a few make the best seller list. However, that few were numbered as 100 by The World Almanac and the Book of Facts when it listed the best sellers for the year of June 1984 and May of 1985.

Man's knowledge is still increasing and evidently at a much faster pace than in ancient days because many textbooks are out-of-date so quickly. Science books are scarcely off the press when newly discovered scientific data makes them obsolete. Inventions are more numerous, especially in the field of electronics. We have talking automobiles, faster jets, undreamed of space vehicles, weather and communication satellites and missile interceptors, etc.

All of this had been known though not experienced or understood, since the first part of the best selling book, the Bible, was written. Many of the mysterious prophecies in the Old Testament are now more easily understood. One says that "men shall become weaker and wiser" and "knowledge shall increase" and "many shall run to and fro" and "there shall be signs (sights) and wonders in the heavens." The one that used to be a real puzzle for me was "woe unto those who give suck in the later days." This was made very clear when the cloud of radiation passed over Poland, and we heard what it did to the mother's milk, and also to the cow's milk.

These things are also told in the New Testament. If you haven't read the 24th chapter of Matthew recently, you may wish to re-read it in the light of today's happenings. Read especially verses 7 and 19.

How has God dealt with us as a nation? It was He who prepared this land for our habitation and guided our forefathers to seek its shores and declare the inalienable rights of men to life, liberty and the pursuit of happiness. Truly our wonderful heritage is our most valuable possession. We may be somewhat less than humble in the knowledge and acceptance of it, but we have shared our heritage with many other peoples in their quest for life and liberty. And we can be justly proud!

Our blessings have been many, and we have shared them with others that we may continue to be blessed as we stand for righteousness and truth.

In this patriotic month of July, may we celebrate our independence by renewing our faith and belief in Almighty God, our all-wise and all-loving Provider, Redeemer and Creator, whose life is eternal. His promise to us, if we live lives worthy of the gospel brought by Jesus Christ, is that we will live eternally too in the kingdom of God.

Patriotism and nationalism doesn't always mean a love and loyalty and general concern, but is sometimes a hollow symbol with only a vague idea of what it means to the masses. A scope too wide is ineffective. Patriotism like charity begins at home. We must develop a responsibility for the happenings in our homes, our cities, our small towns and communities. We learn and practice patriotism in the surroundings where we live before we try to cope with national responsibilities.

No matter how much you love your country and are willing to serve it, patriotism alone cannot save democratic nations because the concept of democracy came from the Bible which also tells us to have love for God and His church which is the ONE TRUE FOUNDATION.

"The gates of hell and the powers of darkness can never prevail against a nation standing 'under God' on such a foundation."

I have read that all United States Marines, from helicopter pilots to jeep drivers, are tested and re-classified annually on their ability to handle a rifle. The ability to handle a gun is a basic requirement or qualification for a marine. Reading the Bible is as basic to a Christian's life as shooting a gun is to a marine. Only by reading the Bible can we learn to handle the great truths therein.

How has God dealt with America? We sing the prayer song, "God Bless America" and that is the way He has dealt with our nation. He has blessed her, guided her and kept her safe in both war-time and peace. And we are still "one nation under God." Here are some mottoes to follow to keep it that way:

Practice what you believe in.

Righteousness exalteth a nation.

Nothing is great if it is not true.

Where there is no vision, the people perish.

Only through hard work do we build character.

When a principle is at stake, compromise is fatal.

It makes a difference whether I do right or wrong today.

Unless we develop loyalty, we cannot find unity and peace.

Continuing with our patriotic theme, let's consider the question, what should be the relation between a nation and God? We have been taught to think that religion is a very personal thing between an individual and his Creator and indeed it is, to the extent that everyone must decide for himself whom he wishes to serve, God or mammon, good or evil.

God also deals with the masses and nations. The Old Testament is a record of God's dealing with a nation. In this history, individuals are constantly being pointed out but they are always individuals from inside that nation. They are the ones chosen to lead that nation's affairs.

In our own nation, U.S.A. we feel that the hand of God is still guiding us as He did the early colonists and settlers as they fled from the old country seeking religious freedom. Here they found freedom in both their political and spiritual life. But even as we feel that our nation is still under the protective hand of God, there is grave danger that it may not remain that way. This is because so many do not fully understand the nature of our freedom.

To some people freedom means nothing more than a protected right to do as they please, and unknowingly, they help to destroy freedom by the way they use it and abuse it.

The big change that our country needs to make right now is in the men and women themselves. We must all realize that it is not the curbing of freedom from without, but the curbing of sin within that we really need.

Our nation needs to repent. It needs to recognize and repent of all its feelings of arrogance and superiority to other nations; of our loss of God, as shown by our terrible crime rate, dope peddling and child abuse, our crooked politicians, lawyers, and even doctors. There are even a few ministers who are wolves in sheep clothing, indulging in greed and crime.

The fact that families have let their children grow up without a knowledge of God except that it is a word to swear by shows how far we have strayed from God's laws. There is a new book on the market for children, and it contains the most profane word ever used. That book is titled The Mulberry Music by Doris Orgel, published by Harper and Row. It is a simple little tale of a child's love for her grandmother who was terminally ill and subsequently died. The taking of God's name in vain on page 112, and thereby breaking one of God's Ten Commandments, will keep that book off of Christian bookshelves. Some of America's children who have inherited more material blessings to enjoy than any children on earth do not know enough to say "Thank You" to God. They have not been taught by their equally ungrateful parents.

We are incredibly lacking in mature philosophy. There are moral, or I should say immoral, standards of behavior in our universe that's as obvious to the trained eye as scientific facts. Sometimes the role that destiny (of our own making) seems to have handed us, can break us as well as make us.

Speaking of safety in troubled times, a minister recently proclaimed, "The only safe place for America is on her knees saying, 'God, be merciful to us sinners.'" David, the Psalmist said, "Blessed is the nation whose God is the Lord."

Freedom will not long be sustained except in an atmosphere where man knows both his affinity and his accountability to God.

The words, ".… Of the people, by the people and for the people" seem to have different meaning to different people. Some think that "for the people" means a regular hand-out from the government and that governments are formed for the sole purpose of benefit and profit to each willing-not-to-work citizen.

Winston Churchill once said, "The inherent vice of capitalism is the unequal sharing of blessings; the inherent virtue of socialism is the equal sharing of miseries." Although many have admired the writings of Winston Churchill and others, we are more concerned with our own system of government and how, without the concern of all Americans, it could be changed so slowly and gradually that "we the people" could awaken someday and wonder what has become of the "of", and "by", and "for".

Remembering opinions of past presidents, we recall J.F. Kennedy saying, "Ask not what your country can do for you, but what you can do for your country." Abraham Lincoln said, "This nation, under God, shall have a new birth of freedom, that government of the people, by the people and for the people shall not perish from the earth." Woodrow Wilson said, "Only free people can hold their purpose and their honor steady to a common end, and prefer the interest of mankind to any narrow interest of their own." He also said, on another occasion, "The world must be made safe for democracy."

This one by Calvin Coolidge seems especially appropriate for today, "Governments are necessarily continuing concerns. They have to keep going in good times and in bad. They therefore need a wide margin of safety. IF taxes and debts are almost more than people can bear when times are good, there will be certain disaster when times are bad."

President William Howard Taft wanted better professional politicians, "If we can develop a class of educated men with nothing else to do but better government we ought to use them; and we ought to use them by having the profession of the politician recognized as essential to the welfare of the Republic." George Washington had been of the same opinion, "Government is not mere advice; it is authority, with power to enforce its laws."

Both George Washington and Woodrow Wilson seemed to have changed their minds afterward, "The aggregate happiness of society, which is best promoted by the practice of a virtuous policy, is or ought to be the end of government." (George Washington) And "No man ever saw the people of whom he forms a part. No man ever saw a government. I live in the midst of the government of the United States, but I never saw the government of the United States." (Woodrow Wilson)

Daniel Webster had an answer for politicians, "Nothing will ruin the country if the people themselves will undertake its safety; and nothing can save it if they leave that safety in any hands but their own."

President Ronald Reagan, as did Franklin Delano Roosevelt, agreed with Webster and both have carried some matters straight to the people. F.D.R. said, "The only sure bulwark of continuing liberty is a government strong enough to protect the interests of the people, and a people strong enough and well enough informed to maintain its sovereign control over its government."

The best government is yet to be! Read about it in Isaiah 9:6 and 7.

In spite of television, books still play an important part in our lives. We cannot learn any standard of conduct without reading a book or being taught by someone else who has read a book. I would say that there are four requirements absolutely necessary for life: food, clothing, shelter and books. The mind must have its food too!

I hope computers never replace books, but if they should and then something destroys the computer's memory, where would we be? Would it be back to square one, and the square wheels again?

However, it seems that when God has something to say to His people, He inspires someone to write a book. He told Jeremiah, "Write in a book all the words I have spoken to you."

A minister, speaking of the Apostle Paul being in jail and sending word to Timothy to bring him some things, and telling him, "And above all bring the parchments" (books in scrolls). And it is in just such books that God's word speaks more consistently and plainly to us than in any other way. Without books, God is silent, justice dormant, philosophy lame, letters dumb and all things in Cimmerian darkness.

The Apostle Paul was a reader. He knew from experience that he could find what he sought in books, and so can we.

Oliver Wendell Holmes said, "A man's mind, when once stretched to a new idea, never goes back to its original dimensions." If the mind is so subject to being stretched by what we read, we should guard well the quality of our reading material. Read only the best books, magazines and literature available for worldly knowledge; and for wisdom, read the Holy Bible daily.

Through the pages of the Bible we really get to know Christ. When we read this book we hear God speaking to us through His prophets. In fact, there can be no real Christian worship, individually or publicly, without the reading of the Bible.

Christians, in very age, because of their dedication and study of the scriptures, have been leaders in the field of education. One great task of every missionary is to teach the people that he wants to help to read.

Some years back there was much ado about someone saying, "God is dead!" Newspapers and magazine articles followed this statement, refuting that assumption. A few books on the subject were written too. God is not dead, but democracy will fail if we forget God and neglect to read His book.

American's greatest need is a revival of the faith that our forefathers had and return to the teachings of the Bible. Franklin, Jefferson, Washington, Lincoln, and even Jimmy Carter publicly declared they had accepted God and His teachings.

We sing about the "Faith of Our Fathers" but do we have it? They were not ashamed of their faith; they were not ashamed to pray; they believed in God! My own parents and grandparents drove for miles to attend all-day song fests and to pray with friends.

A minister once said, "Faith is not a walking question mark, it is a standing conviction!" Storms and stress of life cannot shake or deter the fully dedicated Christian!

• • • • • • • • • • • • • • • • • • • • • • • • • • • • • • • • • • • • • • •

Regarding the International Sunday School Lesson (chosen by the World Council of Churches) for Sunday, May 18, 1986, titled "The Gifts of the Holy Spirit", did you know that a part of the scriptures in that lesson, I Cor. 12:4 through 11, dealing with spiritual gifts has caused one of the great theological debates of the twentieth century?

One of the most confusing things in Bible study is that so many of the words are now obsolete or have changed in meaning. Sometimes two different words are used that have the same meaning. Such words as tongues and languages can mean the same thing. The modern way of saying "diverse tongues" is different languages. Charity also means love. In reading this 12th chapter, if we use the word love where they have charity, and use language where they have tongue, it is much easier to understand. Verse four says that all of the named gifts are from the same Spirit (God) and verse seven says this same Spirit is made manifest to every man.

I didn't have the gift for learning other languages. After two years of Spanish in high school and one in Junior College, I still don't have the gift of speaking the language. I do have the gift for interpreting it – if not spoken too fast. Some gifts are like the one talent given to the man in the parable of the talents; he didn't use it to increase it, and it was taken from him. If you don't use your gifts, you lose the power to use them, perhaps by forgetting.

If each of our fifty states were an independent country and spoke a different language, as did all of those little countries in Bible times, there would be plenty of people in the United States who could speak in diverse kinds of languages.

There are those who believe that God has given them the gift of speaking other languages without any effort of studying on their part. I have friends and acquaintances who believe this. They tell me they don't even know what they are saying until God interprets it and tells them.

I have no quarrel with that. Who am I to say what God does or does not do or say to someone else? Suffice it to say that everyone I know or have ministered unto (cared for) speaks English, and I have no thoughts or requests or desires to speak in a language in which I wouldn't understand what I said to them. I also pray in English and know that my prayers are heard because they are answered. Perhaps not always as quickly or in the exact way expected, but in His own time and in a way often proving more beneficial.

Prayer time is happy time. I am happy when I pray, happy even to have the privilege, but not esthetically so. Sometimes I think that prayer-thoughts may be heard and appreciated more than a lot of emotional and almost hysterical repetition.

Praise Him? Of course! Thank Him? We must! Love Him? Forever! But let's not waste His time by begging for spiritual gifts that we haven't earned and don't need!

It seems to me that we have more use for the word "charity" which means love and caring. "Love beareth all things, love believeth all things, love hopeth all things and love endureth all things." (I Cor. 12:7)

I have been reading the "new, revised and enlarged edition" of the book, <u>The Magic Power of Your Mind,</u> of which Dr. Daniel A. Poling of Christian Herald says, "Here is proof that you can remake your life; use the hidden power within you to achieve success." The book was written by Walter M. Germain. It is a study of psychology the way it was taught about 40 years ago, perhaps earlier. Although I can't agree with the entire contents, it is worthwhile reading and in layman's language.

Also I like books that tell a lot about the author. He was born in Saginaw, Michigan in 1890; he was a business man until 1929, clerk of City Police Department in 1931, Police Inspector in 1934, and stayed with the Police Department for 20 years. During that time he organized and was superintendent of a Crime Prevention division which helped so many people that the American Legion called him "the cop who cared". This caused him to study psychology and write this book to help people and solve their problems. This information should prompt anyone who also likes to help people to read his book.

Earlier psychological theories that the "goodness-badness" and the "knowledge-ignorance" and the "maturity-immaturity" of man is determined by dual or multiple personalities is something strange to me. My belief is that man is motivated by "positive-negative thinking" which develops into positive or negative attitudes and actions. Do you remember this old song? "Accentuate the positive, eliminate the negative and don't bother with Mr. in-between?" Also, have you read Dr. Norman Vincent Peale's popular book, <u>The Power of Positive Thinking?</u>

I believe in the power of suggestion but not through hypnotism or the state of being in a trance or suspended animation. Neither can I believe the case history that states of a woman said to have four distinct personalities. One of them could speak fluently in French, and it was unknown to the other three.

There is a lot of superstition and even some "voodooism" mixed with early psychology. A student of psychology can readily understand why this is so.

If you would like to read this book and your library doesn't have a copy, try the book club, The Family Bookshelf, sponsored by Christian Herald. It may still be in print.

Although theology and philosophy are my favorite subjects, psychology, the study of human behavior, is very interesting too. And in regard to Dr. Poling's quote, I would like to know what, in his opinion, constitutes success.

As a wise man once said, "If a man can write a better book, preach a better sermon, or make a better mousetrap than his neighbor, though he build his house in the woods, the world will make a beaten path to his door." (This saying is generally attributed to Emerson, but it is also claimed by Elbert Hubbard.)

Yet there are some who think that continuous success is not good. Albert Einstein said, "Possessions, outward success, publicity, luxury, to me these have always been contemptible. I believe that a simple an unassuming manner of life is best for everyone, best both for the body and the mind."

God is great! God is all-powerful! He is omnipotent, omnipresent and omniscient! Yet there is one thing that God cannot do; God cannot lie! In the light of His knowledge, which is often overlooked when we are considering His omnipotence, we see the frailty of history that's recorded by un-inspired human historians, and we are gratified by the truth of the inspired word.

This word that was in the beginning with God, the word that was God, said, "I am the Way, the Truth and the Light and no man cometh unto the Father except by me."

That light will not be clouded or darkened by lies, not by men's lies nor by Satan's lies. The word, which is God's eternal truth, tells us that the devil is a liar and has been from the beginning, and also that the human heart is deceitful and wicked above all things – until it is redeemed by the love of God. For by faith we are saved; by unbelief we are lost.

Our disobedience does not destroy God's love for us, but it will prevent us from receiving His blessings until we ask to be forgiven for our sins, which may be sins of omission as well as sins of commission.

God wants us to have an abundant life but in return, He wants our loyalty. How can God abundantly bless an unyielding sinner? He said, "If ye keep my commandments, ye shall abide in my love." (John 15:10) If we cannot believe that, we are doomed. God will not save an unbeliever! We are given the freedom of choice. We can accept and return His love, or we can reject Him and invoke the wrath of God that is to be the final judgment of sinners.

He has said, "Behold! I stand at the door and knock…." You don't have to look for Him; He is always seeking the lost and unbelieving and is as near as a prayer. Yes, only a prayer away! But just one word of caution, He also said, "My spirit shall not always strive with man." There's danger in delay!

King David sinned and felt that the wrath of God was upon him. In his misery, he sang this song, "We are consumed by Thine anger, and by Thy wrath are we troubled. You have set our signs before you, our secret sins are before Thy face. For all our days are passed away in Thy wrath; we spend our days as a tale that is already told."

"The days of our years are threescore and ten; and if by reason of strength they are fourscore years, yet is their strength and labor sorrow; for it is soon cut off and we fly away. Who knoweth the power of Thine anger? Even according to Thy fear, so is Thy wrath."

David repented and again found favor with God and sang happier songs, such as, "I will say of the Lord, He is my refuge and my fortress. My God, in Him will I trust."

Our God is a powerful God and to know Him is to receive part of that power. Power over self, power over thoughts and actions and best of all, power to meet daily problems "head-on" knowing that if you can't solve them, He will! He will solve them in His own good time. Meanwhile, not to worry!

Today I was "spot-reading" or "back-reading" through the Meditations of Marcus Aurelius, a stoic philosopher who was also a Roman emperor who reigned from 161 to 180 A.D. at the close of the period of the good Antonine emperors' and at the time when the Roman empire was making the transition from paganism to Christianity.

One paragraph seemed to stand out from the others and signal to me. I reread it. All of that, I thought, to convey the message of the 11th commandment, found in John 13:34 "Thou shalt love thy neighbor as thyself." How beautiful and explicit his interpretation is:

"Begin this morning by saying to yourself, I shall meet with the busybody, the ungrateful, arrogant, deceitful, envious, unsocial. All of these things happen to them by reason of their ignorance of what is good and what is evil. But I who have seen the nature of the good that it is beautiful, and of the bad that it is ugly, and the nature of him who does wrong, that it is akin to mine, not only of the same blood and seed, but that it participates in the same intelligence and the same portion of divinity; I can neither be harmed by any of them, for no one can fix on me what is ugly, nor can I be angry with my brother, nor hate him. For we are made for cooperation, like feet, like hands, like eyelids, like the row of the upper and lower teeth. To act against one another then is contrary to nature; and it is acting against one another to be vexed and to turn away."

The more we research the writings of the "great ones" in history, the more clearly we can see the Bible messages in them; or at least, we can see that the Bible is the basis for the thoughts and opinions expressed although the writer himself may or may not be aware of it.

Being an avid reader, I belong to four book clubs but still have difficulty finding the right books. So many of them are marked, "explicit sex" or "explicit violence" or "strong language"! I can't imagine the type of minds that derive pleasure or entertainment from reading such books, nor can I imagine anyone wanting to write them.

The irony is that so many of the stories are good when the filth and profanity are taken out. I didn't know that until I received a letter from Family Bookshelf (the book club sponsored by Christian Herald), saying, "Please accept our apology. We think we may have mailed you an uncensored book this month. Please return at our expense for exchange." The saga of three generations I received was "clean." The "bad" book must have been mailed to another club member.

That letter lowered my esteem for today's writers of books and the publishers who buy them and the readers who read them. How can one aspire to heavenly things while a large portion of the mind is still in the gutter?

A publisher, or editor, of romance fiction books returned a manuscript to a Houston writer with this notation: "A good story - well written - we'll buy it if you redo it. Add at least one murder and a couple of rapes."

The tragedy is that the reading public must change before the writers and the publishers will, and meanwhile all small children will be exposed to this trash when the stories are displayed on the television screen.

Much has been written about the "rightness" or "wrongness" of things, things in government, in social and personal affairs, in the schools, in the way children and old people are treated; and, indeed, all opinions are considered in the light of whether that opinion is right or wrong. The old-fashioned word "sin" has almost become obsolete.

Ministers used to preach a lot about sin and sinning, especially about the unpardonable sin which is against God. Other sermon topics were about hell-fire and damnation and the "Wrath of God" that we bring down on our own heads because of our sinful natures. People speak and sing of that "Old Time Religion" and some never seem to notice how people's attitudes toward and about God have changed. Hellfire, damnation and God's wrath is seldom heard from the pulpit anymore. Our God is thought of only as a God of love, and no matter what we do or say, He will always say, "I forgive. I forgive." We leave out all the "if"s that accompany God's promises and dwell on the scriptures that appeal to us.

The prophet Isaiah said, "Behold the day of the Lord cometh, cruel both with wrath and fierce anger, to lay the land desolate; and He shall destroy the sinners thereof out of it." The verse above that one seems to describe an atomic war, speaking of the great and tumultuous noise of the nations gathering together for battle (noise of jet airplanes?), they come from far countries - with weapons of indignation, to destroy the whole land.

"And they shall be afraid: pangs and sorrow shall take hold of them; they shall be in pain as a woman that travaileth; they shall be amazed one at another; their faces shall be as flames." (Isaiah 12:8, radiation burns?)

Will bombs and toxic waste destroy the land on which the atomic radiation falls? Verse 20 sounds that way: "It shall never be inhabited, neither shall it be dwelt in from generation to generation: neither shall the Arabian pitch tent there; neither shall the shepherds make their fold there."

Also Verse 11, "I will punish the world for their evil, and the wicked for their iniquity; and I will cause the arrogance of the proud to cease, and will lay low the haughtiness of the terrible: "Therefore I shall shake the heavens, and the earth shall remove out of her place, in the wrath of the Lord of hosts, and in the day of His fierce anger."

Isaiah was the first of the major prophets and is probably the best known. He lived to be 80 or more, and 60 or more of these years were spent in prophetical labors. Most of his prophecies have already come to pass, including the prediction of the advent of the Messiah. There remains the coming judgment and establishment of God's kingdom. Read chapters 24 through 27. It is hard to understand in some places but becomes easier if we keep up with the religious and political news of all the countries that make up our world today.

No one knows the time of this last prophecy, but the 24th chapter of Matthew and the 21st chapter of Luke tell us what the sign of the time shall be. Jesus said in Luke 21:29, "Behold the fig tree, and all the trees; when they shoot forth leaves, you see and know that summer is nigh; likewise when you see these things come to pass, know that the kingdom of God is nigh at hand."

Is America suffering the consequences of "collective sin?"

Although it would appear that America is still governed "by the people" this is literally not true. Is America governed by a political regime that has bogged down in sin and moral degeneracy, and "we the people" are innocent victims of their manipulations and wrongdoing? Money talks louder to politicians today than ever before. What chance would an Abraham Lincoln or any other "honest" poor man have of winning a campaign for any upper level office in today's system of government?

Government "of the people, by the people, for the people" is still the best system on earth, but there is a great danger of being lulled into a false sense of security induced by those in power to keep the silent majority silent.

It takes courage to be different in today's society. It takes courage to go "back to basics." But we must remind ourselves from time to time that America was founded by people of high moral standards, and many had deep religious convictions of which they were not ashamed to speak.

When I was a child (long, long ago) the family Bible was revered. All public assemblies began with prayer. People wanted to feel that God's presence was with them and that they had his blessing, and that He approved of what they were doing.

Somehow our focus has shifted from God to what we think is our own ingenuity and accomplishments. The natural resources and many other blessings that God so graciously bestowed upon our nation when it was under His law, upheld by our forefathers who loved Him, are now being taken for granted.

Have the words "In God we trust" become merely a symbol and a trademark? Patriotism (pride of country) is a feeling that's coveted by every citizen of the world, but it cannot long be sustained when God is left out.

God is sinless and will not dwell long with sinful people who will not turn to Him. When God moves out, who moves in? The dope peddlers, child abusers, murderers and others, including crooked politicians.

Public opinion is a very persuasive power. Be sure that opinion is true and just and not imparted by some fanatic or fund-raiser on a soap box making promises with no intention of keeping them.

Only the indwelling spirit of God can provide us with the courage to rebel against those in high places who have lost their moral integrity and their sense of justice and fair play.

Daily prayers and Bible reading is the most curative tonic. It is 100% effective! Also we must not consider God's long suffering patience as mere indulgence, because our sins and disobedience will eventually be accounted for, either by forgiveness and remembered no more, or by condemnation and cast into outer darkness, and a loving God leaves the choice to us.

We all like to think of ourselves as nonconformists. We all want to think that we are different from everyone else, that we are unique specimens of humanity, that after we were made the pattern was lost, and there will never be another like us. This is the basic belief of both the superior and inferior complexes in our society.

The truth is that while some are thinking, "There's no one as bad as I am" and others are thinking, "There's no one quite as good as I am," all are striving to be like one another.

Today's youth think of themselves as nonconformists while everything they do and say proves otherwise. They dress alike, have the same hair styles, talk alike, eat the same foods and spend a lot of time together.

Grown-ups, although not quite so openly, show that they are conformists too. Both young and old want to think of themselves as "one of a kind," yet no one wants to appear to be different.

Every successful inventor, painter, writer, civic or spiritual leader, has had to step out of the crowd and dare to be different to gain their goal, and those few who do step out are the courageous ones who change the mediocrity and sameness in the world.

No one person can change the trend that has taken over America today, the trend of violent crimes being committed. There's no need to name them. Everyone who reads the newspapers and listens to TV and radio news, knows how varied and numerous these crimes are. Christians, especially, are concerned about today's lifestyle. Each individual feels helpless, and is probably thinking, "What can I, being only one person, do to help stop the tide of crime before it reaches flood stage?"

"Collective sin" can be abolished by collective thinking and talking and praying. Only one person first had the idea of a "hot line" for runaways to call for help, only one person first had the idea for a place for abused wives and children. Only one idea was needed to start the "crime stoppers" organization, and also for the "neighborhood watch program."

If you have what you think is a good idea for helping to solve a bad situation, don't cast it aside with the question, "What can **one** person do?" There is an inner resource of power that comes to the aid of one who is determined to stand for the right in the face of so much opposition.

No nation can long endure whose peoples violate Godly principles. To fight, and to win others to fight with you against these violations, requires a degree of spiritual stamina that only the indwelling Spirit of God can provide.

Let's see if we can put a "chain reaction" into great effect by talking against pornographic literature and movies. The results could be rewarding.

A beginning and an ending is a continuous repetition all through life. For instance, today, regardless of the date, month and year, is the ending of an age in your life.

Tomorrow a new phase of your life begins. Tomorrow! What a wonderful word is "tomorrow." A word of promise, a word of beginning again, a word of continuity, and a word of hope!

We would be wise, as children of God, if at the close of each day before we close our eyes in sleep, to look back into the past, also to look forward, as much as possible, into the future and through this meditation and prayer, set some attainable and worthwhile goals for ourselves. Make some vows to the Lord, and definitely, place ourselves in the center of God's will.

Often we hear it said, "If only I had my life to live over again, etc." Well, that is out! But, instead of bemoaning our fate, we should consider the fact that we are still alive, and as long as we have breath, we will still have a part of our lives to live for the first time. Just how much we live, and how effectively we live, is left entirely up to us.

None of us know the extent of our days and that is good, and part of the wisdom of God that we don't. But the earthly ending of it is a certainty; and that knowledge should be enough to make us consider the time that we have left quite seriously.

Remember the man of Shelah? He was the Biblical Methuselah who was one of the patriarchs and a Babylonian deity; he lived 969 years (Gen. 5:27). To those who think it is too late to turn their lives around, consider this: we know little about Methuselah, other than he was the seventh generation descendant from Adam and lived longer than any other person. Yet, if he had wasted his life for 900 years, he would still have had 69 years for a new beginning and a good life.

The New Testament gives us a life expectancy of three score and ten years. So if you are sixty years or over and feel that you have neglected God for so long that He won't accept you now for your last ten or more years, consider the parable of the laborers in the vineyard (read it in Matthew: second chapter). The owner went out early in the morning to hire laborers for his vineyard. He found men on the street who agreed to work for a certain sum. Three other times during the day the owner went back on the street and saw men idle and sent them to work in his vineyard.

At the close of the day, the owner paid all of them the same wages, whereupon the earlier workers complained that those who had come in last had worked little more than an hour and had received as much compensation as they had. Similarly, some people who claim to have been Christians all their lives, resent the idea that God might accept death-bed confessions, or others who change late in their lives. But remember the thief on the cross was told, "This day shalt thou be with me in paradise."

It is never too late to resolve that from this day forward, to so live each day, that tomorrow the world will be a better place to live in than it was yesterday.

Most of the world's problems, and also most of its joys, are caused by human emotions. Our emotions are the "feelings" we have as we become involved with day-to-day living and decision making.

The brain requires fine tuning (training) and delicate handling to keep emotions in check. But, of course, there are two exceptions. The person who never shows emotion is said to be unfeeling and hard. Psychiatrists say that this is especially true of the criminal mind that seems completely without feelings or emotions caused, no doubt, from soothing the conscience and keeping a tight rein on emotions for too long a period of time. At the opposite extreme is the person who laughs with hysteria or cries with little or no provocation. The medical profession says this type of person is slightly neurotic, but even those who seem self-composed most of the time, have a few bad moments occasionally.

Good emotions are the result of good health and a clean mind. The "fine tuning" of the mind begins with programming it with clean thoughts and right attitudes. After all, the mind is a highly sensitive computer and its memory can ever be expanding. Although it is a computer, it is not a cold and calculating machine; it has feelings and is housed in an emotional body.

The feelings can be kept on an even keel, or steady course, by relaxation. Relaxation makes it possible to have complete health of body, mind and spirit, and when relaxation is accompanied by meditation and prayer, it is an unbeatable threesome!

Judging from the few times I've watched TV this week (June 1986), it's a mad, mad world out there for expressing feelings, especially in the sports world. If you live in a Houston viewing area and watched the national play-offs of the Houston Rockets, you know what I'm talking about. Emotions were running so high that feelings "got out of hand" and turned into fisticuffs.

The modern trend is to want to live in a state of high excitement where feelings and emotions can run rampant. It is an age of wanting to be "on-the-go" at all times. Time that is not spent in eating, sleeping, working or pleasure seeking is thought to be boring, not relaxing. The bored person is a restless person, therefore he can't relax. Perhaps he, or she, is too "up-tight" to feel the need for relaxation because of a constant state of tenseness, they may think it to be normal.

Only the person who takes time out for complete rest and relaxation, for a few quiet moments alone to speak to God, to wait for the feeling of His presence and the soothing and stilling of frayed nerves, can know that this is the only cure for stress and strain. God said, "Be still, and know that I am God."

Jesus said, "I came that you might have life, and have it more abundantly." An abundant life is a life of joy and good health, supplied with all necessities for happiness. Abundant life means knowing and loving God and keeping His commandments, so that "all of these things shall be added unto" us.

Just as we all have visions for our future, so do we all have memories of the past. How should we handle these memories? How are they related to our visions for the future? We envision the years ahead by seeing in advance what we may become, setting goals and striving for the reality of our mental pictures. These visions must not end as mere daydreams if a goal is to be attained.

Visions can be fleeting, or they can become time consuming. The dreamer must turn into a schemer, and plot and plan to make his dreams come true, and it depends upon the character and strength of the individual, his ability to achieve right attitudes and a clean mind, as to whether memories will help or hinder his accomplishments.

Memories come in all sizes and forms and degrees of remembering. There are the cherished memories of those we have loved and lost. These memories sustain us in many ways and it helps to remember them.

There are memories of past accomplishments that one can take pride in remembering, but one shouldn't spend too much time thinking of past glories, because of the temptation to "rest on our laurels." There are also dark memories of regret. Things one would rather forget that keeps popping up at the most unexpected times, the memory of harsh words spoken in wrath and in haste that cannot be recalled.

Let your memories of yesterdays work for your tomorrows, and use today to sort them out. Put them into two stacks. Stack up the golden memories and bring them out on dark days when the ego needs re-kindling, and they will put joy in your heart.

Take the stack of dark and somber memories, all of the unpleasant experiences of the past, and remember them in a religious sense. There are lessons to be learned from hard experiences. Just as a diamond in the rough is black, so can jewels be found in the darkness of our remembering.

Only by remembering wrong deeds can we think to ask God for forgiveness for them. Wrong deeds are not easily forgotten. None of us, when we really know and take account of ourselves, can look back across our lives and escape from thoughts of wrongdoing. The memory of past sins causes one to turn towards the hope that makes life new. Sins cannot be hidden, covered up or forgotten entirely. They can be forgiven. "Though our sins be red or crimson, forgiveness makes them white as snow." They will be remembered against us no more and then, only then, can we forget them entirely ourselves.

Some people still ask, 'What is sin?' The Bible says, "...for whatsoever is not of faith is sin." I tell myself, "Everyone instinctively knows right from wrong; therefore, right things are Holy and wrong things are sinful!" That simplified it for me.

"Remember thy God and forget not all His benefits!"

Every day, as I grow older, the great mystery of God becomes more mysterious. For instance, how can the father of millions of children, perhaps billions counting all who have gone before us, remember all of our names? Not only our names, but the number of hairs on each child's head? (Matt. 10:30.)

Not only is God the father of Abraham, Isaac and Jacob, but also of every Jack and Jill and Tom, Dick and Harry in the world, including you and me. The population of the earth, also of our own country which opens its doors to all people, has grown so that often we see a familiar face and can't remember the name. Every time this happens to me, I think "How great God is! He knows their name. Also the name of everybody else in this crowded thoroughfare," Or department store, supermarket or wherever it may be.

It helps when you find yourself surrounded by strangers to realize that God knows them and you know God, and that makes you feel that He is there with you.

When I was a child many, many years ago, there were numerous games that children played. Growing up with a lot of cousins who improvised new games or added to old ones, I recollect the words "King's X" and "Tick-A-Lock" being applied to running and chasing games. If one was quitting the game for awhile, he or she, had to yell "King's X," meaning it's not fair to catch me now, the King has excused me. But if just stopping to rest for a moment, one had only to draw a ring around oneself and say "Tick-A-Lock." These rules were always kept by everyone. Whether the ring around oneself was made with a stick on a playground of dirt or sand, or an imaginary ring made on yard grass - you were locked in and couldn't be caught.

Even today, if I find myself alone with masses of people going to and fro, like downtown Houston, I have this feeling that I am in my own little Tick-A-Lock and that God is inside it with me. It's a wonderfully protected feeling.

Another mystery, how can God be everywhere at once? How can He be where I am, and also where you are? We know that He exists, "the earth and the heavens declare His handiwork," and His presence can certainly be felt.

To try to even imagine the intellect of God makes our own reasoning sound like baby's prattle, and just as mixed-up as the little girl who for the first time was trying to say the Lord's prayer: "Our Father who art eleven, how did You know my name?" However, unless you have the faith of a little child, you can in no wise enter into the Kingdom of Heaven. - Luke 18:16-17.

Have you ever drawn an imaginary circle around yourself and shut out everything beyond the circle, and then realize that God is with you inside the circle? If not, try it sometime. It can be a blessed experience at any age. To have and to FEEL the presence of God, exactly where you are!

He said, "Lo I am with you always, even unto the end of the world." Matt.28:20.

How can a civilized world change so much in a little less than 100 years? I have a book written in the late 1800's in which the writer says, "The greatest triumph of the 19th century is not its marvelous progress in inventions; its strides in education; its conquests of the dark regions of the world; the spread of a higher mental tone throughout the earth; the wondrous increase in material comfort and wealth; the greatest triumph of the century is not any nor all of these things: It is the sweet atmosphere of peace that is covering the nations, it is the growing close and closer of the peoples of earth."

When did the sweet atmosphere of peace leave us? And what was the possible cause? Could we have brought it about by forgetting love and remembering only duty? A father may claim that he is "doing his duty to his son" which often means that he is merely furnishing him food, clothing and shelter and, if he can afford it , a set of wheels to keep him out of the way.

The word "duty" by itself is to be respected, but two other words can make it shine with new meaning. Add the words "truth" and "love" and you have an unbeatable trinity. It has been said that "duty creeps to laboriously, love reaches in a moment - as if on the wings of a dove." Modern parental duty is a danger in today's society. People who boast often about doing their duty are often covering up a lack of love.

Many of today's children, trying to cope with a society in which just about anything goes, are having a stormy time trying to keep up with their peers yet stay within the boundaries of what they think parents expect of them. Only parents who really love their children can be a haven and refuge during their storms of stress and uncertainty in adapting to our many-sided environment.

To a youth, things aren't always black or white (right or wrong), neither or they red or green (stop or go), but a whole rainbow of colors in between that causes character changes. These changes can be for the best if there are loving and understanding hearts and hands to help them over the rough spots. However, this lack of love could be what has changed our 20th century.

A lack of love means a lack of God, because God is love. Did you know that Christianity is the only religion that is based on love, not duty? Love is the one great duty assigned to Christians: "This commandment I give unto you, that you love one another, even as I have loved you."

Duty is not lost, rejected or destroyed by Christianity; it is dignified with truth and exalted with hope and all the rough and troubled spots are made smooth by love.

In the Bible, duty is mentioned only four times; no one has counted the hundreds of times the word "love" appears.

• • • • • • • • • • • • • • • • • • • • • • • • • • • • • • • • • • • • • • • •

Once again it is the time of year when children look back over their shoulders to see if "ghosties or beasties or things that go bump in the night" are chasing them. Although they may whittle and carve all day putting a scary face on the pumpkin and place a lighted candle inside to scare the witches and hob-goblins away, they still shriek and run as though something is chasing them.

Are they just having fun, or are they really frightened? I have been told that they really want to be afraid on Halloween, and the only way they can be really scared is to sit in the dark and tell ghost stories until they imagine they see eyes in the darkness. This is hard for me to realize: that children enjoy the excitement of being scared "half out of their wits."

Neither do grown-ups seem afraid of the evil spirits that chase after them. Either they are not afraid of them or else, just indifferent about the existence of evil. If this were not the case, something would be done about it.

All Hallows or All Saint's Day falls on the first of November. It originated as a church festival early in the 7th century when the Pantheon at Rome was consecrated as the "Church of the Blessed Virgin and All Martyrs" and in 1835, Pope Gregory IV officially authorized the custom. The festivity was called All Hallows, All Hallowmas or simply Hallowmas. It is believed that the choice of that day was determined by the fact that November 1, was one of four great festivals of the heathen nations of the north, because it was the policy of the church to supplant heathen observances with Christian observances. The Roman Catholic and the Anglican churches annually celebrate the feast of Hallowmas (Holy Mass) in honor of God and all His saints, the ones that are known and also the unknown.

Halloween (Holy eve.) applies to the night preceding Hallowmas, and is informally observed in the United States with masquerading and pumpkin decorating. Traditionally, it is an occasion for children to play pranks.

People celebrated November 1 long before it became a Christian feast day. It is believed to have originated among the ancient Druids. The exact date is not known, neither the name of it, but it was likely named for their God, Samhain, who was the lord of the dead who called forth hosts of evil spirits. The Druids lit great fires on Halloween, apparently for the purpose of warding off these evil spirits.

To ancient Druids (members of a Celtic religious order of priests, soothsayers, judges, poets, etc. in Britain, Ireland and France) Halloween was the last evening of the year and they regarded it as a time for examining and foretelling things of the future. The Celts also believed that the spirits of the dead arose and visited their earthly homes again on that evening.

After the Romans took Britain they added their traditions. Their Nov.1 feast honored Pomona, their goddess of the fruit trees. Traces of Roman harvest festivals survive as a part of modern custom in both the United States and England. We still have big bonfires, not to scare evil spirits away but for roasting wieners and marshmallows. And we have the harvest fruit of pumpkin for pies and decorating, and apples to put in a tub of water for "bobbing for apples." Happy Halloween!

The most wonderful gift that one can have is love, but first one must have love and respect for oneself - only then can one have love and respect for one's fellowman.

The next two important gifts in a person's life are necessary before one can have the greatest gift that is love: A clean mind and a pure heart are essential to love. When one's heart is cleansed and the mind purified with God's Golden Rule, one becomes born again into LOVE.

It has been told that a footpath on the outskirts of a manufacturing town was covered in muddy slush made of four substances: clay, soot, sand and water. The mixture of these elements made a messy and slimy pathway, but when the four substances were separated and cleansed they became things of beauty.

The clay particles united and, in time, became a clear hard material which separated and gathered to itself only the brilliant blue rays from the light, and it became a lovely sapphire.

The sand mysteriously arranges itself into fine parallel lines and absorbs the blue, green, purple and red rays of sun and light and becomes an opal. The soot, when separated and rid of impurities, becomes the hardest substance in the world: a diamond, reflecting all the light.

The water becomes dewdrops that sparkle in the grass, or a snowflake like a crystalline star. All four are objects of beauty that was once the filth of the earth. The human life is like that too, when we separate ourselves from the filth and dirt that can creep into our hearts and minds. But one must want to change, or it won't happen.

Back in the 1950's, according to a story told in one of the best-sellers of that day, there was a barber's convention being held in a certain city. To attract attention to their association's meeting, and advertise their trade, they decided on the following publicity stunt.

They went to the city's "skid-row" and picked up the worst looking drunk they could find. Taking him back to their hotel, they bathed, shampooed and shaved him. They cut his hair and dressed him in the fashion mode of the day.

They showed "before and after" pictures to promote their business.

The hotel manager became interested in the made-over man who, now that he was sober and fashionably dressed, looked like the perfect gentleman. He said, "I would like to be a part in helping you get started all over again. I will give you a job in another business I own. When can you start?"

"Tomorrow morning," was the reply.

He did not come back the next morning and the manager, who had gone to look for him, found him back on skid-row, sleeping on some old sacks, his new clothing torn and soiled.

Neither clothes and attention, nor anything on the outside can make a gentleman or a lady. It's what is in the inside that counts. Strive diligently for a pure heart and clean mind so that you may abide in love.

"Blessed are the pure in heart: for they shall see God." - Matthew 5:8.

When people in my vicinity think of home, they think of east Wharton County, while people on the other side of the county think of home as west Wharton County. Why east? Why west? Why not, simply, Wharton County? (Who? Me? I live in Wharton County.) Do we, the people of Wharton County, still have "one more river to cross"?

What prompted this subject was a newspaper report of an event which was attended by people from Fort Bend, Brazoria, Matagorda, Harris, Waller, east Wharton County and west Wharton County. Doesn't that sound silly to you? It did to me. Not only did it sound silly, it also sounded like two separate counties. Don't you think that we have been inaccurate long enough? It reminds me of an old, old song about the "East and West...and ne'er the twain shall meet!" And I, for one, don't like the sound of it!

My husband has lived in Wharton County all of his life, and I since 1924. Not long after we married (in 1927), I asked him what caused the unfriendliness between the east and west citizens of the county. (And, believe me, it was much more pronounced at that time.) He thought that the Colorado River, which flows through the county on the western edge of the city of Wharton, was the culprit.

Of course this topic goes a long way back in time and that makes it harder to understand. I wonder if there is anyone still living who can remember when there was no bridge across the river at Wharton? My husband remembers crossing the Brazos on a ferry boat at Richmond, but he can't remember when there wasn't a railroad bridge at Wharton. All traveling between east and west, in the county, was by train for many years.

Some of the earlier settlers who had bought land east of the river, were moving down from Missouri and had to camp on the west side of the river until they could get their wagons across. This, of course, was before the existence of the Colorado Dam and sometimes miles of the countryside was inundated. I have seen the Wharton Junior College area (which was Gifford's Airport) and the Plaza Shopping Center (which was pasture land) covered with several feet of water. We had to turn back home to Iago as there was no way of getting on into town. Also Caney Creek overflowed through the town into homes, and into stores around the courthouse square.

River, terrain and weather may have divided the county earlier, but the division that existed after the dam and modern bridges and transportation was caused, I think, by jealousy and rivalry between the "city fathers" of the two largest towns in the county. Some of those strong feelings may still exist among the old-timers; however, it is diminishing. It is taking people like the Little League coaches and the united youth of the various churches to heal the break.

Changes can be wrought by training the youth and the children. They are our future! Viva Wharton County! United we stand, divided we fall! Old hates and old grudges should be treated like old soiled and dirty garments: taken off and laundered, using The Golden Rule as a cleansing detergent!

When some people think of Christianity their first thought is, "If I become a Christian, I must give up everything that is fun in my life." This line of thinking couldn't be more wrong.

It's true there are a number of things a Christian will not do, things that may be interpreted as fun by non-believers. But to think of Christianity as a long list of "don'ts" that will lead to a dull and boring life is a contradiction of the plain truth. Christians (dedicated ones) live life with a feeling of completeness and fullness, and they enjoy a lot of wholesome fun.

People have "blind spots" which let them see only what they want to see and ignore the rest. Like the scripture says, "Having eyes, they see not; and having ears, they hear not." Sometimes we realize those "blind spots" when we hear stories like, "The Blind Men and the Elephant."

It is an old story, handed down through the ages and told in different ways, but its application to life is easily discerned: Four blind men went to see an elephant. The first touched and felt the elephant's trunk. "Tis plain to see," he said, "this animal is like a snake."

"Not so," said the second man who was holding the elephant's tail, "It's very much like a rope."

"You're both wrong," said the third man who was leaning against the broad side of the animal, "anyone can tell that it is exactly like a wall."

The fourth man was kneeling with his arms around the elephant's leg. He said, "How can all three of you be so utterly mistaken? The elephant is this way and he is very much like a tree trunk."

The story ends by saying, "Each of them were partly right, yet all of them were wrong." This simple little tale so aptly describes our inability at times to grasp the full significance of an eternal truth. Our perspective becomes distorted and we grasp at partial truth and fail to get the real meaning of the whole.

The most identifying quality of Christians is their great capacity for love, their love for God and their love for each other, and their loving regard for all mankind everywhere. It truly distinguishes them from the non-Christian people in the world. Also, the truly dedicated believers will love their enemies and help them if they can.

The works of the world through mankind are listed in Galatians 5:19-21, and the works of the Spirit in Christians are also listed in Galatians 5:22-24. Please read the contrast of these two groups. Which ones do you think have the most fun? You may say, "But they are both extreme." True. They are. But there's no luke-warmness nor middle-ground with the Lord who said, "He that is not for me, is against me."

We hear much these days about people's lack of appreciation. Couples have reported that a "lack of communication" caused them to separate. About nine times out of ten that lack of communication is caused by a lack of expressed appreciation and love for each other.

Not only do we forget to say "Thank you," but we forget, or don't find the time, to do nice things for people who have befriended us (keeping in mind, of course, that the Bible says, "If you love and do things only for the people who love and do things for you, what reward have you?" Even sinners do this. Matt. 5:46.)

If we forget to show kindness and appreciation to family and friends that we love, how can we expect to follow the admonition in the 44th verse? "But I say unto you, love your enemies, bless them that curse you, do good to them that hate you, and pray for them which despitefully use you, and persecute you."

It is the ungodly individuals, the non-believers, who find pleasure in belittling, condemning, ridiculing and berating their spouses. It isn't easy to love an unlovely person, and a tyrant in the house is a burden to all who try to love and maintain a happy home. Tyrants aren't always men, some are women.

So many young people rush into marriage without waiting to see if they are going to be "unequally yoked." This does not mean that I approve of "trial marriages." Far from it! Young people should have longer friendships, not going steady the first week, heavy courtship the next week and marriage on the third. The longer you know a person before marriage, the longer the marriage is likely to last.

Parents complain that children don't appreciate what they do for them. Children complain that parents don't appreciate or understand them. Most of these feelings would disappear if each would only say, "I love and appreciate you; and I need your love and understanding."

What difference does it make whose fault it was? If both parties really love and forgive each other, it will soon be forgotten. When the Heavenly Father forgives our sins, He says that they not only will be washed white as snow, but they will not be remembered against us any more. Can we do less for the people who have sinned against us?

There's so much ingratitude in the world that TV is using it in their commercials. One Tarzan-like man rescues a damsel from alligator infested waters and when he puts her safely ashore, instead of saying "Thank you," she asks him to go back through the dangerous waters to get her towel which she had left on the opposite bank of the river.

Selfishness, greed, ingratitude, inconsideration, lack of appreciation and unpopularity go hand-in-hand and do not make an abundant happy life. Whereas, living by the Golden Rule brings many dividends and many worthwhile friends and a very happy life.

Dr. Norman Vincent Peale, who is very gifted in the telling of incidents that contain profound symbolism regarding his subject matter, was saying that the world's problems could be solved if enough people would get Jesus and His love into their hearts. "It's just that simple," he said, "Jesus with His love and kindness is the answer."

Then he told the story of a father who was sitting at home one evening reading the newspaper. His small son kept talking to him and asking questions to get his attention. In order to have peace and quiet while reading, he said, "Son, here is a jig-saw puzzle of the world. Put this world together, will you? And when you have finished come back and tell me."

Five minutes later the small boy was back with the world put together. The father was amazed at his competency and was very proud of him. He knew that his son was smart, but not quite that smart. He asked him, "Son, how did you get the world together so fast?"

"Dad, it's simple. Anybody can do it."

"Well, I don't know about that, Son; I am not sure that I could do it."

"It was easy, Dad, because on the back side of the puzzle is the picture of Jesus. I put Jesus together and the world came out right."

When our lives become a complicated jig-saw puzzle and we don't know what piece of it to pick up to get it all back together again, perhaps we, too, should try a complete turn-around. Sometimes "turning over a new leaf" and seeing a whole new picture, is the only answer.

How quickly and almost unknowingly one can slip into the seamy side of life. A "sound-off" letter to the editor of a Wharton County newspaper indicated that the writer was furious with the police for what he called, "enforcing some laws and not others." He didn't want the pornographic literature, movie tapes and record albums taken out of the stores. This, he said, was adult entertainment, and adults had a right to buy it.

He defended his right to buy it by saying, "They think sex is dirty. How do they think they got here?"

Oh, if God would only give us the wisdom to say and WRITE the right words that would help people in their misguided thinking. Words that would convince them to "turn their lives over" and see all of the beauty on the other side. Because many a life that had once been beautiful has become sordid and distorted by the wrong influences which, gradually, can dominate one.

If you have become a beautiful butterfly, but continue to live down with the worms, you may turn back into a worm.

A child of God should soar, and not dwell in the depths of degradation!

Much has been said about the spiritual side of man which was made in the image of God; however, one's material possessions are very much a part of one's earthly life. I am not speaking of big cars, mansions and bank accounts, but the little things about the house that one uses often and becomes fond of.

Things that mean a lot to me are the things that have been given to me through the years at Christmas or birthdays or anniversaries. I find it difficult to discard old robes and broken costume jewelry that were given to me by my children.

On my breakfast table there is a large crystal bowl. It has become many things to me: an indoor mail box (sort of an inner-office communication system), a safe for small change and postage stamps, an out-going mail depository (where letters are placed at night for the man of the house to mail when he goes out for the morning paper). If I am coming in late to prepare a meal, it is a place to lay gloves, jewelry, or even a hat, while food is put on the stove or in the microwave oven. In fact, it is a "catch-all" for things that may get misplaced before finding the time to put them where they belong.

This piece of Cambridge crystal is a good and faithful servant and is so much in use that it has been given a name: Cryss. Quite often the answer to questions such as, "Do you know where my wallet is?" or, "Have you seen my car keys?" is "Maybe Cryss has them, or it." And more often than not she does.

Isn't it a fact that simple pleasures are the ones most often remembered? And the simple daily routine that we have while living in a home is what we miss the most when we have to be absent from the home for awhile.

But nothing remains the same forever, and even Cryss is no exception. Because there are times when she puts aside her daily routine of the "good and faithful servant" and becomes a splendid thing of magnificent grandeur. Because there is an inner part for Cryss of which I haven't told you.

Cryss is really a three-part set of bowl, candle-holders and flower frog. There is a tall, graceful, crystal bird with out-spread wings on a round, crystal frog base that fits in the center of the bowl. And when this base is filled with flowers for a special occasion, Cryss is transformed. Her load of daily cares has been removed and she is adorned in splendor, reflecting the light from the candles.

There will be a time when we too, like Cryss, shall put aside our daily cares. When this mortal shall put on immortality and bask forever in eternal brightness, reflecting the light and glory of God.

If everyone lived each day as if that were the last day of life, what would our world be like?

It is no small wonder that this is called "the joyous season of the year." Shops and store windows brilliantly displaying gifts and ribbons and many-colored bows; and gold and silver tinsel and beautiful colored Christmas lights reflecting it all. Big-eyed children looking over the new toys which become more and more advanced every year, from rocket guns to spaceships and computers.

At Christmas time I love to go uptown and sit in my car at the curb and watch the faces of those passing by. It's quite a revelation to see how others accept or reject the Spirit of Christmas.

The story is told of an earnest Christian woman who stopped for a moment to admire a window display of things pertaining to Christmas. Among other things, there was pictured the baby Jesus in the manger at Bethlehem. While she stood there, two other women also paused long enough to see what was attracting her attention. Then she heard one of them say, "Just look at that! They're dragging religion into Christmas!"

People must be told: that apart from the religion which centers in Jesus Christ there would never have been a Christmas. He came to bring peace into the world and was hailed as the Prince of Peace, but somehow people don't seem as interested in peace as they do in material comforts.

Industrial progress and the advances made in scientific methods, new discoveries and inventions that make life easier is the answer to some people's quest or "pursuit of happiness." Some would go to war rather than give up the type of lifestyle to which they have become accustomed. Others would rather endure personal hardship, or, at least, to get by on less, in order to have peace.

Neither industry nor science nor comforts is a savior. Our Savior is the Prince of Peace, but we spend more time and money preparing for war than we do planning for peace.

Many people are enslaved to unhealthy habits and fears and attitudes, yet Jesus came to "set men free" of these very things.

Christmas isn't just for children, although children are extremely important to our world. The worth and sacredness of the little child is a factor that ultimately must be reckoned with by all of the abortionists and child abusers. Once we have subjected ourselves and our political economy to a searching examination, we will discover that human rights are the supreme rights. And the rights of the unborn child is at the center of it.

Jesus said, "Suffer the little children to come unto me and forbid them not, for of such is the Kingdom of heaven." So said the Babe of the first Christmas.

The "news of great joy" that was brought to earth at that time is still with us. Just as the angels sang and told the wondrous news to the shepherds, so will we sing praises in our churches on Christmas morning and pay homage to the Baby who was allowed to be born and to escape the child-killers of His day to bring us God's plan for our redemption and salvation.

It has been said that Longfellow could take a worthless piece of paper, write a poem on it, and make it worth $6,000 - that is genius. That Rockefellow could sign his name to a piece of paper and make it worth millions - that is capital. That Uncle Sam could take gold, stamp an eagle on it, and make it worth $20.00 - that is money. That a mechanic can take material worth $5.00 an make an article worth $50.00 - that is skill. That an artist can take a $5.00 piece of canvas, paint a picture on it, and make it worth $1,000.00 - that is art. That God can take a worthless sinful life, wash it in the blood of Christ, put His spirit in it, and make it a blessing to humanity - that is salvation.

After reading the above on an old church bulletin, I began to think of how seldom we hear the word - salvation. Yet that is what Christianity is all about: A plan for our salvation so that we can be like Him. Christ came, bringing the gospel message which was, if accepted by us, to redeem us from sin so that we may have salvation and eternal life. Salvation is free to all who will accept it. It cannot be bought because the price has already been paid by the shed blood of the One who gave His life for the redemption of our sins. Few people refuse free gifts. If someone who loves you hands you a package saying, "This is a gift that I bought for you." What do you say? Do you ignore the gift and the "would be" giver, or do you accept it gracefully with thanks?

Although salvation is "full and free," one must have faith to accept it. Believe! And have faith in what you believe! However, believing and having faith doesn't mean that there will be no more uncertainties or occasional doubts about things that may happen, but it does mean that the outcome is assured because if you have faith, you will eventually pray-it-through. Remember the scripture? - "According to your faith, so be it unto you."

Someone was inspired to write the following poem about faith:

### FAITH
"I do not know what tomorrow may bring.
Maybe I'll cry. Maybe I'll sing. Maybe I'll be all alone,
like an old woman, like an old stone.
Maybe the storm will claim my land,
maybe I'll feel God's judging hand.
But if I trust that He is with me,
giving me angels that I cannot see'
I will have faith to conquer all,
I will not falter, I will not fall.
I do not know what tomorrow may bring.
Maybe I'll cry. Maybe I'll sing.
If I am on God's side, I will not care,
we will win the battle everywhere!"

As we finish the bookkeeping and close the ledger on 1986, we can only wonder: What will the new year bring?

A new year is similar to "The Land of Beginning Again." It is a time for wiping the slate clean, for turning over a new clean page and starting all over. Some start by making many resolutions they can't keep. Some make only one, they resolve to do better than last year. That is too general to be easily kept. If you have trouble keeping your New Year's resolutions, try making just one or two and be specific.

Here are a couple of good ones: "I resolve to be on time for all appointments this year." and "I resolve not to miss Sunday morning Worship Service for any reason other than illness." As a teen-ager I made that resolution and it changed my life completely. It is as much a part of my routine as shopping on Thursdays and baking on Fridays. Resolutions, if kept, are habit forming, so make good ones.

Whether or not we make it a New Year's resolution, there is one thing we shall all surely do in 1987: we will show by our words and actions that we either know or know not God. The Atheists and Communists and other non-believers seem to be gaining ground and many Christians are growing lukewarm. They want God to prove Himself but instead of demanding that God prove Himself, it might be better to demand of ourselves that we prove Him by getting to know Him.

A Japanese student at Yale accepted Christianity: when he returned to Japan, he found himself an outlaw among his former friends who would have nothing to do with him, because he had turned his back on their faith which was Shintoism. Hounded, sick at heart and desperate, he called an old friend at Yale and asked,

"How can I prove that God is?" The answer came back: "Live three months as if He is."

Three months later the Japanese boy sent his second cable to his friend in New Haven: "It works!"

Do we know our God well enough to know how to speak for Him? The story is told that somewhere along the edge of the Sahara Desert a caravan stopped to rest in the shade of a little group of mud houses. Nearby was a mission station. Under a tree (the only tree in sight), an Arab boy sat with a New Testament in his hand. The master of the caravan, a cynical Arab, sent one of his men over to the youngster with a strange request: if the boy would tell them where they might find God, he would give him an orange. (A rather cheap gift, but cynics aren't usually very generous.)

The boy thought for a moment, considering the offer, then with a broad smile said, "Sir, you go back and tell the man who sent you that I will give him two oranges if he can tell me where God is not found."

The boy was right, "You can find Him everywhere. All the world reveals God's care." And this year of 1987 is in His hands. Let's help Him to make it a good New Year.

· · · · · · · · · · · · · · · · · · · · · · · · · · · · · · · ·

"Finally, brethren, whatsoever things are true, whatsoever things are honest, whatsoever things are just, whatsoever things are pure, whatsoever things are lovely, whatsoever things are of good report; if there be any virtue, and if there be any praise, THINK ON THESE THINGS." - Philippians 4:8.

Thus the Apostle Paul admonished the people in the church at Philippi, Macedonia. Of all the letters sent by Paul, this is my favorite. It was not only a letter of instruction, it was also a love letter. During his three missionary journeys, Paul was an evangelist preacher in many churches throughout the region. To these churches he later wrote letters of hope and encouragement, but, in some unknown way, this letter seems different.

Before going to Philippi (it was here the women of the town held their meetings on the bank of the river with Liddia, the seller of purple), Paul saw a vision. He was in Troas when he saw the vision of a man who said, "Come over into Macedonia and help us." Paul responded to that call and helped to promote good will and Christian fellowship among them. He re-visited the church after that time; twice Luke was with him.

At the writing of this letter, Paul was an old man. He had been arrested and placed under custody of the Praetorian prefect, Burrus when he stopped in Rome. He lived two years in his little "hired house" there. Although he had certain freedoms of going in and out of his little house, he was confined to a certain area. Today he probably would be called a "trusty." Because of his infirmities, which he called his "thorn in the flesh," and his advanced age, this letter to the Philippians was written by Epaphroditus, but Paul dictated it. (Phil. 2:25-30) Also, history tells us that Paul could not write in the Greek language.

The length of this letter, which became one of our New Testament books, is only three pages. Read it with the thought that it was written to you or your church, and experience the warm feeling of love and approval that permeates your entire being. Consider the following quotes from Paul's letter: "I thank my God upon every remembrance of you"........"I have you in my heart." (Verses 22,23, &24)

He further says, in substance, "I struggle between two desires: to die and be with Christ, which is far better, or to abide in the flesh and be of more help to you."

"Whether I come and see you or else be absent, I may hear of your affairs"... "Stand fast in one spirit, striving together for the faith of the gospel"... "Let your conversation be as it becometh the gospel of Christ. Let nothing be done through vain glory, but in lowliness of mind and let each esteem others better than themselves....forgetting those things which are behind, and reaching forth unto those things which are before.... My God shall supply all your needs according to His riches in glory ... I can do all things through Christ who strengthens me!"

What a character! What an example! Paul's advice is sound. We should put God FIRST, others SECOND and ourselves LAST.

The preacher had just finished delivering a hot and scathing sermon on the sin of swearing. During his sermon he stated several times that he knew one of his present hearers was guilty.

The service ended. The worshipers one by one filed out through the door: The first to go was a woman never suspected of using foul language. With a red and angry face she exclaimed, "I will never darken this door again!"

Before the astonished preacher could recover from this blast, another said, "Well, Brother, if I had known you were near last week, I would have been more careful of my language." A third said, "I think that you might at least have come to me privately about it, rather than telling it to the whole church!" A fourth remarked angrily, "I was never so embarrassed in all my life!"

Then came the real culprit. The one at whom the preacher had aimed all of his remarks. With a bland and innocent smile he grasped the hand of the preacher and said, "You certainly did pour it on THEM today!"

It is truly a mystery how a guilt complex can influence both the conscious and the subconscious mind. Of course, not everyone swears or takes the name of God in vain, but nearly everyone does have guilt feelings occasionally, because men and women aren't perfect. However, the conscious can be soothed so many times that it becomes hardened and no longer really cares and pretends that everything is the other fellow's mistake, as did the last speaker in the story.

It doesn't take a dastardly deed to make a person feel guilty: A good housekeeper may feel guilty if she doesn't have her house "spic and span" when her family gets home in the afternoon. A good father who is feeling "out-of-sorts" may feel guilty if he has spoken crossly to his son or daughter or wife. Unanswered letters, visits not made to the ill and "shut-ins," donations to favorite charities forgotten to be mailed, scolding or spanking a small child for misbehavior instead of taking the time to get him interested in something else; forgetting to put food and water out for a pet; any of the above things, plus many more, can cause a twinge of conscience. And the more serious the cause or reason, the greater the feeling of guilt.

Most guilt feelings are caused by doing something different from your regular routine. For instance, the person who is in the habit (a very good habit) of going to church every Sunday stays home one Sunday to watch the last ball game of the season and feels guilty about it until the next Sunday when he is back in church again.

Be glad if you can still feel twinges of conscience and experience guilt feelings. That means there's hope for you yet and your conscience is not dead or hardened. But now is the time to do something about it. It's time to rededicate your life to Christ and Christianity whose teachings bring one nearer to God and a promise of the life to come.

• • • • • • • • • • • • • • • • • • • • • • • • • • • • • • • • • • • • • •

"When you are a mature Christian, you think (not worry) a lot about the fate of the faithless. And if you are also a writer, you do a lot of thinking and searching for the right words that would humbly and un-shockingly remind them of (not the error of their way, because we all err and "fall short of the glory of God.") what lies ahead for people of little or no faith.

"Oh ye of little faith!" is a statement made often in the New Testament to the people of that day. It is recorded all through the scriptures in regard to many phases of skepticism and doubt. (Most Bibles have a concordance in the back. Look up the words: "faith" and "faithful" and "faithless" and "little.")

We can tell about our close friends, but how can we know that acquaintances and others that we see only occasionally have faith? The answer is, we can't! And we aren't supposed to make judgments about the faith of others. We are to live our lives in such a manner, openly expressing our own faith, which will inspire and increase the faith in others.

Outward appearances are much the same and the earthly needs (not desires -there's a big difference) of all people (whether they have faith or not) are the same: ambition, some success, some popularity, and above all the necessities of life: food, clothing and shelter. These are characteristics of all earthlings.

Of what good are food, clothing and shelter in this life if the withering faithless soul is being deprived of the life to come? The person without faith doesn't think of another life, or else doesn't believe that there is a life after death. Either way, their fate is the same.

We should train ourselves to take the' long view of life because the short-sighted are more apt to live just for the moment. Prosperity is really a hindrance to faith in the short-sighted or narrow-minded person. The vision of the "rich young ruler," in the Biblical story, was really of short range.

People in need realize they need God; people with plenty tend to forget God, unless they have developed a good, strong, abiding faith in Him before receiving the plenty. God wants all His children to have "abundantly," but, also, to remember WHO gives it and makes it possible.

The faith of the Christian is a simple faith. It is the faith taught in the Bible; "For by grace are you saved through faith; and that not of yourselves: it is the gift of God." - Ephesians 2:8.

The more faith one has, the more powerful that one becomes. The more powerful faith comes by praying and fasting (Read Matthew 17:20-21.) The Biblical definition of faith: "Faith is the substance of things hoped for and the evidence of things not seen." - Hebrews 11:1. The Bible also tells how faith comes to us: "So the faith cometh by hearing, and hearing by the word of God." We can hear while reading God's word.

Why must we have faith? Because "for whatsoever is not of faith is sin." - Romans 14:23.

We are living in difficult times. I can make that statement without fear of being called a "prophet of doom" because we are all aware of the events and circumstances existing in today's world that threaten our sense of security on both a personal and national level.

Personally we fear the work shortage, the money shortage, the bankruptcy of farmers who will not be growing food anymore, the rising of doctor's fees and hospital bills, and the fear of illness and old age. We fear that our two major political parties may war with each other and divide the nation, and we fear disharmony between the branches of the armed forces of our country.

I have lived through the terms of many presidents (being born three months after our 27th president, William Howard Taft, was elected, but I don't remember him; I do remember the next one, Woodrow Wilson, and the Germans sinking four of our ships and World War I) and I know that many of our later presidents have taken their "party battles "into the White House with them. Earlier presidents did not leave their business of running the government to go on the campaign trail for fellow party members. There was a time when an elected president was president to all of the people, of both parties.

We fear the national economy. So did Herbert Hoover. He encouraged people to spend more and keep money in circulation. "Mr. Herbert Hoover says now's the time to buy, so let's have another cup of coffee, and let's have another piece of pie!" was a line from a popular song of that day. People who have money fear the closing of banks and financial institutions; and especially that the stock market may crash again. (I remember the last time, and of seeing a picture in the paper of a man committing suicide by jumping from a skyscraper window on Wall Street. Others jumped too, but a photographer happened to see this one as he jumped.)

F.D.R. said, "The only thing to fear is fear itself." But why fear at all? The only cure for fear is to have more confidence. And how can we have more confidence except through a Christian faith? However, living the life of a Christian is no guarantee of a soft life during hard times. When it rains it falls on the good and the bad. When there is war or famine or epidemics of illness they involve both the good and the bad.

When there is a bad ruler or leader the people suffer! When there is a lack of scientific medical knowledge the people suffer! Where there is a lack of our Christian heritage the people suffer! All through the years Christians have suffered boycotts, persecution and even martyrdom while Satan has tried to overpower the good in the world. But the early Christians kept their faith and had confidence that God was still in control. That confidence quelled their fears and sustained them in the midst of their trials, sufferings and tribulations.

So, when the nations cry "Peace! Peace! and there is no peace," let's remember that even though some of the good may be sacrificed, no one can conquer the sovereign Lord of history. He will keep His promises!

· · · · · · · · · · · · · · · · · · · · · · · · · · · · · · · · · · · ·

We like to think of the people we love as belonging to us, but we have no right of possession over them. In life, as well as in death, we are the Lord's, and those whom we love also belong to Him - or should.

Why do we fight and work so hard for security? Nothing is gained by wrapping-one's life in a blanket and preserving it for many, many years. Existence, in itself, has neither meaning nor purpose.

Despite our bonds to those we love, and regardless of their security measures to protect us, we must be dedicated to a future that is completely in God's hands. Because only then can we commit ourselves with gladness to doing whatever work the Lord would have us do. Death is a reality, but it does not rule and have domination over us.

To become a Christian and a child of God means turning a page, crossing a new frontier, leaving one land for another - the land of darkness for the land of light, leaving the land of despair for the land of hope, the land of futility for the land of purpose; it even means leaving the land of death for the land of life. We must move into this new land if we expect its contents to be ours.

Life in any new land is a life of discipline and discovery. One of the first things we discover is that others have found this new land too, and we learn from their experience. In this land Christians are related to God and to one another in a very special way.

The world's best known sojourner was probably Abraham: "By faith Abraham, when he was called to go out into a place which he should after receive for an inheritance, obeyed; and he went out, not knowing whither he went."

We know that Abraham entered into, and experienced, a wonderful relationship with God. He was obedient. "When God called him, he answered. And because of his faithfulness, God's promise to him was fulfilled. Today three of the world's great religions reverence his name: Islam, Judaism, and Christianity.

Back in the days when the people were more "God conscious," the prophet Joel said, "Your young men shall see visions and your old men shall dream dreams." The question was asked if that applied to today, and the response was, "Our young men do not see visions, but they dream troubled dreams.'

The youth of today are worried and do have troubled dreams about the future. They worry about the job shortage and whether they can or cannot stay in college. They worry about military duty and the indications of a Third World War which, with modern weaponry, could destroy life as we know it.

People of all ages must turn back to God and really get to know Him. He alone is our salvation. Only through Him can we find peace of mind, and He is the only loved one who can transport us into the new land of promise. *Amen!*

# AFTERWORD

My mother, Esther King, wrote the articles in this book about 25 years ago, and it is impossible for her to read or proof this book now that she is aged and blind. I have attempted to give credit where credit is due for all quotations she used in her writing. However, I could not find references for some of the quotations used, and I apologize to anyone who may have been inadvertently omitted. Most of the quotations came directly from scriptures in the Bible, but may not have book title and chapter/verse listed.

Esther King's wish was that her writing might in some way help others. I hope that her wish comes true. Here are my mother's last words concerning her articles that are in this book.

"I am a believing Christian. I am convinced that God is who He says He was, and that He is who He says He is, and He will be what He said He will be. I believe the Bible is true as written by his disciples right after the crucifixion. I believe He told them 'heaven and earth shall pass away, but my words will never die.'"

"He told them He was the alpha and the omega, (the beginning and the end), but He will not leave you comfortless. Jesus said, 'I will send you a comforter who will comfort you. I go to prepare a place for you, and if I go to prepare a place for you, I will come again and receive you unto myself.'"

"I am what I believe so this book is my biography."